Non-Parametric Econometrics

Practical Econometrics

Series Editors
Jurgen Doornik and Bronwyn Hall

Practical econometrics is a series of books designed to provide accessible and practical introductions to various topics in econometrics. From econometric techniques to econometric modelling approaches, these short introductions are ideal for applied economists, graduate students, and researchers looking for a non-technical discussion on specific topics in econometrics.

Books published in this series

An Introduction to State Space Time Series Analysis
Jacques J. F. Commandeur and Siem Jan Koopman

Non-Parametric Econometrics
Ibrahim Ahamada and Emmanuel Flachaire

Non-Parametric Econometrics

Ibrahim Ahamada
Emmanuel Flachaire

Translated by
Andrew Clark

OXFORD
UNIVERSITY PRESS

OXFORD
UNIVERSITY PRESS

Great Clarendon Street, Oxford OX2 6DP

Oxford University Press is a department of the University of Oxford.
It furthers the University's objective of excellence in research, scholarship,
and education by publishing worldwide in

Oxford New York

Auckland Cape Town Dar es Salaam Hong Kong Karachi
Kuala Lumpur Madrid Melbourne Mexico City Nairobi
New Delhi Shanghai Taipei Toronto

With offices in

Argentina Austria Brazil Chile Czech Republic France Greece
Guatemala Hungary Italy Japan Poland Portugal Singapore
South Korea Switzerland Thailand Turkey Ukraine Vietnam

Published in the United States
by Oxford University Press Inc., New York

First published 2010

British Library Cataloguing in Publication Data
Data available

Library of Congress Cataloging in Publication Data
Library of Congress Control Number: 2010937008

Typeset by SPI Publisher Services, Pondicherry, India
Printed in Great Britain
on acid-free paper by
MPG Books Group, Bodmin and King's Lynn

ISBN 978–0–19–957800–9

1 3 5 7 9 10 8 6 4 2

Preface

The role of econometrics is to bring together economic theory, statistical methods, and observed data. One way of doing so is via regression. In this context, one of the overriding preoccupations of econometricians is finding the right specification of their regression model. The simple reason for doing so is that bad model specifications increase the risk of drawing the wrong conclusions from the analysis of data, with all of the negative side-effects that this would imply.

Standard econometric textbooks set out the properties of various estimators for different specifications of regression models. It is very commonly supposed in these presentations that the form of the relationship linking the dependent to the explanatory variables is known, and that the regression model is correctly specified: we are here in the world of parametric regression models, both linear and non-linear. However, the retained specification may be very dissimilar to the real underlying relationship in certain cases. The appeal of non-parametric and semi-parametric methods is that they relax the specification constraint: no *a priori* relationship is imposed between the explanatory and the dependent variables. In the context of the search for the best specification, these methods have brought new information to the debate, and have caused established regression specifications to be questioned in a number of empirical domains.

Recent developments in non- and semi-parametric estimation have opened up a wide vista of empirical applications across all the domains in which econometrics is applied: Macroeconomics, Microeconomics, Finance, and so on. These new methods can equally be applied to all of the different types of data used by researchers: cross-section, time-series, panel, and qualitative. The goal of this book is to present these new empirical tools so as to encourage their wider use in empirical applications.

Chapter 1 starts by setting out the principles of the estimation of a density. Chapters 2, 3, and 4 cover the simplest of the regression cases, with one dependent variable and one explanatory variable. These chapters describe the different methods of non-parametric estimation: kernel, splines, and wavelets. However, most empirical applications include a number of explanatory variables. Chapter 5 acknowledges this reality, and describes the estimation of semi-parametric regressions. Finally, mixture models are presented in Chapter 6. These introduce unobserved heterogeneity into the estimation of both densities and regression models. Sections marked $*$ are more technical and can be skipped if required.

This book sets out to be a pedagogical piece of work, illustrated by a number of original applications of the techniques at hand. We particularly emphasize the understanding of the methods, the underlying intuition, and how these techniques can be applied in practice. Each chapter includes a certain number of concrete applications of the methods described, as a way of illustrating them and of underlining both the advantages of these new techniques and their limitations. The applications described cover a wide variety of economic topics: economic convergence, income inequality, earnings, the Phillips curve, interest rates, financial markets, inflation, and house prices. An appendix describes how to apply these methods using statistical software. The reader can then reproduce the results in the applications described in this book using the original data.

This book is aimed at advanced undergraduate and graduate students in Economics, Business and Statistics, academic and non-academic readers, and researchers and analysts who use econometrics in firms and public organizations.

We have benefitted enormously from the advice and comments of a number of colleagues while writing this book. In particular, we thank Jean-Marc Bardet, Luc Bauwens, Philippe Bertrand, Russell Davidson, Véronique Delouille, Alain Desdoigts, Jean-Pierre Florens, Philippe Jolivaldt, Hubert Kempf, Mohamad Khaled, Michel Lubrano, Olivier Nũnez, Anne Péguin-Feissolle, Véronique Simonnet, Antoine Terracol, and the editors Jurgen Doornik and Bronwyn Hall. The students in the Nonparametric Econometrics course at the University of Paris 1 Panthéon-Sorbonne also played a crucial part in the development of this work. We are very grateful to them. We are particularly grateful to Andrew Clark, who translated this book into English and, with relevant remarks, largely contributed to improving its quality and readability. We also thank the

Centre d'Economie de la Sorbonne and the Région Provence-Alpes-Côte d'Azur for financial support.

Those who, unbeknownst to them, contributed the most to this book are our families and our children. They provided us with both the desire and the opportunity to carry out our work. This book is dedicated to them: to Muriel, Haris, and Adam, and to Valérie, Rémi, and Tom.

Contents

List of Figures

List of Tables

1

Kernel Density Estimation

1.1 Introduction

Has the gap in wealth between rich and poor countries narrowed or widened over time? Is investment in shares risky? How does the tax system affect the distribution of income between households? A preliminary analysis of the distribution of the variable of interest is often extremely useful to address this kind of question. The probability density function is a fundamental concept in statistics, providing a natural description of a variable's distribution. The analysis of this density clearly reveals certain properties of the variable in question, and yields information that is very likely useful in guiding and deepening the empirical analysis. This chapter is mainly devoted to the estimation of this density function from a data sample and its analysis.

Figure 1.1 shows the estimated density function of GDP per capita in 121 countries across the world in 1988. The data here come from the Penn World Table of Summers and Heston (1991), and have been divided by the mean of GDP per capita over all countries. On the X-axis, the value of 1/2 corresponds to one-half of the world mean of GDP per head, and the value 2 corresponds to twice the world mean. If we consider GDP per head to be a useful measure of a country's wealth, this figure allows us to analyze the world distribution of income. One of the first things that we note is that the density function is bimodal. The existence of two modes suggests that there are two distinct groups: one composed of the "richest" countries, and another consisting of the "poorest". The second mode is much less pronounced than the first, which indicates that the two groups are not of the same size: there are relatively few "rich" countries, and distinctly more "poor" countries. Further, the first mode is located just to the left of the value 0.5 on the X-axis, while the second is found at around 3. We can

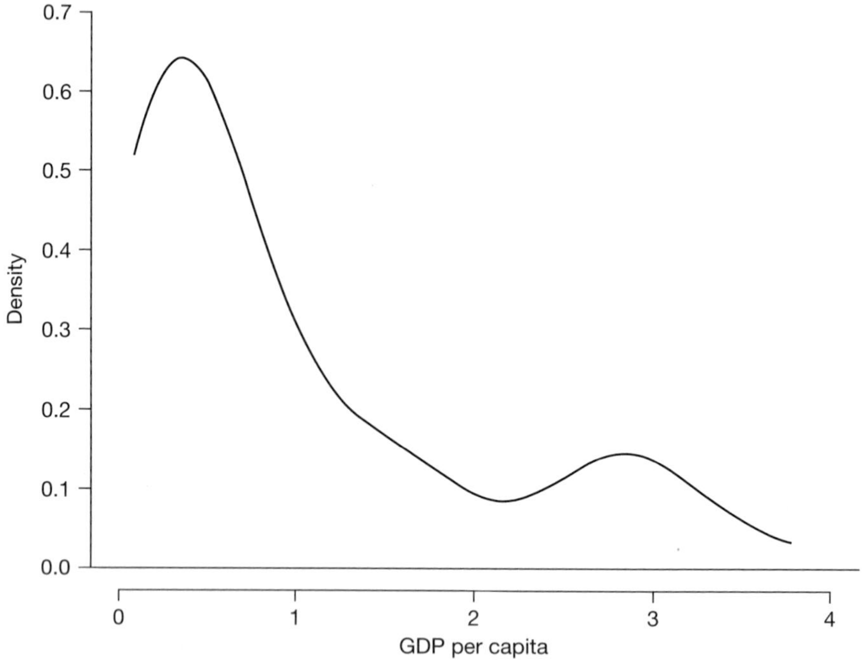

Figure 1.1: Kernel density estimation of the world distribution of income

thus conclude from this figure that, on average in 1988, "rich" countries enjoyed a level of GDP per capita that was around three times the world average, whereas that of "poor" countries was only half of the average level. We can also carry out a dynamic analysis by taking into account data from different years. For example, the same figure using data from 1960 reveals that the distance between the two modes was larger in 1988 than in 1960: the gap between the two groups of countries seems to have grown over time. The in-depth analysis in Quah (1997) considers the question of convergence between groups, but also the persistence of the gap, and the mobility of countries between different groups since the 1960s.

Figure 1.2 presents the estimated density function of daily returns of the CAC 40, the French stock market index, between March 1, 1990 and September 27, 2006. For comparison purposes, we have overlaid a Normal distribution (the dotted line). This distribution of financial returns is Leptokurtic: compared to the Normal distribution, the peak is more pointed and the extremities are thicker. As such, the probabilities at the extremes and in the middle of the distribution are greater than those in the Normal distribution. This shape is commonly observed in data from

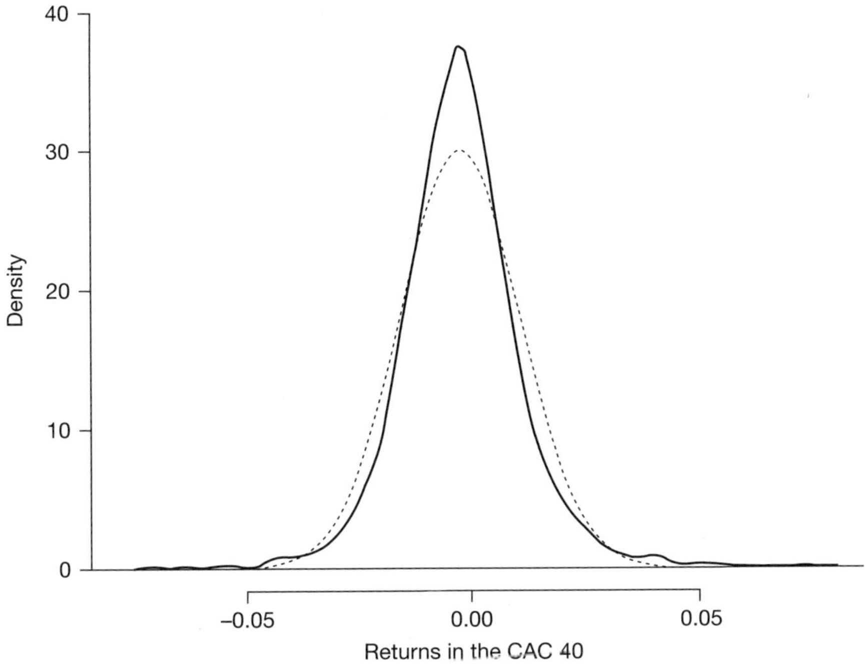

Figure 1.2: Kernel density estimation of daily returns in the CAC 40

financial markets, where extreme movements are more common than the Normal distribution would predict. This is one of the reasons for which ARCH (AutoRegressive Conditional Heteroskedasticity) regression models are often used in finance: the predicted returns from ARCH models are often Leptokurtic.

Figure 1.3 depicts the distribution of household *gross* and *net* income, that is, before and after taxes, in 1998 (equivalent income in 1000 Italian Lire). Both income measures are expressed in logarithms. In this figure, there is no very clear difference between the form of the two density functions: a simple shift would appear to suffice to move from one density function to the other. A shift in a logarithmic scale corresponds to a percentage change in the variable of interest. As such, the horizontal displacement that is evident in Figure 1.3 reveals a multiplicative effect on the distribution of income (of x%). In other words, the tax system in Italy affects the concentration of income distribution (the location of log-income distribution) but has no impact on the shape of the income distribution across the population. The tax system thus seems to deduct the same proportion of income from all households (Fiorio, 2008).

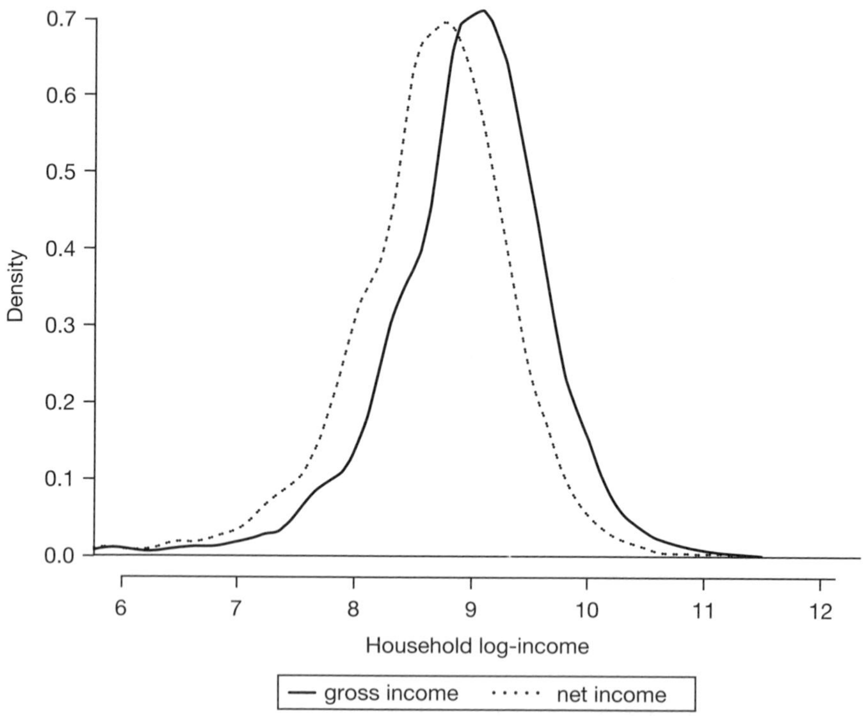

Figure 1.3: Kernel density estimation of Italian household incomes

All of the conclusions from the three examples above could have been reached by other means; however, the estimated density function is an ideal tool for the illustration of the properties of the data at hand, as it is easily understood by non-statisticians. The estimation of the density functions in the examples above was carried out by kernel methods with an automatic choice of the smoothing parameter. The following sections present this non-parametric density estimation method, and describe its statistical properties. More information is available in Silverman (1986), as well as Härdle (1989), Scott (1992), Wand and Jones (1995), Simonoff (1996), Bowman and Azzalini (1997), and Pagan and Ullah (1999).

Section 1.2 presents the standard methods for the estimation of a density, and Section 1.3 the Kernel estimation methods. The choice of the smoothing parameter is addressed in Section 1.4, and adaptive Kernel methods are described in Section 1.5. Finally, Section 1.6 considers the case of multivariate analysis.

1.2 Standard Density Estimation Methods

First of all, we restate the definition of a probability density function. If we say that a random variable Y has a probability density function of f, this means that for any real values a and b, the probability that Y falls between a and b is:

$$P(a < Y < b) = \int_a^b f(y)\,dy \quad \text{for any } a < b.$$

The function f has the following properties: it takes only non-negative values, it is integrable, and its integral from $-\infty$ to $+\infty$ is equal to 1. If we have available a sample of data, which we suppose to have come from an unknown density function, then the calculation of the estimated density function will appeal only to the observed data to hand. A number of different approaches are then possible. In this section, we consider the parametric estimation of this density function and the estimation by histogram, which are very often used in practice.

1.2.1 *Parametric Estimation*

If the density function is known up to k parameters, written as $f(y;\theta)$, the estimation of the density boils down to estimating the vector θ, which consists of k unknown parameters. This is the parametric approach, which requires the prior specification of a family of distributions from which the data sample is supposed to have been obtained.

Consider, for example, that we have a sample of n observations, $y_1, \ldots, y_n$, obtained from a Normal distribution, with mean μ and variance σ^2. The density function of the Normal distribution $N(\mu, \sigma^2)$, evaluated at x, is given by:

$$f(x;\mu,\sigma) = \frac{1}{\sigma\sqrt{2\pi}} \exp\left(-\frac{(x-\mu)^2}{2\sigma^2}\right).$$

The estimation of the density function is equivalent to obtaining estimates of the parameters μ and σ using the sample of data. One classic method consists in specifying the joint density of the sample and calculating the parameter values which maximize this function. In other words, we choose the parameters which maximize the likelihood of observing the actual values in the data sample. This is the method of Maximum Likelihood. If the observations are independently and identically distributed, the joint density function of $y_1, \ldots, y_n$ is equal to the product of the individual densities:

$$f(y; \mu, \sigma) = \prod_{i=1}^{n} f(y_i; \mu, \sigma).$$

The estimation of the density therefore requires the maximization of this function with respect to the parameters μ and σ. It is simpler to maximize the logarithmic transformation of this function, called the log-likelihood:

$$\ell(y; \mu, \sigma) = \log f(y; \mu, \sigma) = \sum_{i=1}^{n} \log f(y_i; \mu, \sigma).$$

This is the sum of the individual log-densities. The solution of the two maximizations is identical, as the logarithmic transformation is positive and monotonic, but the analytical resolution of the log transformation is much simpler. In our case, with a family of Normal distributions, the parameter values which maximize the log-likelihood are the mean and the variance of our data sample. Different examples can be presented with different probability distributions. The resolution of the problem may then be more complicated, but the same principle applies for other families of parametric distributions.

The main drawback of this approach is that we have to suppose the data are drawn from a given family of distributions f. If this hypothesis does not hold, then the estimated density function can differ substantially from its real value. For example, the estimated Normal distribution in Figure 1.2 is obtained from a parametric estimation of the density under the *a priori* hypothesis that the data were indeed distributed normally. This curve is markedly different from that which results from a non-parametric estimation, which latter reveals a pronounced Leptokurtic distribution. Here, the hypothesis underlying the parametric estimation seems very strong, and ignores one of the notable properties of financial markets.

The advantage of non-parametric estimation is that it makes no such *a priori* hypotheses regarding the form of the density function. As such, it is much more flexible than the parametric approach. Non-parametric estimation lets the data themselves determine the shape of the density, without constraining the function to belong to any particular family of distributions.

1.2.2 *Histograms*

Histograms are without doubt the oldest non-parametric density estimators, and the most widely used. Constructing a histogram from a sample of n observations, $y_1, \ldots, y_n$, consists in dividing the data up into different groups or intervals, and then counting up the number of observations that are found in each interval. The estimator of the density, evaluated over y, is written as follows :

$$\hat{f}(y) = \frac{1}{n} \times \frac{\texttt{number of observations in the interval of } y}{\texttt{width of the interval}}. \qquad (1.1)$$

The numerator in this equation corresponds to the number of the observations, $y_1, \ldots, y_n$, which are situated in the interval of y in question. The implementation of this estimator requires two choices to be made: the point of origin of the division of the data, and the number of distinct intervals.

The choice of the point of origin is not anodyne, and can have a substantial impact on the form of the histogram. Figure 1.4 depicts two estimations of GDP per head across different countries in 1988. Both histograms contain the same number of intervals (which is chosen by default by the statistical package used here). The difference between the two panels of Figure 1.4 comes from the choice of the point of origin: the panel on the left uses the point of origin of 0 on the X-axis, while that on the right uses the value −0.5. The resulting impression given by the two histograms is far from being the same. In one case there is only one mode, while in the other two modes are apparent. As such, it is difficult to conclude as to which one of the two provides the best representation of the underlying distribution. While the kernel estimation (Figure 1.1) yielded a clear conclusion, this is no longer the case for the estimation by histogram (Figure 1.4).

The choice of the number of intervals affects the degree of smoothing in the histogram. In the limiting case where there is only one interval, the histogram is completely smooth, and consists of only one value over the entire interval of the data.[1] At the other extreme, when an infinity of intervals are used, the histogram is anything but smooth, taking values that are either zero or close to zero, or close to $+\infty$.[2] The choice of the number of intervals obviously has an enormous impact on the graphical

[1] There are n observations in the interval, and the width of the interval is $\max(y) - \min(y)$.

[2] With intervals that are infinitely small, the value given by (1.1) is infinitely large if the numerator is a whole number different from zero.

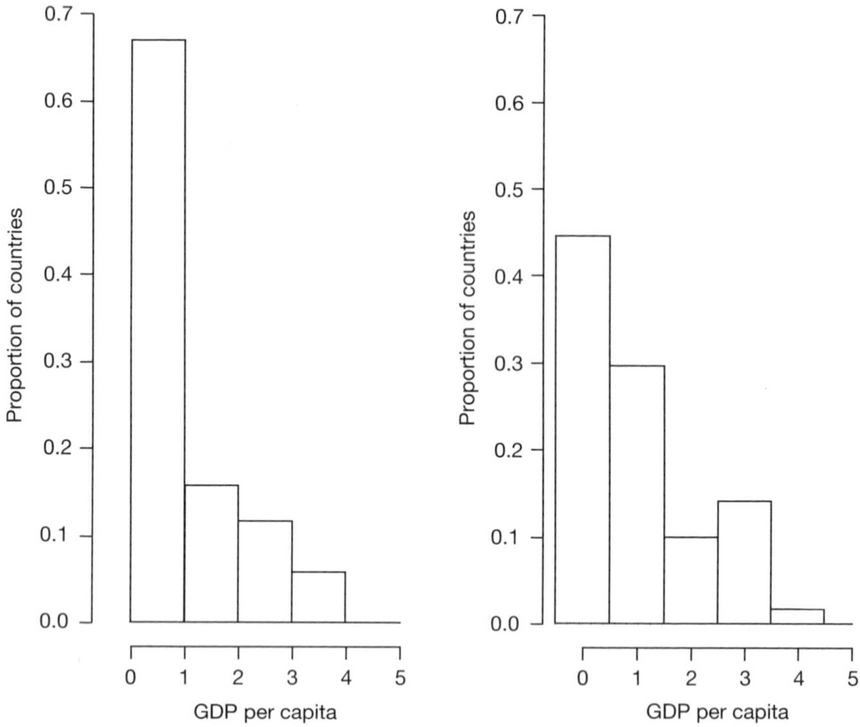

Figure 1.4: Histograms

representation in the histogram. The number of intervals chosen needs to be such that a sufficient number of observations fall in each interval, and that the histogram best depicts the different aspects of the distribution. In practice, the number of intervals is often determined visually.

Histograms are often very useful as a first stab at the portrayal of the data. Nonetheless, more sophisticated techniques may be used to overcome the shortcomings listed above, and to reveal more clearly the intrinsic properties of the data. Before we broach these new techniques, it will be useful to rewrite the density function of the histogram. In most cases, intervals of the same width are used. Consider the partition of the data into m distinct intervals of the same width: $(z_k; z_{k+1})$, for all $k = 1, \ldots, m$, with $m < n$ and $z_{k+1} - z_k = h$. The estimator of the density function by histogram (1.1) is equivalent to:

$$\hat{f}(y) = \frac{1}{nh} \sum_{i=1}^{n} I(z_k < y_i \leq z_{k+1}) \qquad \text{for } k \text{ such that } z_k < y \leq z_{k+1}, \qquad (1.2)$$

where $I(.)$ is an indicator function, equal to 1 if its argument holds and zero otherwise.

1.3 Kernel Estimation

The main characteristics of non-parametric estimation via histograms are as follows: (1) the graphical representation of the data is not smooth; (2) the representation depends on the choice of the point of origin; (3) the representation also depends on the number of intervals used. The first two of these points can be dealt with by using kernel estimation, with the dependence on the number of intervals boiling down to the choice of a smoothing parameter. We present in this section the kernel estimator of the density function, before moving on to the question of the automatic selection of the smoothing parameter.

1.3.1 *The Naive Estimator*

One of the main drawbacks of the representation of data by histogram is the choice of the point of origin. To avoid having to make this kind of arbitrary choice, the naive estimator considers intervals that may overlap, rather than being separate from each other. The principle here is to estimate a density function at one point by counting the number of observations which are "close" to this evaluation point. For a sample of n observations, $y_1, \ldots, y_n$, the naive density estimator is given by:

$$\hat{f}(y) = \frac{1}{nh} \sum_{i=1}^{n} I\left(y - \frac{h}{2} < y_i < y + \frac{h}{2}\right), \tag{1.3}$$

where h is the width of the intervals and $I(.)$ is an indicator function, equal to 1 if its argument holds and zero otherwise. In this equation, the estimate of the density at point y is given by the proportion of observations which are within a distance of $h/2$ or less from point y. The global density is obtained by sliding this window of width h along all of the evaluation points.

This estimator can be compared to that in a histogram with intervals of width h. If the evaluation point y of the density function corresponds to the center of one of intervals of the histogram, the evaluation given by the naive estimator (1.3) at this point is exactly the same as that given by the histogram (1.2). However, for all other points which do not correspond to the center of an interval, the naive estimator produces a different figure.

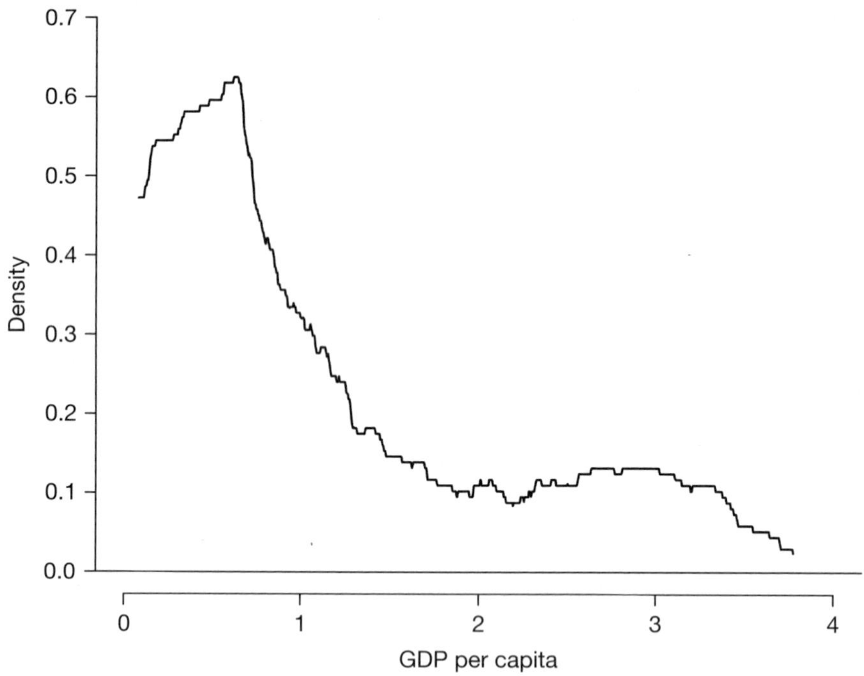

Figure 1.5: Naive estimator

Figure 1.5 presents the naive estimation of the density of GDP per capita across different countries in 1988. Compared to the estimation by histogram (Figure 1.4), the naive estimator reveals much more detail about the curvature of the density function. As the estimation is carried out at all points, and not by separate intervals, the problem of the choice of the point of origin disappears. The choice of the interval width, which is $h = 0.3286$ in Figure 1.5, allows us to choose the degree of smoothing: larger values of h produce smoother functions, while much smaller values of h produce curves that are not smooth at all. The value of h has to be large enough to ensure that there is a sufficient number of observations per interval, but small enough to avoid over-smoothing the resulting function. Optimal choice criteria (described later on) or visual inspection can be used to determine a satisfactory value of h. This value will depend on the number of observations that we have to hand, and will typically be smaller the more data we have available.

Figure 1.5 also shows, however, that the naive estimator is not differentiable at all points: as was the case for the histogram, the graphical representation is a step function. To obtain an estimator which is differentiable at all points, with a completely smooth graphical representation, we appeal to kernel estimation. To do so, it is useful to rewrite the naive estimator as follows:

$$\hat{f}(y) = \frac{1}{nh}\sum_{i=1}^{n} w\left(\frac{y - y_i}{h}\right) \qquad \text{where} \qquad w(x) = \begin{cases} 1 & \text{if } |x| < \frac{1}{2} \\ 0 & \text{otherwise.} \end{cases} \tag{1.4}$$

The function $w(.)$ can be represented by a rectangle. As such, this estimator is the sum of rectangles, of width h and height $(nh)^{-1}$, placed around each of the observations.

1.3.2 *The Kernel Estimator*

The kernel estimator is a generalization of the naive estimator which allows us to overcome the problem of differentiability at all points. Equation (1.4) clearly shows that this problem comes from $w(.)$: this function allocates a weight of 1 to all of the observations which belong to the interval centered on y, and zero weight to the other observations. The principle of kernel estimation is simple: rather than giving all observations in the interval the same weight, the allocated weight is greater the closer the observation is to y. In other words, the transition from 1 to zero in the weights is not carried out abruptly, but rather gradually. The kernel estimator is obtained by replacing the weighting function $w(.)$ in (1.4) by a kernel function $K(.)$:

$$\hat{f}(y) = \frac{1}{nh}\sum_{i=1}^{n} K\left(\frac{y - y_i}{h}\right). \tag{1.5}$$

In order for $\hat{f}(y)$ to conserve the properties of a density function, the kernel function has to satisfy the following condition:

$$\int_{-\infty}^{\infty} K(x)\, dx = 1. \tag{1.6}$$

Any density function satisfies this condition. As such, symmetric probability density functions are generally used. These imply that the same weight is assigned to all observations that are situated at the same distance from y. Amongst the many possible different choices, we present a number of the functions that are commonly used in practice.

The Gaussian kernel corresponds to the choice of the standard Normal distribution:

$$K(x) = \frac{1}{\sqrt{2\pi}} e^{-\frac{x^2}{2}}. \tag{1.7}$$

The Epanechnikov (1969) kernel is a second-degree polynomial, adjusted to satisfy the properties of a density function:

$$K(x) = \begin{cases} \frac{3\left(1-\frac{x^2}{5}\right)}{4\sqrt{5}} & \text{if } |x| < \sqrt{5} \\ 0 & \text{otherwise.} \end{cases} \tag{1.8}$$

This latter has the advantage of being analytically simple; it also has optimality properties, which we will describe in the following section.

The triangular kernel can be written as:

$$K(x) = \begin{cases} 1 - |x| & \text{if } |x| < 1 \\ 0 & \text{otherwise.} \end{cases}$$

The rectangular kernel is given by:

$$K(x) = \begin{cases} \frac{1}{2} & \text{if } |x| < 1 \\ 0 & \text{otherwise.} \end{cases}$$

This corresponds to the naive estimator, as defined in equation (1.4), with a normalized weighting function.

These different kernels are depicted in Figure 1.6. The Gaussian and Epanechnikov kernels are fairly similar: both are symmetric around zero and diminish gradually as we move away from zero. The difference between them is that the Gaussian kernel always takes on positive values, even though these are extremely small outside of the $[-3; 3]$ interval, whereas the Epanechnikov kernel yields values of zero outside of $[-\sqrt{5}; \sqrt{5}]$. The triangular kernel is not always differentiable; it does, however, diminish gradually with the distance from zero, which is not the case for the rectangular kernel. Silverman (1986, Chapter 3) discusses the effect of kernel choice on the density estimation. The results suggest that this choice actually has relatively little impact. In practice, the Gaussian and Epanechnikov kernels are the most often used.

In general, the kernel function is normalized; that is, the variance is set equal to 1. This implies that the parameter h plays the role of the variance in the estimation of the density in (1.5). As such, the Gaussian kernel puts little weight on observations that are a distance of over $3h$ away from the reference point, while the Epanechnikov kernel assigns

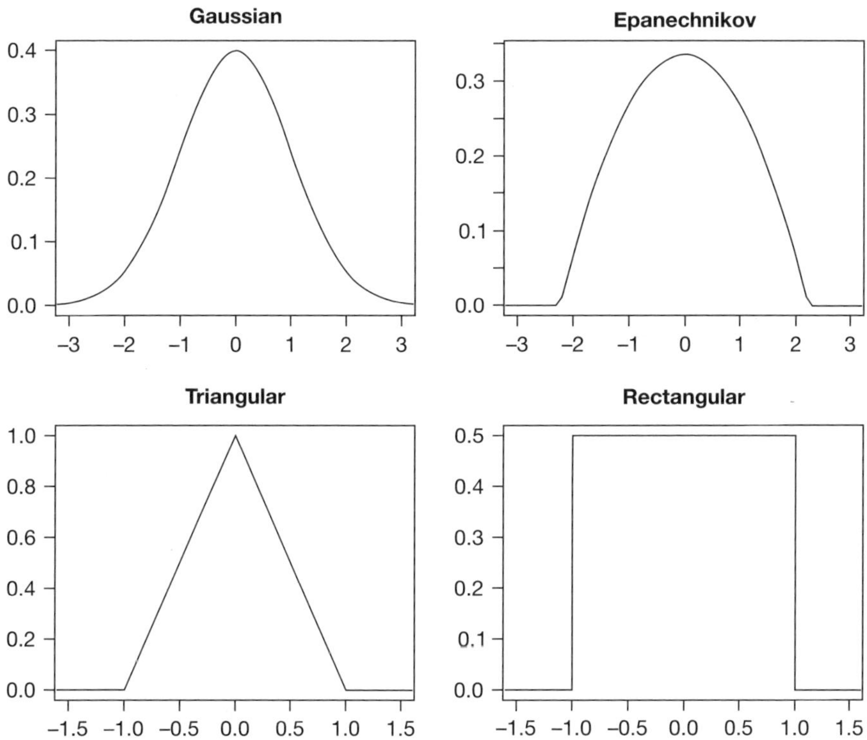

Figure 1.6: Kernel functions

zero weight to observations that are a distance of over $h\sqrt{5}$ away from the reference point. This parameter corresponds to the choice of the interval width, as noted above, and determines the degree of smoothing of the estimation. This is often called the choice of smoothing parameter or bandwidth selection.

Kernel estimation thus requires the specification of the kernel $K(.)$ and the smoothing parameter h. While kernel choice does affect the estimation of the density, the literature suggests that this effect is only small, with the empirical results being similar for different choices of $K(.)$. On the contrary, the results are sensitive to the choice of the bandwidth h. The effect of different choices of the kernel and bandwidth is illustrated in Figure 1.7. This shows kernel estimates of the density function of GDP per head across different countries in 1988, with values $h = 0.1643$ and $h = 0.6572$ and with Gaussian and Epanechnikov kernels. The two different values of the bandwidth provide very different figures: with $h = 0.1643$ we distinguish three modes and the highest value is around

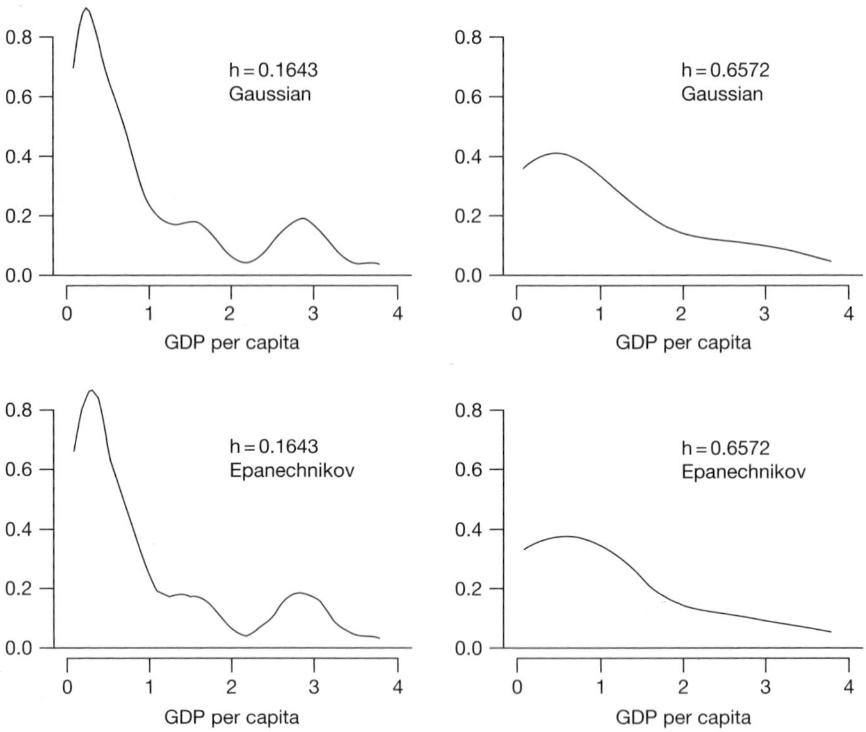

Figure 1.7: Kernel and bandwidth sensitivity

0.9; for $h = 0.6572$ only one mode is apparent and the highest value is around 0.4. The choice of h is thus central to the graphical representation of the estimated density function. Compared to the estimation of Figure 1.1 in the introduction, which corresponds to $h = 0.3286$, a value of h that is half as large ($h = 0.1643$) produces far more fluctuations, while many details disappear with a value of h that is twice as large ($h = 0.6572$), producing a function that is much smoother. The question of which value of h is the most appropriate is a particularly thorny one, and is dealt with in the following section.

1.4 Bandwidth Selection

One simple way of choosing the smoothing parameter is to do so visually, by depicting a number of graphical estimations of the density corresponding to different choices of h. This is satisfactory in certain cases.

Nonetheless, it is often preferable to be able to call on a less subjective method, which will automatically choose the value of the smoothing parameter. This section is devoted to the description of these methods.

The optimal bandwidth is that which yields an estimated density as close as possible to the true density. In other words, we should choose the value of h which minimizes the distance between $\hat{f}(y)$ and $f(y)$.

Considering the estimation of the density function at *one specific point* y, a natural candidate is the mean squared error (MSE). This is given by the mean distance between the estimated and the true values:

$$\text{MSE}(h) = E\left([\hat{f}(y) - f(y)]^2\right),$$

where $\hat{f}(y)$ is the estimated density at the point y for a bandwidth selection of h. We choose the value of h which minimizes this expression. The preceding equation can be decomposed into two terms:

$$\text{MSE}(h) = \left(E[\hat{f}(y)] - f(y)\right)^2 + \text{Var}[\hat{f}(y)].$$

The first corresponds to the bias of the estimator (squared) and the second to its variance. If the value of the smoothing parameter is too large, then the estimator tends to over-smooth the function; this produces larger values of the bias (the first term). On the contrary, a smoothing parameter that is too small will not smooth enough, and will produce an estimator that varies a great deal (the second term). The minimization of the bias thus goes hand-in-hand with maximal variance ($h = 0$); equally, minimizing the variance produces maximum bias ($h = \infty$). Minimizing the mean squared error corresponds to a trade-off between the bias and the variance of the estimator.

In practice, we are interested in the precision of the estimation *at all points*, and not only at one specific point. We thus consider the integral of the MSE over all possible values of y: the *mean integrated squared error* (MISE):

$$\text{MISE}(h) = E\left(\int [\hat{f}(y) - f(y)]^2 dy\right).$$

This represents the *global* precision of the density estimator. We choose h to minimize this measure. Note that, as the elements of the integral cannot take on negative values, we can inverse the expectation and the integral and write $\text{MISE}(h) = \int \text{MSE}(h)dy$. The equation above can thus be decomposed into two terms:

$$\text{MISE}(h) = \int \left(E[\hat{f}(y)] - f(y)\right)^2 dy + \int \text{Var}[\hat{f}(y)]dy.$$

The first term corresponds to the different biases for all possible values of y, and the second to all of the variances of the density estimator. This measure also represents a trade-off between the bias and the variance of the estimator.

The use of the MISE criterion requires the evaluation of an expectation which depends on the true density function. Consequently, we often use an approximation to this criterion, called AMISE, which is obtained from asymptotical arguments. Silverman (1986, Chapter 3) shows that the value of h which minimizes the AMISE criterion is as follows:

$$h_{opt} = \left[\left(\int x^2 K(x) dx \right)^{-\frac{2}{5}} \left(\int K(x)^2 dx \right)^{\frac{1}{5}} \right] \left[\left(\int f''(y)^2 dy \right)^{-\frac{1}{5}} \right] n^{-\frac{1}{5}}, \quad (1.9)$$

where $K(x)$ is the kernel function, $f''(y)$ is the second derivative of the density function, and n is the sample size. This result underlines that bandwidth selection depends on the choice of kernel, which appears in the first set of square brackets, the true density function, which appears in the second set of square brackets, and the sample size. A number of useful observations can be made regarding this formula:

1. The optimal value of the smoothing parameter depends on the number of observations available: h_{opt} tends towards zero as the size of the sample, n, increases, but only at a relatively slow speed, of the order of $n^{-1/5}$.

2. The second derivative of a function measures the variation in the slope of the function. If this derivative is zero over an interval, then the curve is locally straight, while a positive (resp. negative) value indicates that the slope is increasing (resp. decreasing) and that the function is convex (resp. concave). A function which varies only little thus produces a relatively low value of $\int f''$, while a function which moves around a great deal will be associated with a relatively high value of $\int f''$. In a sense, the term in the second set of square brackets is a measure of the speed at which the true density varies. We expect h_{opt} to be smaller for a density which varies substantially, and to take on a much larger value for a density which varies only a little.[3]

3. The density estimator depends on the choices of bandwidth h and kernel $K(x)$. We can then pose the question of the best choice of kernel when the bandwidth chosen is h_{opt}. To answer this question, we rewrite

[3] This relation is negative due to the negative exponent on the second factor between square brackets.

the expression of MISE above using the definition of h_{opt}, and then determine the choice of $K(x)$ which minimizes the resulting function, if this is possible. Silverman (1986) shows that it is possible to solve this last stage analytically, due to the fact that $K(x)$ only appears in the first term in square brackets in the expression for h_{opt}. The Epanechnikov kernel is shown to possess this optimality property.

The choice of bandwidth thus finally depends on the sample size and the way in which the true density fluctuates. This result might be considered as rather frustrating, as it requires us to know the true density before we can calculate h_{opt}.

1.4.1 *Rule of Thumb*

One natural way of developing an automatic selection method which is usable in practice is to use a reference distribution. If we retain the Normal distribution with variance of σ^2 as the reference distribution and a Gaussian kernel, we can calculate the optimal smoothing parameter (1.9) as:

$$h_{opt} = 1.059\,\sigma n^{-\frac{1}{5}}. \tag{1.10}$$

See Silverman (1986, Chapter 3) for more details. One quick way of calculating this parameter is to replace σ by the standard deviation of the sample data, which is an estimator of σ. One drawback of the standard deviation of the data is that it is very sensitive to outliers in the sample. This is typically the case when the sample is of small size, or if the true density is characterized by thick tails, as was the case in the daily CAC 40 returns example in the introduction. We may then prefer to use an alternative estimator of dispersion which is more robust to outliers. This is the case with the interquartile range, defined as the distance between the third and first quartiles, $q_3 - q_1$. We then have:

$$h_{opt} = 1.059\,\frac{q_3 - q_1}{1.349}\,n^{-\frac{1}{5}},$$

where the value of 1.349 corresponds to the interquartile range of the standard Normal distribution, $N(0, 1)$. These two automatic choices of bandwidth work well in practice when the true density is close to that of the reference distribution, that is, to the Normal distribution. However, this is no longer necessarily the case if the true density is distant from the Normal distribution. Silverman (1986) analyzed the performance of automatic bandwidth choices when the true density is not close to being Normal. The results led him to propose the following *rule of thumb*:

$$\hat{h}_{opt} = 0.9 \min\left(\hat{\sigma}; \frac{\hat{q}_3 - \hat{q}_1}{1.349}\right) n^{-\frac{1}{5}}, \qquad (1.11)$$

where $\hat{\sigma}$ is the standard deviation of the data, and $\hat{q}_3$ and $\hat{q}_1$ are respectively the third and first quartiles calculated from the data. This rule boils down to using the minimum of the two preceding options, replacing the value of 1.059 by 0.9 to reduce the risk of over-smoothing the function. This rule works well in numerous cases. Nonetheless, when the true density is multi-modal and very asymmetric, it tends to over-smooth the distribution.

1.4.2 *Plug-in Method*

The only unknown quantity in the MISE criterion is the second derivative of the density function, f''. Rather than using a reference distribution in equation (1.9), the *plug-in* approach consists of replacing $f''(y)$ by a prior non-parametric estimate, and then choosing the h that minimizes this function. This choice of bandwidth does not then produce an empirical rule as simple as that proposed by Silverman, as it requires numerical calculation. For more details, see Sheather and Jones (1991).

1.4.3 *Cross-validation*

There has now been a substantial amount of work on the selection of bandwidth by cross-validation. While a number of different approaches are possible, we limit our discussion to the most commonly used method, *cross-validation by least squares*. For more details and the presentation of other methods, see Silverman (1986), Pagan and Ullah (1999) and Loader (1999a), amongst others.

Rather than minimizing the mean integrated squared error (MISE), the underlying idea of *cross-validation by least squares* is to minimize the integrated squared error (ISE). In other words, we use the same criterion, but not expressed in terms of expectations. The advantage of the ISE criterion is that it provides an optimal formula for h for a given sample. The counterpart is that two samples drawn from the same density will lead to two different optimal bandwidth choices. Despite the conceptual difference between the MISE and ISE criteria, the use of one rather than the other to choose h makes practically no difference in terms of performance

(Grund et al., 1994). The ISE solution consists in finding the value of h that minimizes:

$$\text{ISE}(h) = \int [\hat{f} - f]^2\, dy = \int \hat{f}^2\, dy - 2\int \hat{f} f\, dy + \int f^2\, dy,$$

where, for simplicity, f and $\hat{f}$ correspond to $f(y)$ and $\hat{f}(y)$. The last term in this equation does not contain h and thus plays no role in the minimization. Furthermore, the term $\int \hat{f} f\, dy$ is exactly $E(\hat{f})$. Let $\hat{f}_{-i}$ be the estimator of the density based on the sample containing all of the observations except for y_i. An unbiased estimator of $E(\hat{f})$ is given by $n^{-1}\sum_{i=1}^{n} \hat{f}_{-i}$. The minimization of the ISE criterion thus requires us to minimize the following expression:

$$\text{CV}(h) = \int \hat{f}^2\, dy - \frac{2}{n}\sum_{i=1}^{n} \hat{f}_{-i}.$$

This method is also called *unbiased cross-validation*, as $\text{CV}(h) + \int f^2 dy$ is an unbiased estimator of MISE. The value of h which minimizes this expression, denoted by $\hat{h}_{cv}$, converges asymptotically to the value that minimizes the MISE.

One drawback of the automatic selection methods evoked in this section is that they do not work very well when the true density is characterized by long or thick tails. The sample then contains a lot of observations in some places, but very few in others, notably in the tails. To take into account this considerable variation in the density of data in different areas of the sample, what are called "adaptive" methods have been developed. These are described in the following section.

1.5 Adaptive Methods

The kernel method requires the prior choice of the smoothing parameter, also known as the bandwidth, which remains constant at all points where the distribution is estimated. This constraint can be particularly onerous when the concentration of data is markedly heterogeneous in the sample. For example, the distribution of daily returns in the CAC 40, as depicted in Figure 1.2, exhibits a peak in the middle and long tails. There is therefore considerable heterogeneity in the concentration of the data: many observations take on values close to zero, while large numbers in absolute value are much less common. As such, it would seem intuitively attractive to use a larger bandwidth to estimate the tails of the density than to estimate its middle. The use of a constant bandwidth produces both over-smoothing of the function where the data is concentrated, and not enough smoothing where the data are sparse. Kernel methods, as presented above, then over-smooth the middle of the distribution, and under-smooth the ends.

Adaptive methods have been developed to deal with this problem, which allow the bandwidth to vary as a function of the local concentration of the data. We will present two such approaches in this section: the methods of the nearest neighbor and the adaptive kernel.[4]

It is worth emphasizing that fixed-bandwidth kernel estimation does work well in many cases, and has the advantage of being simple, intuitive, and possessing well-known statistical properties. As such, Silverman (1986) recommends the use of adaptive methods only if the estimation of the tails of the distribution is an issue.

1.5.1 *Nearest Neighbors*

The principle of the nearest-neighbors method is to determine the bandwidth such that each interval contains the same number of observations. This principle contrasts with that of the naive estimator, where bandwidth is fixed and where the number of observations per interval plays a role. The *a priori* choice here is over the number of observations k that each interval should contain, rather than the size of the intervals h.

Consider the density function estimated at a point y, and the absolute distance of the observation i from this point: $d(y) = |y_i - y|$. We rank the distances of each point from y in ascending order, such that:

$$d_1(y) \leq d_2(y) \leq d_3(y) \leq \cdots \leq d_n(y).$$

This ranking allows us to establish, for example, that k observations are at a distance of at most $d_k(y)$. Consequently, we expect that the interval

$$[y - d_k(y); y + d_k(y)]$$

will contain k observations. If we apply the definition of the naive estimator of equation (1.3) to this interval, with $h = 2d_k(y)$, we obtain the *nearest-neighbor estimator* of the density function:

$$\hat{f}(y) = \frac{k}{2nd_k(y)}. \tag{1.12}$$

[4] Other approaches are not described, such as penalized maximum likelihood, and decomposition into orthogonal series. For more details, see Silverman (1986) and Pagan and Ullah (1999).

Evaluated at one particular point, the nearest-neighbor estimator is identical to the naive estimator. For each value of k in equation (1.12) we can find a value of h in equation (1.3) that yields the same result. It is when we consider the estimation of a number of different points of the density function that the two methods yield different results. Towards the middle of the distribution, where we typically find a greater number of observations, $d_k(y)$ will be smaller than in the tails of the distribution. The nearest-neighbor estimator helps us to avoid the problem of under-smoothing of the tails.

As was the case for the naive estimator, the nearest-neighbor estimator is not differentiable everywhere. In equation (1.12), the numerator refers to the number of observations in each interval: a weight of 1 is assigned to each observation in the interval, and a weight of zero to the other observations. As for the standard kernel estimator, we can consider a *generalized nearest-neighbor estimator*, defined as follows:

$$\hat{f}(y) = \frac{1}{2nd_k(y)} \sum_{i=1}^{n} K\left(\frac{y - y_i}{2d_k(y)}\right), \tag{1.13}$$

where $K(.)$ is a kernel function. This is none other than a kernel estimator evaluated at point y with a bandwidth of $2d_k(y)$.

The degree of smoothing is determined by the number of nearest neighbors, k. It is not possible to obtain a rule of thumb by minimizing the MISE and taking the reference distribution to be Normal, as was the case for the kernel estimator Silverman (1986). We can select k by comparing the results obtained with a number of different values, and choosing that which appears to be the most satisfactory in the light of the application and its context. In any case, the value of k has to be much smaller than the size of the sample, and $k \approx n^{1/2}$ is often used as a starting value.

The main difference from the kernel estimator is that the bandwidth now depends on y. In other words, the denominator of $\hat{f}(y)$ depends on y in equations (1.12) and (1.13) via the distance function $d_k(y)$. This has important implications for the properties of the nearest-neighbor estimator (1.12), and produces the following drawbacks:

1. *Differentiability*: the estimator depends on an absolute value function, $d_k(y)$, which is continuous but is not differentiable at all points. Consequently, the nearest-neighbor estimator is not differentiable at any point where $d_k(y)$ is not differentiable.

2. *Over-evaluation of tails*: in equation (1.12), the numerator is always non-zero, even if we evaluate the function at a point that is far removed

from the minimum or maximum values found in the observations. We therefore need to consider the behavior of the denominator to analyze how the tail diminishes towards zero, for a given sample size of n. At a point y which is less than the minimum value in the data, we have $d_k(y) = y_{(k)} - y$, where $y_{(k)}$ is the kth observation of the ascending-ranked sample. Consequently, $\hat{f}(y)$ tends towards zero as y moves away from $y_{(k)}$ at a speed of y^{-1}, that is, extremely slowly.[5] The same analysis also applies to the right-hand tail. We thus expect the nearest-neighbor estimator to over-estimate the tails so that they seem to be thicker than they are in the true distribution.

3. *This is not a density function*: one consequence of the over-estimation of the tails described above is that $\int_{-\infty}^{\infty} \hat{f}(y)dy$ is infinite.[6] Were this estimator to be a density, its integral would be equal to 1.

The generalized nearest-neighbor estimator does not resolve these problems. It depends on $d_k(y)$, which is a continuous function, but not everywhere differentiable. The generalized nearest-neighbor estimator is not differentiable at the points where $d_k(y)$ is not differentiable. The problem of the over-estimation of tails, which are thus too thick, is not completely overcome by the generalized estimator either. If the kernel is symmetric and quickly assigns small values within the interval and zero values outside of it, the tails of $\hat{f}(y)$ diminish more quickly as $d_k(y)$ rises. However, the exact behavior here depends greatly on kernel choice, and nothing guarantees that $\int_{-\infty}^{\infty} \hat{f}(y)dy$ will be equal to 1.

The three main problems of (generalized) nearest-neighbor estimation—non-differentiability at some points, a tendency to over-estimate tails, and the lack of density-function properties—are all overcome by adaptive kernel estimation.

1.5.2 *Adaptive Kernel Estimation*

Adaptive kernel estimation combines the advantages of the simple kernel and nearest-neighbor estimates. The estimator is constructed in the same way as in the simple kernel approach, but with a smoothing parameter that varies according to the degree of concentration of the data. Before we present the adaptive kernel estimator, we consider the special case of the variable kernel method.

[5] As $k/2n$ is constant, $\hat{f}(y)$ tends towards 0 when y tends towards $-\infty$ at a speed of y^{-1}.

[6] We have: $\int_{-\infty}^{y_{(1)}} \hat{f}(y)dy = \int_{-\infty}^{y_{(1)}} k[2n(y_{(k)} - y)]^{-1}dy = [-k(2n)^{-1} \log(y_{(k)} - y)]_{-\infty}^{y_{(1)}} = +\infty$, where $y_{(1)}$ is the smallest observation.

Let $d_k(y_i)$ be the distance to point y_i of its kth nearest neighbor, then the *variable kernel estimator* is defined as:

$$\hat{f}(y) = \frac{1}{n}\sum_{i=1}^{n} \frac{1}{hd_k(y_i)} K\left(\frac{y - y_i}{hd_k(y_i)}\right). \tag{1.14}$$

The bandwidth, or smoothing parameter, is decomposed into two elements, h and $d_k(y_i)$. The local degree of smoothing depends on the parameter h, while the relationship to the local concentration of the data is given by the parameter k in the function $d_k(y_i)$.

The main difference from (generalized) nearest-neighbor estimation is that the distance to the kth neighbor is independent of the point y where the function is evaluated. This latter is expressed in terms of the distance around the point y_i, that is, uniquely between observations in the sample. Consequently, the drawbacks associated with nearest-neighbor estimation are overcome. The variable kernel estimator is a density function, differentiable at all points, that does not over-evaluate the tails of the density.

In the equation (1.14), the function $d_k(y_i)$ measures the sensitivity of the bandwidth to the local density of observations. Methods other than nearest neighbor can also be used to specify this function. The *adaptive kernel estimator* is defined as follows:

$$\hat{f}(y) = \frac{1}{n}\sum_{i=1}^{n} \frac{1}{h\lambda_i} K\left(\frac{y - y_i}{h\lambda_i}\right),$$

where λ_i is a parameter that varies with the local concentration of the data. An estimate of the density at point y_i, denoted by $\tilde{f}(y_i)$, measures the concentration of the data around this point: a higher value of $\tilde{f}(y_i)$ denotes a greater concentration of data, while smaller values indicate lighter concentrations. The parameter λ_i can thus be defined as being inversely proportional to this estimated value $\tilde{f}(y_i)$:

$$\lambda_i = \left[\frac{g}{\tilde{f}(y_i)}\right]^{\alpha},$$

where g is the geometric mean of $\tilde{f}(y_i)$ and α is a parameter that takes on values between 0 and 1. The parameter λ_i is smaller when the density is greater (notably towards the middle of the distribution), and larger when the density is lighter (in the tails of the distribution). The function $\tilde{f}(y_i)$ is called the "pilot" estimator, which needs to be calculated in a first stage, before we calculate the adaptive estimator. For instance, an estimator of the density by kernel or nearest-neighbor method can be used. The results do not seem to be very sensitive to this choice of the "pilot" (Breiman et al., 1977; Abramson, 1982; and Silverman, 1986); the simple kernel estimator is thus often employed in practice.

The global degree of smoothing is captured by the parameter h, while the sensitivity to local concentration in the data depends on α. Adaptive kernel estimation requires the *a priori* choice of these parameters:

- Choice of α: Abramson (1982) shows that the bias in the estimation of the density function is reduced by the choice of $\alpha = 1/2$.[7] His empirical results suggest that this choice produces satisfactory results. Note that the particular case of $\alpha = 0$ corresponds to the simple kernel estimator, as we then have $\lambda_i = 1$, and that the variable kernel estimator corresponds to $\alpha = 1$ with the nearest-neighbor method used for the "pilot".
- Choice of h: as the estimator is not particularly sensitive to the choice of the "pilot", we can carry out the analysis considering λ_i to be fixed. The rule of thumb used to choose h for the simple kernel estimator would then appear to be a natural choice—see (1.11), even if the theory underlying this rule does not apply directly to the adaptive method. In addition, visual adjustment is sometimes useful.

Figure 1.8 reproduces on the left-hand side the results from the kernel estimation of daily returns in the CAC 40 in Figure 1.2, based on a fixed bandwidth h chosen according to Silverman's rule of thumb. The right-hand side shows the results from adaptive kernel estimation, with $\alpha = 1/2$ and h again chosen according to Silverman's rule of thumb. In both cases, the Gaussian kernel is used. The adaptive kernel estimation produces smoother tails than does standard kernel estimation, and a peak that is somewhat higher (at 39.13, as opposed to 37.51). We can see here the drawbacks of simple kernel estimation in the context of distributions with long tails: the estimator tends to over-smooth the middle of the distribution, but under-smooths the tails, and thus produces a bias in the center of the distribution and too much variability at the extremes. Figure 1.8 shows that these drawbacks are attenuated by adaptive kernel estimation.

[7] More precisely, he shows that a term is suppressed in the Taylor expansion approximation of the bias. This is not the case with a simple kernel estimator.

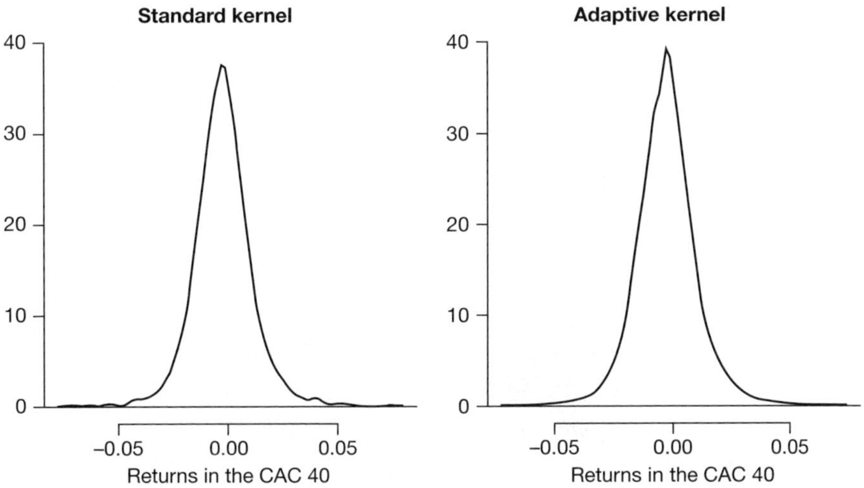

Figure 1.8: Adaptive kernel estimator

1.6 The Multivariate Case

Up to now, we have considered the estimation of the density of one single variable. In many cases, it is nonetheless useful to estimate the joint density of a number of variables. We therefore now turn to the estimation of density in a multivariate context.

The question of the potential convergence of countries to the same level of income has generated a great deal of discussion, and the non-parametric estimation of a bivariate density has played an important role in the empirical analysis of movements over time in the cross-country income distribution (Quah, 1993, 1997; Desdoigts, 1994, 1996; Durlauf et al., 2005). Figure 1.9 shows the results of bivariate kernel estimation of the joint density of GDP per head across 121 countries in 1978 and 1988. The GDP per head figures are divided by the world mean GDP per head that pertained in the year in question, as in Figure 1.1. This figure shows how the world income distribution evolved between 1978 and 1988. It is evident that the probability of jointly observing lower values of GDP per head in 1978 (X-axis) and 1988 (Y-axis) is fairly high (Z-axis). This means that a country with relatively low GDP per head in 1978 had a substantial probability of remaining a low GDP per head country in 1988. On the other hand, the probability of observing a high value of GDP per head in 1978 and a low value in 1988 is only small: a country with relatively high

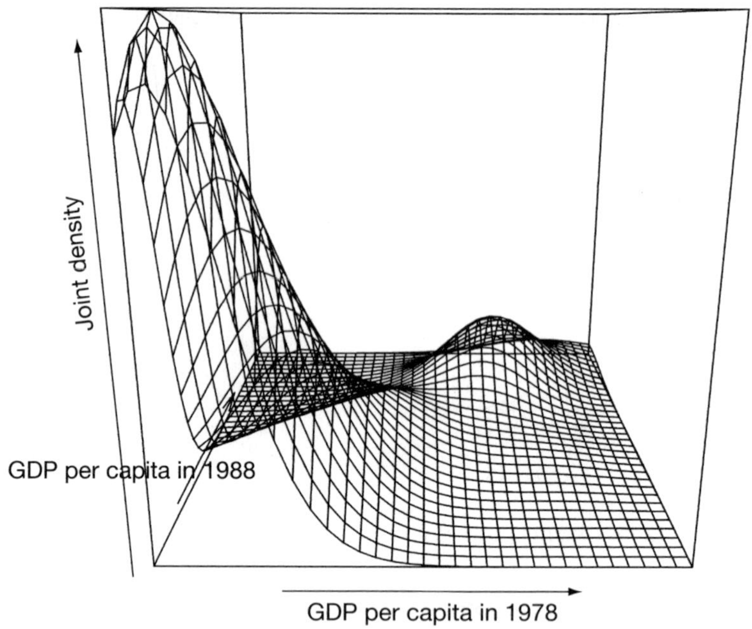

Figure 1.9: Bivariate kernel density estimation (density plot)

GDP per head in 1978 ran only a small risk of having low GDP per head in 1988. Overall, we can see that poor countries in 1978 were pretty likely to remain poor in 1988, and richer countries in 1978 mostly remained rich in 1988. This result is depicted graphically by the fact that the points in the graph are concentrated around the 45-degree line in (X-axis, Y-axis) space.

The results from bivariate estimation are often represented in two dimensions. Figure 1.10 depicts the results from the bivariate estimation of GDP per capita in 1978 and 1988 as contour lines. These provide a "bird's eye view" of Figure 1.9, with the contour lines joining the points for which the density has the same value. These contour lines present the shape of the density in a two-dimensional picture. This type of figure is often used in topography as a way of representing the three-dimensional shape of terrain in a horizontal map. The closer the contour lines are to each other, the steeper the slope. This figure shows that the density is very concentrated around the diagonal 45-degree line, which indicates that the (relative) levels of GDP per capita in 1978 are very similar to those in 1988. The figure also reveals the existence of two modes. The fact that these modes are distinct from each other, and that both are situated on the 45-degree line, suggests that they act as "basins of attraction". As such,

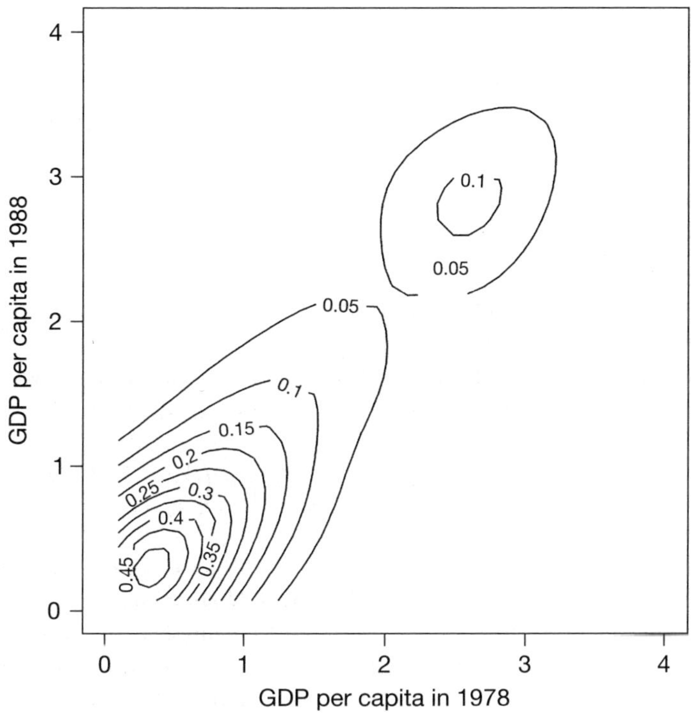

Figure 1.10: Bivariate kernel density estimation (contour plot)

all countries do not converge to the same level of income over time, with poor countries showing little tendency to catch up with rich countries.

This section presents the method of multivariate kernels. Although we will see that the extension of kernel estimation to many dimensions is simple, practical applications rarely go beyond two dimensions. This can be explained by the graphical ease of interpretation of results in two dimensions, whereas those in higher dimensions are more difficult to visualize. However, the main reason is that datasets with a very substantial number of observations are required for the reliable estimation of multivariate densities. This phenomenon is known as the *curse of dimensionality*, which determines the principal limits of non-parametric methods.

1.6.1 *Multivariate Kernels**

We will first consider the two-dimensional case, that is, a sample with two variables y_1 and y_2 for which we have n observations. The extension of the naive estimator—defined in equation (1.3)—to two dimensions requires us to reason in terms of pairs of observations rather than in single observations. We therefore count up the proportion of pairs of observations (y_{1i}, y_{2i}) which are situated close to the pair of points at which the density is evaluated:

$$\hat{f}(y_1, y_2) = \frac{1}{nh^2} \sum_{i=1}^{n} \left[I\left(-\frac{h}{2} < y_{1i} - y_1 < \frac{h}{2}\right) I\left(-\frac{h}{2} < y_{2i} - y_2 < \frac{h}{2}\right) \right].$$

The product of the indicator functions $I(.)$ serves to define a square of size h, centered on the reference point (y_1, y_2).

To produce a smoothed estimator, as in the univariate case, we replace the indicator function by a kernel:

$$\hat{f}(y_1, y_2) = \frac{1}{nh^2} \sum_{i=1}^{n} \left[K\left(\frac{y_{1i} - y_1}{h}\right) K\left(\frac{y_{2i} - y_2}{h}\right) \right], \qquad (1.15)$$

where $K(.)$ has the properties of a density, and can be the Gaussian or Epanechnikov kernel, defined in (1.7) and (1.8). The weights assigned to the pairs of data are therefore smaller the farther they are from the reference pair. However, the product of two univariate kernels does not necessarily lead to the same weight being assigned to two points that are equidistant from the reference point. To overcome this drawback, we consider a bivariate kernel:

$$\hat{f}(y_1, y_2) = \frac{1}{nh^2} \sum_{i=1}^{n} K\left(\frac{y_{1i} - y_1}{h}, \frac{y_{2i} - y_2}{h}\right), \qquad (1.16)$$

where $K(.)$ is a bivariate density function, with a single mode and radially symmetric.

The Gaussian bivariate kernel is based on the standard bivariate Normal distribution:

$$K(x_1, x_2) = (2\pi)^{-1} \exp\left(-\frac{x_1^2 + x_2^2}{2}\right).$$

This function is equal to the product of two standard Normal distributions (cf. 1.7). As such, the use of the multivariate Gaussian kernel or the product of two univariate Gaussian kernels yields the same results.

The bivariate Epanechnikov kernel is defined as follows:

$$K(x_1, x_2) = \begin{cases} 2\pi^{-1}(1 - x_1^2 - x_2^2) & \text{if} \quad x_1^2 + x_2^2 < 1 \\ 0 & \text{otherwise.} \end{cases}$$

This expression is not equal to the product of two univariate Epanechnikov distributions (cf. equation (1.8)). Consequently, the use of the multivariate Epanechnikov kernel or the product of two univariate Epanechnikov kernels does not produce the same results. It is only the bivariate Epanechnikov kernel which assigns a weight to points which diminish, in a symmetric and circular way, with the distance from the reference point. Panel (a) of Figure 1.11 depicts the contours of the product of two univariate Epanechnikov kernels, while panel (b) shows those from the bivariate Epanechnikov kernel. In the bivariate case, it is clear that all points on the same contour line are equidistant from the center. This is not the case for the product of two univariate Epanechnikov kernels.

The use of one single smoothing parameter h implies that we use the same value for the evaluation of the closeness to y_1 and to y_2. However, if the degree of dispersion of the data is very different in y_1 and y_2, it is preferable to appeal to two different smoothing parameters, h_1 and h_2. Panel (c) of Figure 1.11 shows the contours associated with a bivariate Epanechnikov kernel with two separate smoothing parameters,

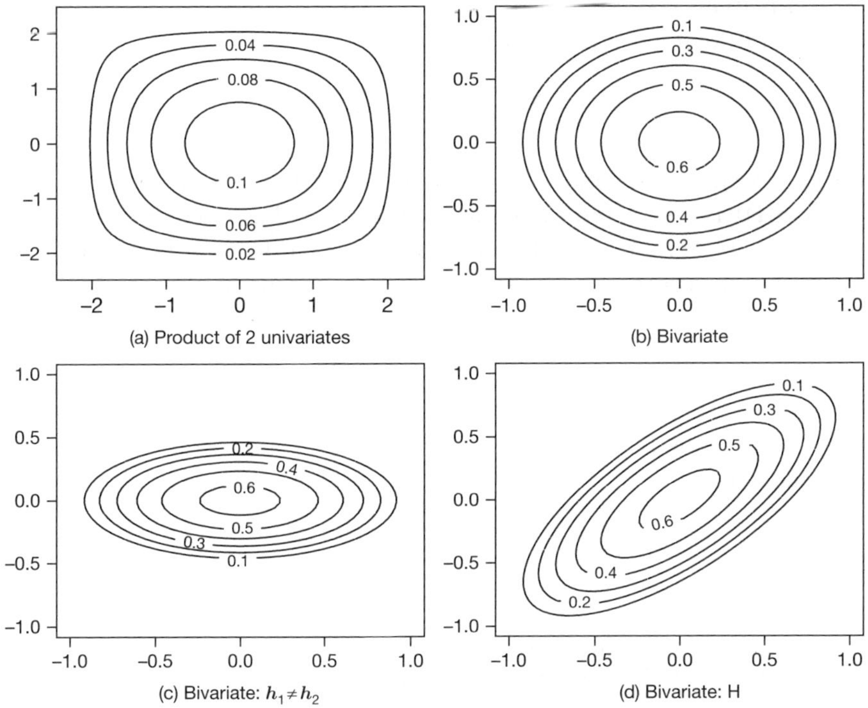

Figure 1.11: The bandwidth in the multivariate case with Epanechnikov kernels

$K(x_1/h_1, x_2/h_2)$ with $h_1 = 1, h_2 = 1/2$. The use of two separate smoothing parameters produces contours of the weighting function that are ellipses rather than concentric circles.

In addition, if the two variables in question are strongly correlated with each other, we can take this into consideration by using a matrix-smoothing parameter H,[8] with four elements:

$$\mathrm{H} = \begin{pmatrix} h_1 & h_{12} \\ h_{21} & h_2 \end{pmatrix},$$

where $h_{21} = h_{12}$. A smoothing parameter which is identical in all dimensions corresponds to $\mathrm{H} = h\mathcal{I}$, where $\mathcal{I}$ is the identity matrix, whereas the diagonal matrix $\mathrm{H} = \mathrm{diag}\{h_1, h_2\}$ corresponds to two distinct smoothing parameters. Panel (d) of Figure (1.11) depicts the contour lines associated with a bivariate Epanechnikov kernel with matrix smoothing containing off-diagonal elements $\mathrm{H} = \{1, \sqrt{1/2}; \sqrt{1/2}, 1\}$.[9] Taking correlation into account via the off-diagonal elements produces ellipses that are adjusted for the correlation between the two variables y_1 and y_2.

The extension to the d-dimensional case is immediate, via the use of multivariate kernels in d dimensions. We can thus write the general formula of the *multivariate kernel estimator*:

$$\hat{f}(\mathbf{y}) = \frac{1}{n} \sum_{i=1}^{n} \frac{1}{\det(\mathrm{H})} K\left(\mathrm{H}^{-1}(\mathbf{y} - \mathbf{y}_i)\right),$$

where $\mathbf{y}$ is a d-dimensional vector, consisting of the variables $y_1, y_2, \ldots, y_d$, and $\det(\mathrm{H})$ is the determinant of H.[10] For $d = 2$ and $\mathrm{H} = h\mathcal{I}$ we have the bivariate kernel estimator defined in equation (1.16). If $\mathbf{x}$ is a d-dimensional vector, the Gaussian kernel is based on the multivariate Normal distribution:

$$K(\mathbf{x}) = (2\pi)^{-d/2} \exp\left(-\frac{\mathbf{x}^\top \mathbf{x}}{2}\right).$$

The Epanechnikov kernel is based on the following multivariate distribution:

$$K(\mathbf{x}) = \begin{cases} (2c_d)^{-1}(d+2)(1 - \mathbf{x}^\top \mathbf{x}) & \text{if} \quad \mathbf{x}^\top \mathbf{x} < 1 \\ 0 & \text{otherwise,} \end{cases} \tag{1.17}$$

[8] The matrix H is symmetric and positive definite.

[9] The figure shows $K(\mathrm{H}^{-1}\mathbf{x})$ based on the multivariate Epanechnikov kernel, defined in (1.17).

[10] H is symmetric positive definite and thus its determinant is strictly positive.

where c_d is the volume of the unit sphere of dimension d ($c_1 = 2, c_2 = \pi, c_3 = 4\pi/3$).

The choice of the smoothing parameter is more complex in the multivariate case. This is so in particular as the visual evaluation of different parameter values becomes considerably more difficult in more than two dimensions. Above two dimensions, the choice of smoothing parameters is thus determined by automatic selection rules. These can be developed as natural extensions of those in the univariate case. The plug-in and cross-validation methods are based on kernel estimations of the density, and their extension to the multivariate case is immediate with the use of multivariate kernels. Their use becomes nonetheless more complex as it requires the calculation of the derivatives of multivariate distributions and a great deal of numerical calculation. It is also possible to determine rules of thumb by appealing to a reference distribution, as we shall see below.

Taking the reference distribution to be multivariate Normal $N(\mu, \Sigma)$, where the covariance matrix is diagonal $\Sigma = \text{diag}(\sigma_1^2, \ldots, \sigma_d^2)$, we obtain an empirical rule of thumb that is as simple as that in the univariate case. The minimization of an approximation to the MISE produces an optimal bandwidth $\text{H} = \text{diag}(h_1, \ldots, h_d)$ as follows:

$$h_j = \left(\frac{4}{d+2}\right)^{\frac{1}{d+4}} n^{-\frac{1}{d+4}} \sigma_j, \tag{1.18}$$

where $j = 1, \ldots, d$. With $d = 1$ we reproduce Silverman's rule defined by (1.10). Scott (1992) notes that the first element of this equation always takes on values between 0.924 and 1.059, and proposes the following *rule of thumb*:

$$\hat{h}_j = n^{-\frac{1}{d+4}} \hat{\sigma}_j,$$

where $\hat{\sigma}_j$ are the standard deviations calculated from the data. The same analysis cannot be carried out to yield a rule of thumb in the case of a covariance matrix with non-zero off-diagonal elements in the reference distribution. Nonetheless, equation (1.18) suggests that H is proportional to $\Sigma^{1/2}$. We can thus generalize *Scott's rule of thumb*, by considering:

$$\hat{\text{H}} = n^{-\frac{1}{d+4}} \hat{\Sigma}^{1/2}.$$

The empirical application of this rule is analogous to: (1) transforming the data such that their covariance matrix is the identity matrix; (2) estimating the density with a sole smoothing parameter of $h = n^{-1/(d+4)}$; and (3) transforming the estimated density to bring it back to the original scale. This prior transformation of the data is simple and very useful for the practical estimation of a multivariate density. It allows us to use a single smoothing parameter in the estimation of the density, while taking into account the different concentrations of the data across the dimensions and any correlation between the variables.

1.6.2 *The Curse of Dimensionality*

The expression *curse of dimensionality* refers to the fact that the number of observations required to guarantee a certain degree of reliability rises explosively with the number of dimensions. In other words, the convergence of the density estimator to the true function is much slower as the number of dimensions rises. In practice, the number of observations required for the satisfactory estimation of a multivariate density of more than two dimensions is enormous, and often exceeds the number of observations that are available.

We can illustrate this problem by considering a heterogeneous population of men and women. The number of men in this population is greater than the number of men who are aged around 35. This latter is equally (much) greater than the number of men aged around 35 who play sport, are around 1.80 meters tall, earn more than 80,000 euros per year, and have an IQ greater than average. To simplify matters, we call this latter group the "Prince Charmings". It is obvious that, as we increase the number of characteristics (dimensions), the fewer observations we will find that are close to the reference point. To obtain a reliable estimate of the proportion of individuals with these different characteristics, we require a representative sample of the population, that contains a sufficient number of individuals with the required characteristics. To estimate the proportion of the "Prince Charmings", we thus require a sample that is much larger than that we would need to estimate the proportion of men, if we require the same degree of precision. If the sample is too small, we may (erroneously) conclude that there are actually no "Prince Charmings".

More formally, Silverman (1986) has calculated the number of observations necessary for a Gaussian kernel to produce estimations of the same quality, evaluated at the single point of zero, when the true density is a standard Normal distribution. As the estimation is evaluated at a single point, the quality criterion used is the fact that the MSE should be less than 0.1. The number of observations required to produce the same quality of estimation, as a function of the number of dimensions,

Table 1.1: Number of observations required to produce the same quality of estimation

Number of dimensions	Number of observations required
1	4
2	19
3	67
4	223
5	768
6	2,790
7	10,700
8	43,700
9	187,000
10	842,000

Source: Silverman (1986).

is given in Table 1.1. The numbers in this table speak for themselves. Only four observations are required in the univariate case, whereas five times more are necessary in the bivariate case, almost 17 times more in three dimensions, and almost a million observations once we reach ten dimensions. These results apply to the case of estimation at a single point, zero, which corresponds to the center of the distribution. We are thus in the best of all possible worlds, in the sense that we have a greater number of observations at the center of the distribution than at its ends, but also in the sense that the Normal distribution is unimodal and homogeneous.[11] In other words, the figures given in Table 1.1 would need to be even higher for the estimation of the density in the tails of the distribution, or if the distribution were to be less homogeneous than the Normal distribution.

The curse of dimensionality is the most serious problem of non-parametric estimation methods. The estimation of a univariate density already requires a substantial number of observations to ensure satisfactory estimation at every point of the distribution. To produce the same quality, the estimation of a bivariate density requires a much larger number of observations. Beyond three dimensions, the number of observations required for reliable estimation is so large that non-parametric estimation is almost never used in empirical applications.

[11] The graph of the Normal density function is bell-shaped, with a peak at the mean.

2

Kernel Regression

2.1 Introduction

In this chapter we will consider the estimation of a regression model with two variables. In parametric econometrics, the relationship between the dependent variable and the explanatory variable is specified via a parametric form. Various different functional forms can be used, and there is no general rule for the choice of one particular form over another. For example, logarithmic transformations of one or more variables are often used, as are power functions and interactions between the regressors, in order to take possible non-linear relationships into account. If the model specification used is appropriate, the parametric approach produces impressive results. However, if the specification is incorrect, the estimation and test results will be erroneous. This is the classic problem of a mis-specified regression model. As such, it is useful to be able to appeal to methods which approximate the relationship between the variables without having to impose any parametric specification. This is precisely what non-parametric methods do.

Non-parametric econometrics allows us to determine the nature of the relationship between y and x, but without having to make any *a priori* hypotheses regarding the specification. Consider the non-parametric regression below:

$$y = m(x) + \varepsilon, \tag{2.1}$$

where y is the dependent variable, x is the explanatory variable and ε an error term. In this model, the function $m(.)$ specifies the relationship between the two variables, and it is this function that is estimated. As it does not make any *a priori* hypotheses regarding the form of function $m(.)$, the non-parametric approach is robust to any error in the specification of the model. Nonetheless, the advantage of this robustness comes at the cost of less precise estimation than that which would pertain from a parametric approach, given that the latter is correctly specified. We here find again the classic trade-off in econometrics between estimation robustness and efficiency. In addition, one advantage of the parametric approach is that all of the information is summarized in the model parameters, which can often be given an economic interpretation. In non-parametric estimation, the formulation of the relationship is not given by any algebraic formula, and is most often presented as a graphical representation. The interpretation of the results can be more difficult to set out, and cannot be summarized by only a small number of parameters. As such, as far as it is possible, the appropriate use of non-parametric techniques is to reveal the relationship between two variables, and from this to infer the fitting parametric relationship.

To illustrate the non-parametric estimation of a regression model, we consider the specification of the relationship between earnings and labor-market experience. The labor-economics literature often suggests modeling this relationship in the following way:

$$\log(\text{Earnings}) = \alpha + \beta\,\text{Education} + \gamma\,\text{Experience} + \delta\,(\text{Experience})^2 + \varepsilon, \quad (2.2)$$

where the "Education" variable corresponds to the number of years of education, and the "Experience" variable to the number of years of labor-force experience (Mincer, 1974). At a given level of education, the relationship between the log of earnings and experience is concave and quadratic, if $\gamma > 0$ and $\delta < 0$. This reflects that earnings rise with labor-force experience, but at a decreasing rate until they reach a peak, beyond which they start to decline.

If we consider individuals who have the same level of education, then the "Education" variable is a constant and will no longer appear in the regression (2.2). This allows us to examine the following non-parametric model:

$$\log(\text{Earnings}) = m(\text{Experience}) + \varepsilon. \quad (2.3)$$

Figure 2.1 shows the results of a non-parametric estimation of the function $m(.)$ using the kernel method, for working men with the general baccalaureate as their highest-achieved qualification.[1] The data here come from the 1998 Labour Force Survey conducted by the French National

[1] Earnings here are monthly, and experience is calculated by subtracting the age at which the individuals finish their education from their current age.

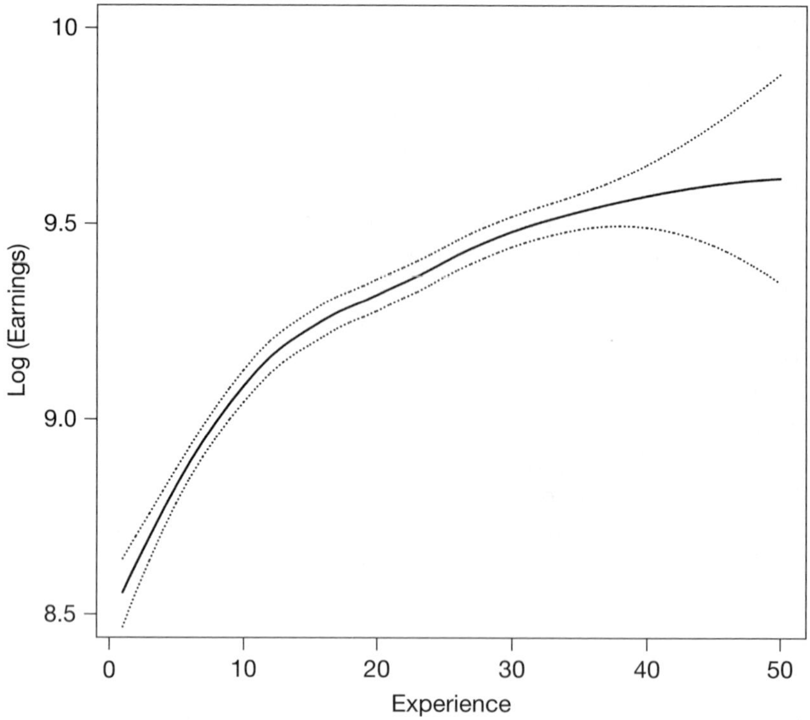

Figure 2.1: An earnings equation

Institute for Statistics and Economic Studies (INSEE). The 95% confidence intervals in this figure are represented by dotted lines. The graph suggests a relationship in three parts: up to just over ten years of experience, there is a strong linear relationship with earnings; then, up to around 35 years of experience, there is another linear relationship, but this time much less strong; last, beyond 35 years, there is no significant positive or negative relationship. In other words, the effect of experience on earnings is largest during the first ten years, and no visible effect is found for experience beyond 35 years. The results shown in this figure thus suggest that a concave function, which can be specified by the addition of a squared term in equation (2.2), is perhaps not particularly appropriate.

A better parametric specification might be obtained via the use of a higher-degree polynomial. For example, we could consider a quartic model, which consists in adding experience terms to the power three and four to model (2.2). In this dataset, quartic estimation produces predicted

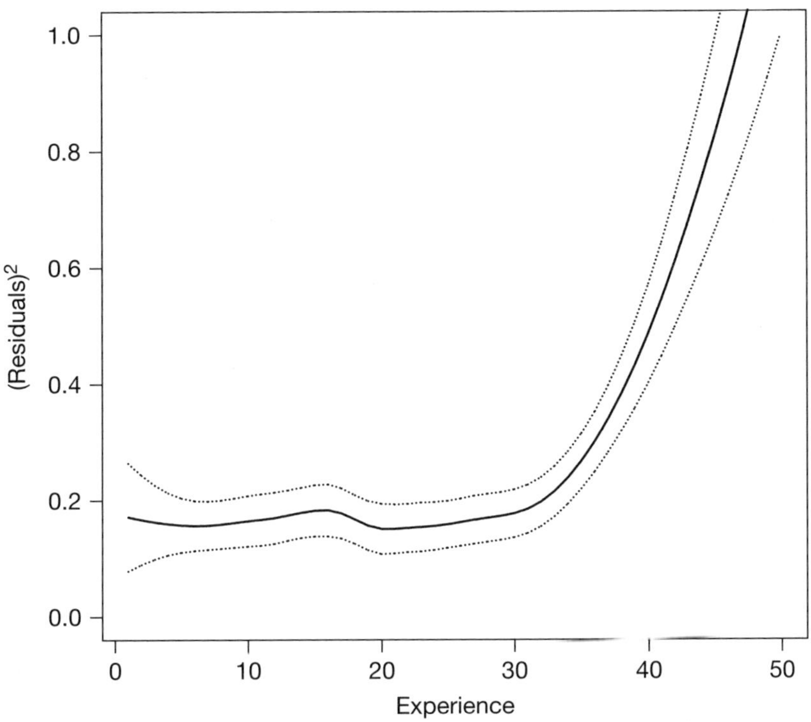

Figure 2.2: Heteroskedasticity

values that are very close to those resulting from the non-parametric estimation, despite the fact that the estimated coefficients on the two new regressors are not significantly different from zero with student *t*-statistics.[2] This empirical result is consistent with those of Murphy and Welch (1990), who suggest that the quartic formulation is often the most appropriate. In their results, quadratic estimation of the relationship between earnings and experience is often inappropriate, and leads to considerable bias in the estimated parameters.

Non-parametric regressions can also be used to detect the presence of heteroskedasticity in a regression model. If we suppose that the gaps between earnings levels are not the same for different levels of experience, then the conditional variance of the error term is heteroskedastic. This

[2] This phenomenon reveals the presence of considerable collinearity, which comes from the addition to the model of various powers of the same variable which itself only takes on a relatively small number of discrete values. The regressors are thus strongly correlated between themselves, which renders the estimation of the associated parameters very imprecise.

heteroskedasticity can be detected by estimating the following equation in a non-parametric manner:

$$\hat{\varepsilon}^2 = g(\text{Experience}) + \eta,$$

where $\hat{\varepsilon}$ is the vector of errors from the model in (2.3) and η is white noise. If there is no heteroskedasticity, then the function $g(.)$ will be constant, represented graphically by a flat line. Figure 2.2 shows the results of the non-parametric estimation of the function $g(.)$ by the kernel method. The 95% confidence intervals are depicted by the dotted lines. For example, in Figure 2.2 the point g(10) = 0.163 indicates that the variance of earnings for all those with ten years of experience is 0.163. This graph does suggest that there is some heteroskedasticity in the model: the variance appears constant over the first 30 years of experience, but rises sharply thereafter. In other words, the gaps between earnings (at a given level of experience) are pretty much the same over the first 30 years of labor-market activity, but increase notably in the later years of activity.

Many different methods have been developed to estimate the non-parametric relationship between two variables. The method of Nadaraya and Watson is one of the most commonly employed. It was the revelation of a number of disadvantages of the Nadaraya-Watson estimator which led to the development of the method of local polynomials, which will be discussed below. Additional reading can be found in the work of Härdle (1989), Wand and Jones (1995), Fan and Gijbel (1996), Loader (1999b), Pagan and Ullah (1999), and Li and Racine (2006).

The sections below present the estimation of regressions by local polynomials. Section 2.2 first considers the kernel estimator of Nadaraya and Watson, and then section 2.3 discusses the drawbacks of this estimator, and considers estimators that are locally linear or quadratic. The choice of the smoothing parameter appears in section 2.4, and the calculation of confidence intervals and statistical tests are discussed in section 2.5.

2.2 The Nadaraya-Watson Estimator

In the non-parametric regression model (2.1), the function $m(.)$ characterizes the conditional expectation of y given x. If the hypothesis $E(\varepsilon|x) = 0$ holds, we can rewrite this model as follows:

$$E(y|x) = m(x).$$

If both y and x come from a bivariate Normal distribution, then the mean of the conditional density of y given x is $E(y|x) = \alpha + \beta x$, with

$\alpha = \bar{y} - \bar{x}\beta$ and $\beta = \text{cov}(x, y)/\text{var}(x)$, where $\bar{y}$ and $\bar{x}$ are the means of y and x, respectively. In other words, the linear model and estimation by Ordinary Least Squares (OLS) yield the best unbiased estimator. However, if the joint distribution of y and x is not bivariate Normal, this linear specification of the conditional expectation is no longer necessarily appropriate, and the OLS estimator may be biased and inconsistent. Non-parametric econometrics proposes the direct estimation of the function $m(.)$, without making any *a priori* assumptions about the functional form. With the objective of estimating the conditional expectation of y given x, a number of different approaches—both intuitive and formal—lead to the non-parametric estimator proposed by Nadaraya (1964) and Watson (1964). This estimator falls within the framework of the kernel estimation of a density, discussed in section 1.3, and can be viewed as an extension of the latter to a simple regression setting.

2.2.1 *From the Discrete to the Continuous Case*

We first consider that x is a discrete variable, taking on only a few different values. The estimation of the conditional expectation of y given x can be carried out simply by keeping the observations for a given value of x and calculating the corresponding average value of y. If y is earnings, for example, and x is a male/female dummy variable, we calculate the average earnings of men for one value of x and that of women for the other. It is, however, clear that this approach is fairly limited. In particular, it cannot be used when x is continuous or takes on a great number of distinct values: in this case, to have sufficient observations for each value of x, we would require an extremely large dataset.

If x is continuous or takes on many distinct values, it is possible to calculate a *naive estimator*, the principle of which is to calculate the mean value of y for values of x which are "close" to the reference value. Given a sample (y_i, x_i), with $i = 1, \ldots n$, observation x_i is defined as being close to the reference value of x if it is situated at a distance of less than $h/2$ away, where h is a constant. The number of observations that are close to x is thus given by

$$n^* = \sum_{i=1}^{n} I\left(-\frac{h}{2} < x - x_i < \frac{h}{2}\right).$$

The naive estimator of $m(x)$ is defined as follows:

$$\hat{m}(x) = \frac{\sum_{i=1}^{n} I\left(-\frac{1}{2} < \frac{x-x_i}{h} < \frac{1}{2}\right) y_i}{\sum_{i=1}^{n} I\left(-\frac{1}{2} < \frac{x-x_i}{h} < \frac{1}{2}\right)}.$$

This consists in calculating the sum of the y_i's, keeping only observations for which the values of x_i are close to x. The same weight of $1/n^*$ is assigned to all of these observations.

This estimator is consistent if h falls to zero as the size of the sample rises. As Section 1.3 noted for the case of the density, the function $m(.)$ is discontinuous due to the use of the indicator function $I(.)$: this latter assigns a weight of 1 to all observations with a value of x_i which is sufficiently close to x, and a weight of zero to all other observations. Consequently, two observations that are very close to each other may have very different weights if they are situated at opposite sides of one bound of the $(x - h/2, x + h/2)$ interval. Rather than giving the same weight to all of the observations in the same interval, a kernel method can be used, consisting in assigning a weight which is larger the closer the observation is to x.

The Nadaraya-Watson estimator consists in calculating the weighted average of the y_i's, assigning a weight that is larger the closer is x_i to x. This implies the replacement of the indicator function in the naive estimator by a kernel function $K(.)$:

$$\hat{m}(x) = \frac{\sum_{i=1}^{n} K\left(\frac{x-x_i}{h}\right) y_i}{\sum_{i=1}^{n} K\left(\frac{x-x_i}{h}\right)}. \tag{2.4}$$

This estimator produces an approximation of $m(.)$, producing a smoothed graphical representation. Any kind of probability density function can be used for the kernel. Gaussian and Epanechnikov kernels are commonly used. These kernels are discussed in Section 1.3. The Nadaraya-Watson estimator depends on the choice of the kernel and of the smoothing parameter, h. As in the case of the density, the choice of kernel has relatively little impact, producing very similar results in many cases. On the contrary, the results are sensitive to the choice of bandwidth, and a number of optimal choice-methods have been developed in this respect, which we shall discuss below. Note that for the choice of $h = \infty$, the Nadaraya-Watson is the sample mean $\hat{m}(x) = n^{-1} \sum_{i=1}^{n} y_i$. At the other extreme, $h = 0$, the estimator is $\hat{m}(x_i) = y_i$.

The Nadaraya-Watson estimator can be written as below:

$$\hat{m}(x) = \sum_{i=1}^{n} w_i(x)\, y_i, \qquad \text{where} \qquad w_i(x) = \frac{K(\frac{x-x_i}{h})}{\sum_{i=1}^{n} K(\frac{x-x_i}{h})}.$$

This can also be considered as the weighted sum of all of the y_i's, with weights that depend on the distance of the individual x_i's from the point x under consideration. The choices of kernel and bandwidth h determine the points close to the reference point x which are taken into account for the calculation of the conditional mean.

2.2.2 *Formal Derivation*

It is possible to derive the Nadaraya-Watson estimator more formally, using the definition of a conditional expectation:

$$E(y|x) = \int_{-\infty}^{+\infty} y\, f(y|x)\, dy.$$

In the preceding chapter, we considered the estimation of a probability density via non-parametric methods. The idea developed here consists in rewriting the equation above in terms of unconditional densities, so that we can appeal directly to non-parametric density estimation methods. By definition, we know that a conditional density is the ratio of a joint density and a marginal density: $f(y|x) = f(x, y)/f(x)$. Given that $f(x) = \int_{-\infty}^{+\infty} f(x, y)dy$, we can rewrite the equation above as:

$$E(y|x) = \int_{-\infty}^{+\infty} \frac{y\, f(x, y)}{f(x)}\, dy = \frac{\int_{-\infty}^{+\infty} y\, f(x, y)dy}{\int_{-\infty}^{+\infty} f(x, y)dy}. \tag{2.5}$$

This conditional expectation can be estimated if we have an estimator of the joint density of x and y. The bivariate kernel estimator, discussed in (1.16), can be used to this end.

We now show that, if we use the product of two univariate kernels (1.15) rather than a bivariate kernel (1.16) to estimate the joint density, the estimator of (2.5) corresponds to the Nadaraya-Watson estimator presented in (2.4). Consider the estimation of the joint density by the product of two univariate kernels:

$$\hat{f}(x, y) = \frac{1}{nh^2} \sum_{i=1}^{n} K\left(\frac{x - x_i}{h}\right) K\left(\frac{y - y_i}{h}\right).$$

If we use this latter to estimate equation (2.5), we have:

$$\int_{-\infty}^{+\infty} \hat{f}(x, y)dy = \frac{1}{nh^2} \sum_{i=1}^{n} \left[K\left(\frac{x - x_i}{h}\right)\right] \underbrace{\left[\int_{-\infty}^{+\infty} K\left(\frac{y - y_i}{h}\right) dy\right]}_{=1}. \tag{2.6}$$

The second term in square brackets equals 1, as the kernel function has the same properties as a probability density function (see (1.6)). With respect to the numerator, we have:

$$\int_{-\infty}^{+\infty} y\hat{f}(x,y)dy = \frac{1}{nh^2}\sum_{i=1}^{n}\left[K\left(\frac{x-x_i}{h}\right)\right]\underbrace{\left[\int_{-\infty}^{+\infty} yK\left(\frac{y-y_i}{h}\right)dy\right]}_{=y_i}.$$

The second term in square brackets here is the expected value of the kernel function, which is a symmetric probability density function, centered around y_i and with variance of h^2. This term thus equals y_i. It is thus obvious that the ratio of these two terms gives the Nadaraya-Watson estimator defined in (2.4). This result can equally be shown in the case where the estimator of the joint density is calculated via a *symmetric* bivariate kernel (see Pagan and Ullah 1999).

The denominator of the Nadaraya-Watson estimator is an estimator of $f(x)$ (see (2.5) and (2.6)). The Nadaraya-Watson estimator thus cannot be calculated for all of the values of x for which $f(x) = 0$. The regression estimation will equally be very imprecise when carried out at points for which $f(x)$ is close to 0. As such, the Nadaraya-Watson estimator can only be usefully evaluated for x values where the density $f(x)$ is sufficiently large. It cannot therefore be used to predict out of sample values of x, contrary to parametric estimators.

2.3 Local Polynomials

Regression estimation via local polynomials is based on a local approximation to a polynomial. The Nadaraya-Watson estimator assumes that the regression function is locally constant (polynomial of order 0). The idea of the local linear estimator is to fit locally a straight line (polynomial of order 1), and not the constant. Instead of fitting locally linear functions, one can fit quadratic functions (polynomial of order 2); this is the idea of the local quadratic estimator. We shall see below that this extension to polynomials of order 1 and 2 allows us to avoid two potential sources of bias that are inherent in the Nadaraya-Watson estimator.

2.3.1 *Local Linear Estimators*

A first source of bias in the Nadaraya-Watson estimator comes from the unequal spacing of observations in the sample. To show this, we consider a simplified case: the function $m(.)$ is a straight line close to the point x_2, passing through five observations. Panel (a) of Figure 2.3 depicts a close-up of this function in the neighborhood of x_2. In the first instance, we ignore the observations (y_A, x_A) and (y_B, x_B) in this figure. The Nadaraya-Watson regression estimator evaluated at x_2 is a weighted sum of y_1, y_2, and y_3. As the points x_1 and x_3 are equidistant from x_2, the kernel function assigns an equal weight to y_1 and y_3. The largest weight is given to y_2. It follows that the weighted sum is given by $\hat{m}(x_2) = y_2$. The kernel estimator provides a good estimation of the regression at x_2. We now introduce the points (y_A, x_A) and (y_B, x_B) so that five points are now taken into consideration in the calculation of the weighted mean, which are now no longer equidistant. The observation y_2 remains that with the largest weight, and y_1 and y_3 still have identical weights. The "new" observations y_A and y_B have positive weights. As both of these values are larger than y_2, the weighted mean of the five points will also be larger than y_2. In other words, the kernel estimator is positively biased, as $\hat{m}(x_2) > y_2$.

This type of bias is likely to be particularly important when we estimate the regression at the extremities of the distribution. If we evaluate the regression at the point x_{min}, the smallest observation in the sample, the weighted mean of the points in the neighborhood of x_{min} will only include points y_i which are all larger than y_{min} if the regression line is positive, or all smaller if the regression line is negative. The Nadaraya-Watson estimator is thus biased. Analogously, the same nature of bias holds when we evaluate the regression at the largest point in the sample, x_{max}.

This bias, which is due to the unequal spacing of observations, can be eliminated by adopting a different approach to that taken by Nadaraya and Watson. Considering panel (a) of Figure 2.3, we can see that the

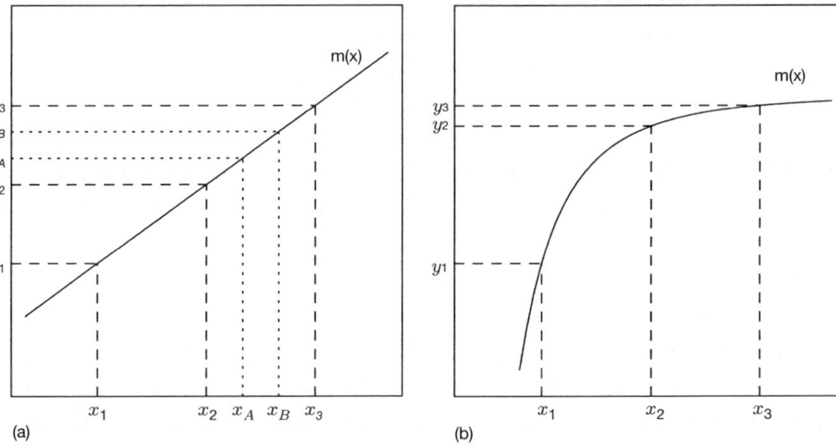

Figure 2.3: The limitations of the Nadaraya-Watson estimator

estimation by least squares of the linear regression $y_i = \alpha + \beta x_i + \varepsilon_i$, from which we can calculate the predicted value $\hat{y}_2 = \hat{\alpha} + \hat{\beta} x_2$, yields $\hat{y}_2 = y_2$. The estimation of $m(x_2)$ in this way does not suffer from the bias described above. This allows us to define the principle of local linear estimation at the point x as follows: we estimate a linear regression via Ordinary Least Squares over the observations which are "close" to x, and then calculate the predicted value from this regression model at x. The weights are determined by the kernel function, and are larger the closer the observations are to x.

The local linear estimator evaluated at x corresponds to the estimate of the parameter α in the regression

$$y_i = \alpha + \beta\,(x_i - x) + \varepsilon_i,$$

obtained via Weighted Least Squares, with weights $K(\frac{x_i - x}{h})$. In other words, the estimator results from the minimization of the following function:

$$\underset{\alpha,\beta}{\text{Min}} \sum_{i=1}^{n} K(\tfrac{x_i - x}{h})\,[y_i - \alpha - \beta\,(x_i - x)]^2. \tag{2.7}$$

Using the principle of the estimation of a Weighted Least Squares model, the local linear estimator evaluated at x corresponds to the OLS estimate of the parameter α in the regression:

$$\sqrt{K(\tfrac{x_i - x}{h})}\,y_i = \alpha\sqrt{K(\tfrac{x_i - x}{h})} + \beta\sqrt{K(\tfrac{x_i - x}{h})}\,(x_i - x) + \varepsilon_i.$$

This estimation is carried out separately for each value of x for which we wish to obtain an estimate of $m(x)$. The local estimation of this regression corresponds to a local approximation of a polynomial of degree 1.

Note that the Nadaraya-Watson estimator corresponds to (2.7) with $\beta = 0$. Setting the first derivative of this function (with $\beta = 0$) equal to 0 yields (2.4). This thus corresponds to the OLS estimator of α in the above regression with $\beta = 0$. In other words, the Nadaraya-Watson estimator is based on a local approximation to a polynomial of degree 0.

2.3.2 *Local Quadratic Estimators*

The second potential source of bias in the Nadaraya-Watson estimator comes from any concavity or convexity in the $m(.)$ function. To illustrate this, we return to the simple case discussed previously, but with a $m(.)$ function which is concave in the region of the point x_2 and three equally spaced observations. Panel (b) of Figure 2.3 shows a close-up of this function in the region of x_2. The Nadaraya-Watson estimator of the regression evaluated at x_2 is the weighted mean of the values y_1, y_2, and y_3. In the calculation of this mean, the point y_2 has the largest weight, with y_1 and y_3 having equal, smaller, weights. As soon as there is any concavity in the $m(.)$ function, this weighted mean will be smaller than y_2. As such, the Nadaraya-Watson estimator produces a biased estimate of $m(x_2)$, with the estimate being too low in the case of concavity of $m(.)$. Analogously, the estimate is too high when $m(.)$ is convex. The estimator is unbiased only when $m(.)$ is linear.

This bias, which stems from the non-linearity of $m(.)$, can be reduced by using an approach similar to that in the local linear estimation described above. To take any local concavity or convexity of $m(.)$ into account, we can appeal to a local quadratic approximation rather than a local linear approximation. The principle of local quadratic estimation at the point x is as follows: we estimate a quadratic regression using Ordinary Least Squares over the observations which are "close" to x, and calculate the predicted value of the regression model at x. The weights are determined by the kernel function: these weights will be larger the closer the point is to x.

The local quadratic estimator evaluated at a point x corresponds to the Weighted Least Squares estimation of α in the regression below, with the weights $K(\frac{x_i-x}{h})$:

$$y_i = \alpha + \beta\,(x_i - x) + \gamma\,(x_i - x)^2 + \varepsilon_i.$$

In other words, the estimator results from the minimization of the following function:

$$\underset{\alpha,\beta,\gamma}{\text{Min}} \sum_{i=1}^{n} K(\tfrac{x_i-x}{h})\,[y_i - \alpha - \beta\,(x_i - x) - \gamma\,(x_i - x)^2]^2.$$

Using the principle of the estimation of a Weighted Least Squares model, the local quadratic estimator evaluated at x corresponds to the OLS estimate of the parameter α in the regression:

$$\sqrt{K(\tfrac{x_i-x}{h})}\,y_i = \alpha\sqrt{K(\tfrac{x_i-x}{h})} + \beta\sqrt{K(\tfrac{x_i-x}{h})}\,(x_i - x) + \gamma\sqrt{K(\tfrac{x_i-x}{h})}\,(x_i - x)^2 + \varepsilon_i.$$

This estimation is carried out separately for each value of x for which we wish to obtain an estimate of $m(x)$. The local estimation of this regression corresponds to a local approximation of a polynomial of degree 2.

For comparison purposes, panel (a) of Figure 2.4 depicts the estimates given by local polynomials of degrees zero, 1, and 2 of the earnings equation of Figure 2.1. The comparison of the Nadaraya-Watson estimator (degree 0) to the local linear estimator (degree 1) reveals a gap between the two that is larger towards the ends of the distribution. As such, the difference in the results from the two methods is the largest precisely at the points where the Nadaraya-Watson estimator performs poorly (see the preceding subsection). A comparison of the local linear estimator (degree 1) with the local quadratic estimator (degree 2) reveals a somewhat different degree of curvature. However, the difference between the two curves is not that large.

2.3.3 *Generalization and the Estimation of Derivatives*

The estimation of the derivatives of the regression function is often useful in empirical applications. For example, the effect of a change in x on the dependent variable is given by the first derivative of the regression function $m(x)$ (which is equivalent to the estimated coefficient on the explanatory variable in the simple linear model). The second derivative provides an indication of the curvature of the regression line. One natural approach to the calculation of these two values is to estimate $m(x)$ and then calculate the derivatives. If we suppose that h tends towards zero as the sample size rises, then the definitions of the first and second derivatives yield:

$$\hat{m}'(x) = \frac{1}{2h}\left[\hat{m}(x+h) - \hat{m}(x-h)\right]$$

and

$$\hat{m}''(x) = \frac{1}{(2h)^2}\left[\hat{m}(x+h) - 2\hat{m}(x) + \hat{m}(x-h)\right].$$

An alternative and more powerful method results from the reconsideration of estimation by local polynomials.

The extension of the estimation to local polynomials of higher degrees is carried out by adding additional terms to the function that is minimized:

$$\underset{\alpha,\beta,\gamma,\ldots,\delta}{\text{Min}} \sum_{i=1}^{n} K\left(\tfrac{x_i - x}{h}\right)\left[y_i - \alpha - \beta\,(x_i - x) - \gamma\,(x_i - x)^2 - \cdots - \delta(x_i - x)^p\right]^2.$$

One advantage of the local polynomial estimator is that it allows the simple evaluation of the derivatives of $m(x)$. To do so, it is useful to remark that the expression above can be obtained by replacing the function $m(x_i)$ in $\sum_{i=1}^{n} K(.)[y_i - m(x_i)]^2$ by a Taylor approximation:

$$m(x_i) \approx m(x) + m'(x)(x_i - x) + \frac{m''(x)}{2}(x_i - x)^2 + \cdots + \frac{m^{(p)}(x)}{p!}(x_i - x)^p,$$

for x_i in the neighborhood of x. This allows us to show that the derivatives of $m(x)$ can be written as a function of the estimated parameters from local polynomial estimation, as below:

$$m(x) = \alpha, \quad m'(x) = \beta, \quad m''(x) = 2\gamma, \ldots \text{and} \quad m^{(p)}(x) = p!\,\delta.$$

Hence, estimation by local polynomials produces direct estimates of the derivatives of the regression function from the estimated coefficients.

2.4 Bandwidth Selection

The previous chapter showed that the kernel estimation of a density was very sensitive to the choice of bandwidth or smoothing parameter (Section 1.4). It is therefore to be expected that the estimation of non-parametric regressions, which is based on kernel methods, is equally sensitive to this choice. As an illustration, panel (b) of Figure 2.4 represents the local quadratic estimator of the heteroskedastic earnings equation (see Figure 2.2), for different bandwidth values. With a smoothing parameter that is twice as large as the default value, the estimated function is smoother; when this parameter is half as large as the default value, the function is much less smooth. As the gaps between the curves can be considerable, the choice of this parameter is crucial.

For the estimation of a density, we were able to determine a satisfactory rule of thumb which enabled us to choose the smoothing parameter

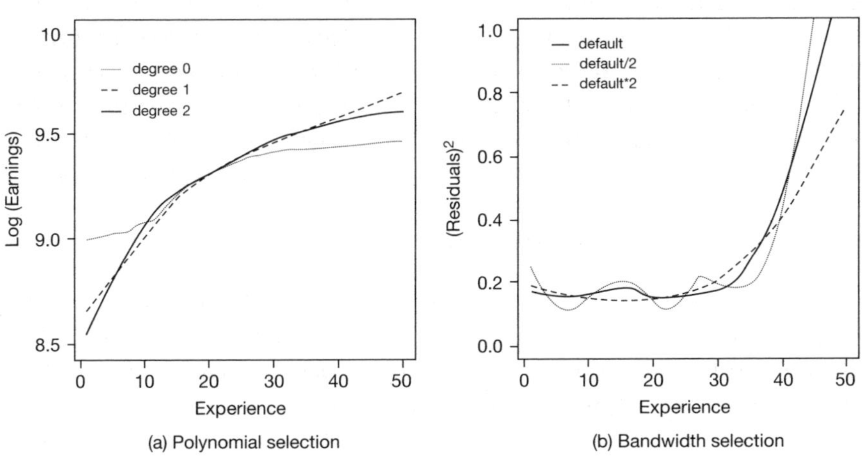

Figure 2.4: Sensitivity of local polynomial estimators

automatically. In this section, we will explain why this is no longer possible in the case of regression estimation. We then present an approach which produces satisfactory results based on the principle of cross-validation.

2.4.1 *Rule of Thumb*

The optimal bandwidth is that which produces an estimated regression function which is as close as possible to the true regression function. A number of different criteria can be applied to make this choice, including the mean integrated squared error:

$$\mathrm{MISE}(h) = E\left[\int [\hat{m}(x) - m(x)]^2 dx\right].$$

For the estimation of a density, we saw that the minimization of an approximation to this criterion produced an optimal value of h which depends on the true density. Silverman proposed a rule of thumb which replaces this unknown function by the Normal distribution. The plug-in method has also been suggested, which consists in replacing the true density by an initial non-parametric estimate, based on Silverman's rule of thumb: see Section 1.4 for a detailed discussion.

In the case of the estimation of a regression function, the minimization of an approximation to this criterion produces the following optimal value of h:

$$h_{opt} = c\, n^{-1/5}.$$

This expression is proportional to $n^{-1/5}$, with a constant c which depends on a number of unknown quantities, including the true density of x and the true regression function. Even if we choose the Normal distribution as the reference distribution instead of the density of x, it is much more difficult to replace the regression function $m(x)$ by an appropriate reference function. It is for this reason that there is no rule of thumb as simple and as powerful as that which exists in the case of the estimation of a density.

2.4.2 *Cross-validation*

The cross-validation method proposes the minimization of the following criterion as a way of choosing the appropriate bandwidth:

$$\mathrm{CV}(h) = \frac{1}{n}\sum_{i=1}^{n} [y_i - \hat{m}_{-i}(x_i)]^2, \tag{2.8}$$

where $\hat{m}_{-i}(.)$ is the regression function estimated over the sample of all of the observations except x_i. This is a criterion similar to that of Ordinary Least Squares, which selects the parameter values which minimize the sum of squares of the residuals. However, in order for this criterion to apply to the automatic selection of h, we have to estimate the regression function at x_i while removing the observation x_i from the sample. If we do not remove this observation, then the criterion is always minimized at $h = 0$, as in this case we have $\hat{m}(x_i) = y_i$ if the values $x_1, \ldots, x_n$ are all distinct from each other.

Experience teaches us that it is unwise to blindly follow any one method of automatic bandwidth selection. Even though the cross-validation method often leads to good results, it does sometimes produce very inappropriate smoothing values. As far as is possible, it is advisable to resort to the graphical representation of the regression functions corresponding to different values of h. Visual inspection is often an extremely useful tool in avoiding inappropriate solutions.

2.5 Confidence Intervals and Statistical Tests

In order to calculate a confidence interval or the critical value of a test statistic, we need to know the probability distribution of the estimator or the test statistic in question. In general, this latter distribution is unknown in finite samples, and we fall back on an approximation to it. While it is possible to use asymptotic arguments in the non-parametric case, these are often poor approximations to the true distribution, and it is preferable to use bootstrap methods, which give better results.

The underlying principle of the bootstrap method is relatively simple. In empirical work, econometric analysis determines a regression model, and it is supposed in general that this model is correctly specified. This latter supposition signifies that the true mechanism which generated the data, with specific parameter values and unknown distributions, is that specified in the regression model. The objective of econometric analysis is to provide the best possible estimate of this underlying mechanism. Bootstrap analysis consists in constructing an artificial Data Generating Process (the *bootstrap DGP*), replacing the parameters and the unknown distributions in the model by their empirical estimates. The distribution of the test statistic derived from this artificial process is used as an approximation to the true statistical distribution. This *bootstrap distribution* is often obtained by simulations, and is used to calculate confidence intervals and critical values for statistical tests. If the bootstrap DGP is sufficiently close to the true mechanism which generated the observed data, then the data generated by the bootstrap DGP will equally be similar to the observed data. Also, the critical values calculated from bootstrap data will be close to those which pertain in the true distribution, so that inference is reliable. The following articles provide a useful introduction to bootstrap methods: Horowitz (2000), MacKinnon (2002), Davidson and MacKinnon (2006), as well as the textbooks by Efron and Tibshirani (1993), Davison and Hinkley (1997), and Chernick (2007).

In this section, we first analyze confidence intervals, before considering the question of testing parametric against non-parametric models.

2.5.1 *Confidence Intervals*

Once we have obtained an estimate of the regression function, a natural question that follows is how close this estimator is to the true regression function. One way of answering this question is to calculate confidence intervals around the estimated regression function.

Under certain regularity conditions, it is possible to show that the Nadaraya-Watson estimator of the $m(.)$ function is asymptotically Normally distributed:

$$\sqrt{hn}\,[\hat{m}(x) - m(x)] \rightarrow N\left(b, \frac{v\sigma_\varepsilon^2}{f(x)}\right),$$

where $f(x)$ is the marginal density of x, $v = \int K^2(u)du$ and σ_ε^2 is the variance of the error term. The coefficient b corresponds to the asymptotic bias of the non-parametric estimator, which depends on a number of unknown quantities:

$$b = \frac{wh^2}{2}\left(m''(x) + 2m'(x)\frac{f'(x)}{f(x)}\right),$$

where $w = \int u^2 K(u)du$. This relationship suggests that this bias is particularly large towards the extremities of the distribution ($f(x) \approx 0$) and where the function has the highest variance (greater values of $m''(x)$). The presence of this bias complicates the calculation of confidence intervals.

A first approach is to calculate confidence intervals which correct for this bias. To do so, we need to estimate m'', which can be undertaken via non-parametric kernel estimation (Härdle and Bowman, 1988). Two distinct smoothing parameters are then used: a first to estimate the m function, and a second to estimate its second derivative, m''. Nonetheless, even if m' can be estimated consistently, the choice of the appropriate smoothing parameter remains complicated.

A second approach is to use a smoothing parameter which is smaller than that proposed by the automatic choice methods. This use of a small h serves to under-smooth the function. As such, the bias is smaller but the variance is larger. For a small enough value of h, we can conclude that the bias is negligible compared to the variance, and can approximate the confidence interval via the following formula:

$$\hat{m}(x) \pm 1.96\sqrt{\frac{v\hat{\sigma}_{\varepsilon}^{2}}{nh\hat{f}(x)}},$$

where $\hat{f}(x)$ is the kernel estimator of the density of x and $\hat{\sigma}_{\varepsilon} = n^{-1}\sum_{i=1}^{n}(y_i - \hat{m}(x_i))^2$. This underlines that the appropriate choice of bandwidth is not determined in the same way for the estimation of the regression function as for the estimation of the associated confidence intervals.

A third approach, often used in practice, is to appeal to bootstrap techniques (Efron, 1979). This has the distinct advantage of providing reliable results in finite samples, and of automatically correcting for the bias without having to calculate the latter explicitly. A number of different ways of implementing the bootstrap have been proposed in the literature (Härdle and Bowman, 1988; Härdle and Marron, 1991; Neumann and Polzehl, 1998; Claeskens and Van Keilegom, 2003). However, the underlying principle is always the same: (1) an initial estimation is used to calculate the residuals; (2) these residuals are then used to generate new samples based on random draws (resampling); and (3) new estimations of the regression function result from the analysis of these newly generated samples. The set of estimates of the regression function allows us to measure the variation in the estimated values, and thus to calculate confidence intervals.

A bootstrap confidence interval can be obtained as follows:

1. Select an optimal smoothing parameter via cross-validation: h_{opt}.
2. Re-estimate the regression with a larger value for the smoothing parameter, so that the function is over-smoothed (ex: $h^{+} = 1.1\, h_{opt}$), and then save the new values: $\hat{m}_{h^{+}}(x)$.
3. Re-estimate the regression with a smaller value for the smoothing parameter, so that the function is under-smoothed (ex: $h^{-} = 0.9\, h_{opt}$), and then save the residuals: $\hat{\varepsilon}_i = y_i - \hat{m}_{h-}(x_i)$.

4. Generate a bootstrap sample from the data-generating process:

$$y_i^* = \hat{m}_{h^+}(x_i) + \hat{\varepsilon}_i \, \eta_i^*.$$

where η_i^* is a random draw from a probability distribution with zero mean and variance equal to 1.

5. Estimate the regression model over the bootstrap sample (y^*, x) with the optimal smoothing parameter h_{opt}, which yields the estimate $\hat{m}(x)^*$.

6. Repeat the two preceding stages many times. The 95 % confidence interval results from the calculation of the 0.025 and 0.975 quantiles of the empirical distribution of the values of $\hat{m}(x)^*$ (the bootstrap distribution). This approach is called the *percentile* method.

Note that the residuals are calculated from an under-smoothed estimation of the regression function, and are then added to an over-smoothed estimate of the regression function to produce the bootstrap sample. The under-smoothing is not essential, but does produce residuals from an estimation of the regression function where the bias is reduced (Yatchew, 2003). The over-smoothing is essential, as it ensures that the bias of the initial estimator and that from the bootstrap estimator are the same (Härdle and Marron, 1991). The method used here is that of the *wild* bootstrap (Wu, 1986; Beran, 1986; Liu, 1988), which is valid in the presence of heteroskedasticity in the errors of the regression model. The term η_i^* is a random draw from some distribution with zero mean and variance of 1; the results may be sensitive to the choice of this distribution, however. Two distributions are often used: that proposed by Mammen (1993),

$$\eta_i^* = \begin{cases} (1-\sqrt{5})/2 & \text{with probability} \quad p = (1+\sqrt{5})/(2\sqrt{5}) \\ (1+\sqrt{5})/2 & \text{with probability} \quad 1-p, \end{cases}$$

and that of Rademacher (Davidson and Flachaire, 2008; Flachaire, 2005a),

$$\eta_i^* = \begin{cases} +1 & \text{with probability} \quad 1/2 \\ -1 & \text{with probability} \quad 1/2. \end{cases}$$

Another method, called *percentile-t*, often produces more precise results. Rather than calculating a new estimation $\hat{m}(x)^*$ for each bootstrap sample, we instead calculate $t^* = [\hat{m}(x)^* - \hat{m}(x)]/\hat{s}(x)^*$, where $\hat{s}(x)^*$ is the estimated standard error of $\hat{m}(x)^*$. The bootstrap distribution of t^* is supposed to be an estimate of $t = [\hat{m}(x) - m(x)]/\hat{s}(x)$. The confidence interval includes the values of $m(x)$ such that $q_{.025} \leq t \leq q_{.975}$. Calculating these inequalities yields the following confidence interval:

$$[\hat{m}(x) - q_{.975}\,\hat{s}(x)\,;\,\hat{m}(x) - q_{.025}\,\hat{s}(x)],$$

where $q_{.025}$ and $q_{.975}$ are the 0.025 and 0.975 quantiles of the empirical distribution of t^* calculated for each sample. In this approach, the bootstrap distribution is an approximation to the distribution of t, which is an asymptotic pivot; that is, its asymptotic distribution does not depend on the unknown parameters and distributions of the regression model. In general, this property guarantees better results than those from the *percentile* approach, where the bootstrap distribution is an approximation to the distribution of $\hat{m}(x)$, which is not an asymptotic pivot (Beran, 1986).

2.5.2 *Parametric vs Non-parametric Models*

A correctly specified parametric model is always better than a non-parametric model, due to its superior estimation and inference properties. However, it is often difficult to justify any *a priori* choice of functional form for a parametric model. To help us to overcome this problem, non-parametric estimation is a useful tool to check whether a given parametric specification is appropriate. If we can show that the difference between a parametric and a non-parametric model is not statistically significant, then we can suppose the parametric model to be an appropriate one.

The graphical depiction of two estimators of a regression function often provides valuable information regarding the distance between them. We can construct a statistic to test this degree of conformity, with the following hypotheses:

$$H_0 : y = m(x, \beta) + \varepsilon \qquad \text{vs} \qquad H_1 : y \neq m(x, \beta) + \varepsilon,$$

where $m(x, \beta)$ is a known function which depends on a vector of unknown parameters β, and which specifies the parametric model. When the unconstrained model (H_1) is estimated non-parametrically, that is, without the *a priori* specification of a regression model, then the test will have the advantage of being robust to a mis-specification. As an illustration, consider that these tests concern the following hypotheses:

$$H_0 : y = \beta_0 + \beta_1 x + \varepsilon \qquad \text{vs} \qquad H_1 : y = \beta_0 + \beta_1 x + \beta_2 x^2 + \varepsilon,$$

while the real model is actually: $y = \beta_0 + \beta_1 x + \beta_3 x^3 + \varepsilon$. It is entirely possible that a parametric test statistic (a t-statistic) would not reject the null hypothesis ($\beta_2 = 0$), even though the model under this hypothesis is not the appropriate one. On the contrary, a test statistic based on the alternative $H_1 : y = m(x) + \varepsilon$ would likely reject the null hypothesis model.

We denote by $m(x, \hat{\beta})$ the predicted values from parametric estimation and $\hat{m}(x)$ the predicted values from non-parametric estimation of the regression. One measure of the distance between the two predicted values is given by the following criterion:

$$\int \left(\hat{m}(x) - m(x, \hat{\beta})\right)^2 dx.$$

This provides a measure of the distance between the two predicted values at every point. Härdle and Mammen (1993) note that the non-parametric estimator is biased, while the parametric estimator is not. They propose the use of an empirical version of this criterion, which introduces an artificial bias in the parametric element due to the replacement of $m(x, \hat{\beta})$ by

$$\hat{m}(x, \hat{\beta}) = \frac{\sum_{i=1}^{n} K(\frac{x-x_i}{h})\, m(x, \hat{\beta})}{\sum_{i=1}^{n} K(\frac{x-x_i}{h})}.$$

Härdle and Mammen (1993) then propose the following test statistic:

$$T_n = \sqrt{h} \sum_{i=1}^{n} \left(\hat{m}(x_i) - \hat{m}(x_i, \hat{\beta})\right)^2 \psi(x_i), \tag{2.9}$$

where $\psi(x_i)$ is a weighting function that is chosen by the econometrician, which controls for any heteroskedasticity (the areas where there are relatively few observations are given less weight). They show that this test statistic is asymptotically Normal, but that this latter is not a good approximation to the true distribution of the test statistic in finite samples. They thus recommend the use of *wild* bootstrap methods to calculate the critical values or the P-values.

A bootstrapped P-value can be obtained as follows:

1. Estimate the non-parametric regression model $\hat{m}(x)$, and the parametric regression $m(x, \hat{\beta})$, and calculate the T_n statistic (2.9).
2. Save the residuals from the parametric model: $\hat{\varepsilon}_i = y_i - m(x_i, \hat{\beta})$.
3. Generate a bootstrap sample from the following data-generation process:

$$y_i^* = m(x_i, \hat{\beta}) + \hat{\varepsilon}_i\, \eta_i^*,$$

which respects H_0, and where η_i^* is a random draw from a probability distribution with mean of zero and variance of 1.

4. Use this bootstrap sample to calculate a bootstrap test statistic T_n^*, in the same way as the initial statistic T_n.
5. Repeat the two preceding stages many times. The P-value is the percentage of the bootstrap statistics T_n^* which are greater than the value of the initial statistic T_n.

This *wild* bootstrap method is robust to heteroskedasticity in the error term of the regression model. As in the calculation of confidence intervals, η_i^* is a random draw from the distribution proposed by Mammen (1993) or from Rademacher's distribution.

Other methods have been proposed in the literature. More details on non-parametric regression models are provided in, for example, Härdle (1989), Yatchew (2003), Li and Racine (2006), as well as the articles cited in Hsiao et al. (2007) and Racine and Parmeter (2008).

3

Spline Regression

3.1 Introduction

One simple way of taking the non-linearity of a regression equation into account is to split the sample into a number of segments and then estimate a linear relationship for each of them. Spline regression is based on this principle, and can be seen as an extension of the linear model. Presented as such, this approach corresponds to piecewise linear regression, which can be estimated by Ordinary Least Squares. Piecewise regression takes non-linearity into account but does not guarantee the differentiability of the regression function at all points. The particularity of spline regression is to estimate polynomials rather than straight lines in each segment, chosen such that the estimated function is continuous and differentiable at the junctions of the polynomials. These junction points are called *knots*. The splines are defined such that the estimated function is smooth everywhere. The results of spline estimation are sensitive to the choice of the number of knots and their position. To minimize the influence of these choices on the results, we introduce a penalizing parameter: this is the case of penalized splines, which are the subject of this chapter.

Our first application is the estimation of a Phillips curve. The underlying idea of such a curve, which was widespread in the 1960s, was that it was possible to reduce the unemployment rate if we were prepared to accept higher inflation. To check whether this relationship holds empirically, we consider the following non-parametric model:

$$y = m(x) + \varepsilon, \tag{3.1}$$

where y is the inflation rate and x is the unemployment rate. The monthly American data run from January 1960 to March 1970, and are available

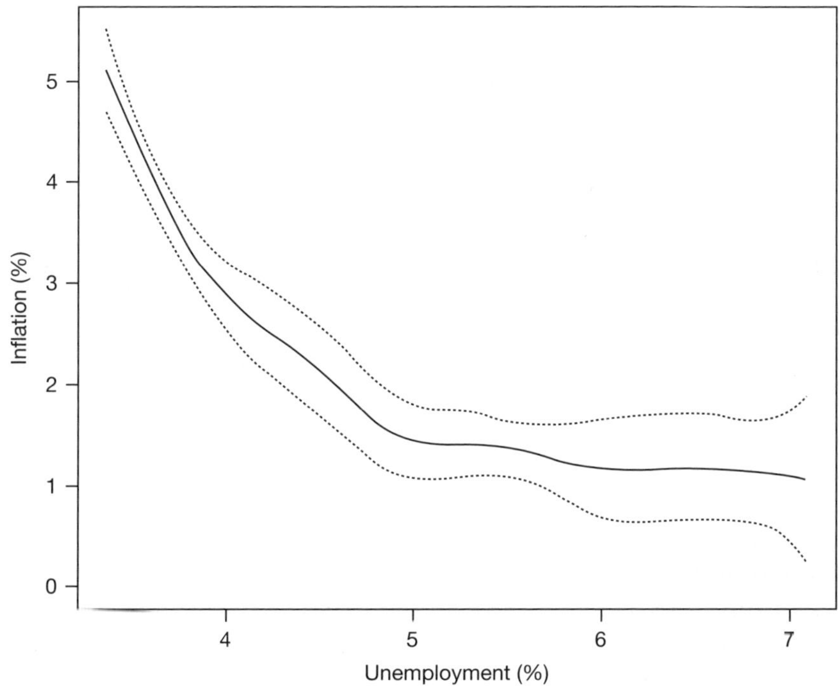

Figure 3.1: The Phillips curve: the unemployment–inflation trade-off

on the website of the Federal Reserve Bank of St Louis.[1] Figure 3.1 presents the regression results from penalized spline estimation of the relationship between unemployment and inflation, as well as the 95% confidence intervals. The estimation results are consistent with the results in Phillips (1958). First, we note that there is a negative relationship between unemployment and inflation. Moreover, this relationship is not linear, being much flatter when the unemployment rate is greater than 5% and much stronger when unemployment is under 4%. There does thus seem to be a trade-off between unemployment and inflation, which relationship was then somewhat challenged in the 1970s by the joint appearance of higher rates of both unemployment and inflation.

The second application concerns the relationship between short-term and long-term interest rates. The dynamics of interest rates of different terms has attracted a great deal of attention in finance. For a long time,

[1] The inflation rate here corresponds to the variable CPIAUCSL (Consumer Price Index For All Urban Consumers: All Items; *percentage change from one year ago*) and unemployment corresponds to the variable UNRATE (Civilian Unemployment Rate).

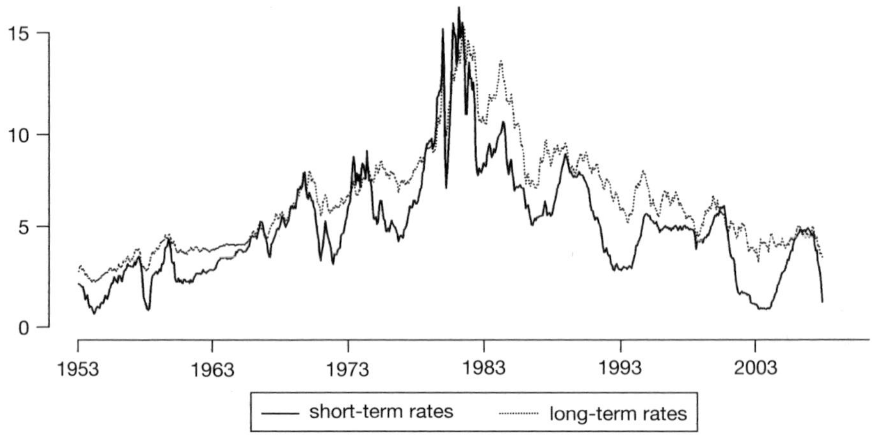

Figure 3.2: The dynamics of interest rates

the most widely used models in this literature were linear, such as AR, ARMA, or ARIMA.[2] The use of such models implies in particular that the relationship between short-term and long-term interest rates is linear.[3] On the contrary, empirical work has underlined the non-linearity of this relationship. For example, Figure 3.2 shows the monthly values of the short-term interest rate (3 months) and the long-term interest rate (10 years) in the USA, from April 1953 to March 2008.[4] This figure suggests that long-term rates are less responsive to short-term rates when these latter are higher. As noted by Pfann et al. (1996), the relation between the two rates is different when the short-term rate is higher and more volatile, that is, between 1979 and 1982. To represent this non-linearity, we estimate (3.1), with y being the long-term interest rate—corresponding to the returns on Government Bonds—and x being the short-term interest rate—reflecting the monetary policy of the Central Bank. Figure 3.3 shows the results of this penalized spline estimation and the associated 95% confidence intervals. The estimated relationship is non-linear, with the slope of the function being flatter for higher values of the short-term

[2] AR: autoregressive; ARMA: autoregressive moving average; ARIMA: autoregressive integrated moving average.

[3] The long-term interest rate y_t is modeled as a weighted average of agents' expectations of the short-term rate, $y_t = \frac{1-\alpha}{1-\alpha^n} \sum_{i=0}^{n-1} \alpha^i E_t(x_{t+i})$, where α is a discount rate and n is the long-term maturity. The term $E_t(x_{t+i})$ designates the expectation of the short-term rate expressed at date t for the future period $t+i$. For $i = 0$, we have $E_t(x_{t+i}) = x_t$. If expectations are based on a linear autoregressive model such as AR, ARMA, or ARIMA, then y_t is a linear function of x_t.

[4] These data come from the website of the Federal Reserve Bank of St Louis. The long-term interest rate is the GS10 variable (10-Year Treasury Constant Maturity Rate), and the short-term rate is the TB3MS variable (3-Month Treasury Bill: Secondary Market Rate).

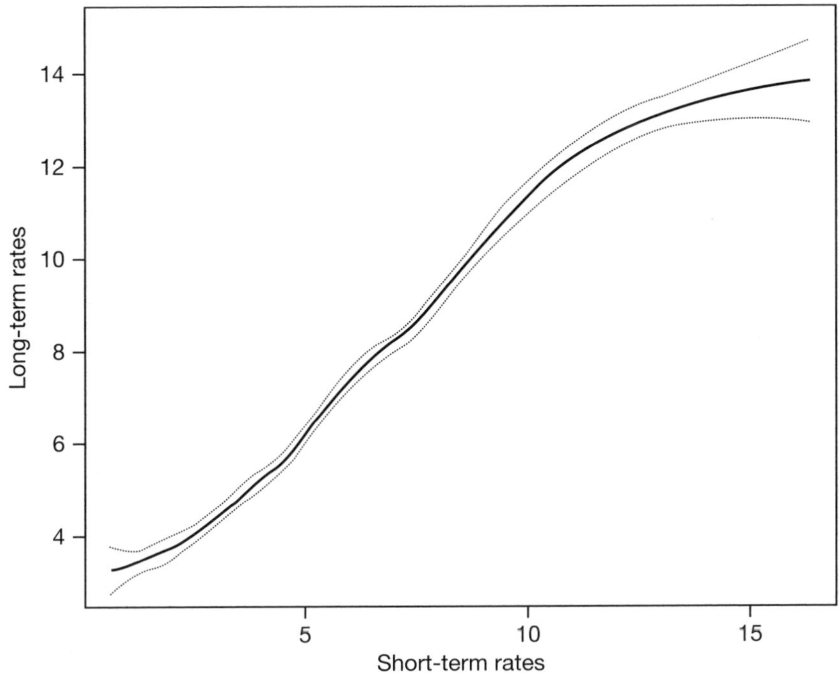

Figure 3.3: The relationship between short-term and long-term interest rates

interest rate. This is similar to the results in Pfann et al. (1996), which led them to use the SETAR model[5] in order to better capture the non-linear dynamics of the structure of interest rates.

In this chapter, we will present the non-parametric estimation of a simple regression model by the method of penalized splines, illustrated by the preceding examples. The first section will discuss splines as an extension of the linear model, and we will then introduce the concept of penalized splines. This will allow us to demonstrate that this is a projective estimation technique, which requires the use of a base. The following section then discusses the choice of an appropriate base. The last section presents the choice of parameters: the number and position of the knots, and the penalization parameter. Further reading on this topic can be found in, amongst others, the work of Wahba (1990), Green and Silverman (1993), Eubank (1999), Loader (1999b), de Boor (2001), Marsh and Cormier (2001), Gu (2002), and Ruppert et al. (2003).

[5] Self-Exciting Threshold AutoRegressive.

3.2 Principles

The first appealing property of splines is that they can be considered as piecewise polynomial estimators. The second is that it is possible to minimize the impact of a certain number of arbitrary choices, via penalized spline estimation. This section presents the principle of this non-parametric method.

3.2.1 *An Extension of the Linear Model*

To demonstrate the non-linearity of the relationship between short-term and long-term interest rates, Pfann et al. (1996) estimated the following piecewise linear model:

$$y = \beta_0 + \beta_1 x + \beta_2 (x - \kappa)_+ + \varepsilon, \tag{3.2}$$

where β_0, β_1, and β_2 are unknown parameters, ε an error term, and $(x - \kappa)_+$ a function which is equal to $x - \kappa$ if this expression is positive and 0 otherwise, with $\kappa = 10.8$.[6] This model produces two straight regression lines, which meet at κ, with different slopes. For values of x less than κ, the regression line has a slope of β_1; for values of x greater than κ, this slope is $\beta_1 + \beta_2$. Panel (a) of Figure 3.4 depicts the OLS estimation results of this model, which can be compared to those previously presented in Figure 3.3. The figure shows an estimated piecewise linear relationship. The estimated β_2 coefficient is statistically significant ($\hat{\beta}_2 = -0.42910$, standard error = 0.08958), implying that the slope of the second linear segment of the regression is significantly different from the slope of the first. This reflects the non-linearity of the relationship between the two variables.

From a geometric point of view, OLS estimation of a linear regression model is equivalent to an orthogonal projection of the dependent variable y in the space of the regressors. In other words, the regressors in the model (3.2) can be seen as representing a base, defined by the following functions:

$$\iota\,,\ x\,,\ (x - \kappa)_+,$$

where ι is the unit vector. Estimation is a projection on this base of functions, and the model parameters are the coordinates of y in this base. We thus refer to projective estimation methods over a pre-defined base.

[6] In their article, Pfann et al. (1996) use the same data as we used in the introduction to this chapter, but from January 1962 to June 1990.

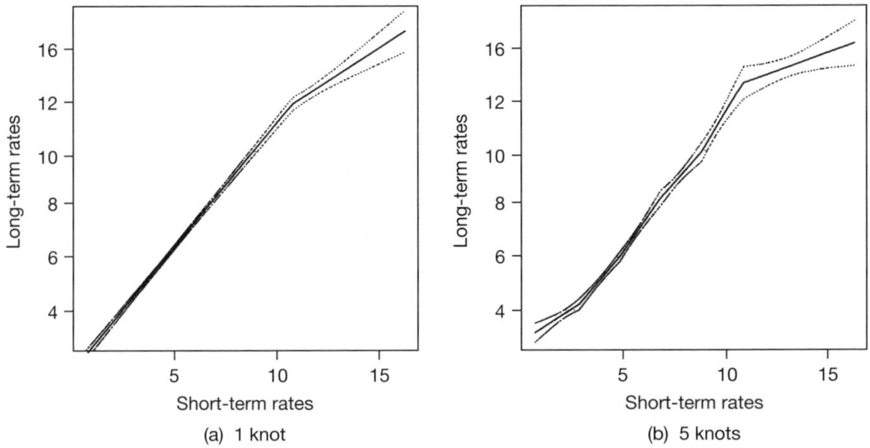

Figure 3.4: Piecewise linear models

The above regression model can be extended to include more than two segments, by choosing the number of junction points or knots beforehand. For the prior choice of q knots, the base is defined by the following functions:

$$\iota,\ x,\ (x-\kappa_1)_+,\ (x-\kappa_2)_+,\ldots,\ (x-\kappa_q)_+. \tag{3.3}$$

The projection of y over this base of functions is equivalent to estimating the following piecewise linear model:

$$y = \beta_0 + \beta_1\, x + \sum_{j=1}^{q} \beta_{1j}\,(x-\kappa_j)_+ + \varepsilon. \tag{3.4}$$

Panel (b) of Figure 3.4 depicts the estimation results of this model for $q = 5$ pre-defined knots: $\kappa_1 = 2.8$, $\kappa_2 = 4.8$, $\kappa_3 = 6.8$, $\kappa_4 = 8.8$, and $\kappa_5 = 10.8$. The resulting relationship is non-linear, and bears a close resemblance to that in Figure 3.3. This example illustrates the potential of piecewise linear estimation to recreate a distinctly non-linear function, by the simple addition of extra terms such as $(x-\kappa_j)_+$ to a linear regression.

The estimated functions in Figure 3.4 do not have continuous first derivatives: they jump discretely at the knots. To avoid this, we appeal to functions that are different from $(x-\kappa_j)_+$ to define the base. We then refer to *spline* functions, which can be linear, quadratic, cubic, or of some other form. Let $b_0(x,\kappa),\ldots,b_r(x,\kappa)$ be the spline functions which define the base, where κ is a vector of q pre-defined knots, then the *spline regression model* can be written as follows:

$$y = \sum_{j=0}^{r} \beta_j \, b_j(x, \kappa) + \varepsilon. \tag{3.5}$$

The OLS estimation of this model produces estimated parameters $\hat{\beta}_j$, for $j = 0, \ldots, r$, which correspond to the coordinates of y in the chosen spline base.[7] The appropriate choice of this base produces an estimator with continuous first derivatives, as in Figure 3.3. The following section discusses the choice of the base.

3.2.2 *Penalized Splines*

The approach described above requires the prior choice of the number of knots and their position. The estimation results are sensitive to this choice: the two panels of Figure 3.4 show that the estimated regression is notably different according to the choice of two or five knots. Automatic selection methods for the number and position of these knots have been developed, but these are relatively complex and demanding in terms of computer time. The problem is that, for a given number of knots, there is a very large number of possible regression models. These different methods are compared in Wand (2000).

To minimize the influence of knot number and position, a different approach is to constrain the estimation of the parameters in (3.5). The estimation by *penalized splines* of the regression (3.1) consists in decomposing the function $m(x)$ in a spline base function; that is, to rewrite the model as in (3.5), and then to choose parameter values (β_j, for $j = 0, \ldots, r$) which minimize the following criterion:

$$\sum_{i=1}^{n} [y_i - m(x_i)]^2 + \lambda \int [m''(x)]^2 dx, \tag{3.6}$$

where n is the number of observations and $\lambda > 0$. This criterion corresponds to a minimization with a Lagrange multiplier. In other words, we minimize the previous argument (the sum of the square of the residuals), but under the constraint that $\int [m''(x)]^2 dx < C$, where C is positive. This constraint depends on the second derivative of the function, which reveals the variation in the slope of the function. The term $\int [m''(x)]^2 dx$ is thus a measure of the speed at which the function $m(x)$ varies. A function which varies only little will yield a small value for this term, while a

[7] Piecewise linear regression (3.4) is a particular case of model (3.5), for which $b_0(x, \kappa) = \iota$, $b_1(x, \kappa) = x$, $b_2(x, \kappa) = (x - \kappa_1)_+, \ldots, b_r(x, \kappa) = (x - \kappa_q)_+$.

function which varies greatly will yield a larger value. Estimation by penalized splines corresponds to an OLS estimation where we constrain the speed at which the function varies. A sound choice of C, or equivalently of λ, produces an estimation of the function which does not vary overmuch.

Spline estimation of parameters is a distinct modification of OLS estimation. Given the parameter vector $\beta = [\beta_0, \beta_1, \ldots, \beta_r]$ and the spline function base $X = [b_0(x, \kappa), b_1(x, \kappa), \ldots, b_r(x, \kappa)]$, the model (3.5) can be written as $y = X\beta + \varepsilon$. Furthermore, we can express the penalization term as a function of the parameters and of the base: $\int [m''(x)]^2 dx = \beta^\top S\beta$, where S is a matrix that depends on the components of the base X.[8] The estimation of the model (3.5) via the minimization of the criterion (3.6) is therefore the same thing as the minimization of:

$$\sum_{i=1}^{n}(y_i - X_i\beta)^2 + \lambda\beta^\top S\beta,$$

which is solved by:

$$\hat{\beta} = (X^\top X + \lambda S)^{-1}X^\top y.$$

The parameter λ in this expression is fixed. This plays the role of a smoothing parameter, and allows us reach a compromise between the distance to the data (the first term in 3.6) and the overall evenness of the function (the second term). In the last section, we will present various methods of choosing this parameter, according to a number of optimality criteria.

3.3 The Choice of the Spline Base

The first stage in spline estimation of the regression model (3.5) consists of the choice of a base of functions. The choice of this base is guided by the properties that we would like it to satisfy. In general, we would like the variations in the $m(x)$ function not to be too abrupt at the junction points, as they are in the case of piecewise linear estimation (Figure 3.4). As such, we require the first derivative of the function to be continuous. A number of different bases satisfy this property. In this section, we present power function bases, and then B-splines.

[8] For the linear base (3.3), S is a diagonal matrix $S = \text{diag}\{0, 0, 1, \ldots, 1\}$ with $q + 2$ elements.

3.3.1 *Power Function Bases*

One particularly simple way of moving beyond piecewise linear regression consists in adding x^2 terms to the base (3.3) and replacing the $(x-\kappa_j)_+$ terms by their squares $(x-\kappa_j)_+^2$. The $(x-\kappa_j)_+^2$ functions have a continuous first derivative. It therefore follows that any linear combination of the functions:

$$\iota,\ x,\ x^2,\ (x-\kappa_1)_+^2,\ (x-\kappa_2)_+^2, \ldots, (x-\kappa_q)_+^2,$$

will also have a continuous first derivative. As a result, the use of this *quadratic* spline base allows us to estimate (3.5) with smooth transitions at the knots $\kappa_1, \ldots, \kappa_q$. Another advantage of the utilization of this base is that the approximation within each segment is carried out using a polynomial of degree 2, which allows us to pick up any concavity or convexity in the function between two knots.

The above base can be generalized by using truncated power functions of order p. A spline base of degree p is written as:

$$\iota,\ x, \ldots, x^p,\ (x-\kappa_1)_+^p,\ (x-\kappa_2)_+^p, \ldots, (x-\kappa_q)_+^p. \tag{3.7}$$

The choice of this base to estimate the model (3.1) leads us to write the *spline regression model of order p* as follows:

$$y = \beta_0 + \beta_1 x + \cdots + \beta_p x^p + \sum_{j=1}^{q} \beta_{pj} (x-\kappa_j)_+^p + \varepsilon. \tag{3.8}$$

The function $(x-\kappa_j)_+^p$ has a continuous derivative of order $p-1$. As such, the choice of this spline base of degree p ensures that the derivative of order $p-1$ of the $m(x)$ function in (3.1) is continuous. In practical terms, *cubic spline* functions are often used ($p = 3$). These guarantee the continuity of the first derivative $m'(x)$ and the second derivative $m''(x)$, and permit change of concavity of $m(x)$ between two knots.

As an example, suppose that the estimation of the model (3.1) with the base of cubic spline functions ($p = 3$) produces the following results:

$$\hat{m}(x) = 2 + x - 2x^2 + x^3 + (x-0.4)_+^3 - (x-0.8)_+^3.$$

This shows that the estimated function $\hat{m}(x)$ has coordinates of $(2, 1, -2, 1, 1, -1)$ in the cubic spline base, with knots of 0.4 and 0.8. The estimated function can be rewritten as:

$$\hat{m}(x) = \begin{cases} 2 + x - 2x^2 + x^3 & \text{if} \quad x < 0.4 \\ 2 + x - 2x^2 + x^3 + (x - 0.4)^3 & \text{if } 0.4 \le x < 0.8 \\ 2 + x - 2x^2 + x^3 + (x - 0.4)^3 - (x - 0.8)^3 & \text{if} \quad x \ge 0.8 \end{cases}$$

It is easy to check that the first and second derivatives of this function are continuous at the knots. This way of writing the results underlines that the function is an approximation via three third-order polynomials over adjacent segments, with the passage from one segment to another being smooth; that is, practically imperceptible at the junction points, as shown in Figure 3.5.

3.3.2 *B-spline Bases*

A second commonly used solution is that of *B-spline* bases. Contrary to those described above, these bases have the advantage of being defined over a compact support. In other words, the functions that define this base are strictly local: they take on values of zero outside of a number of adjacent knots. This property is useful inasmuch as it allows local solutions to the estimation and simplifies the numerical calculations.

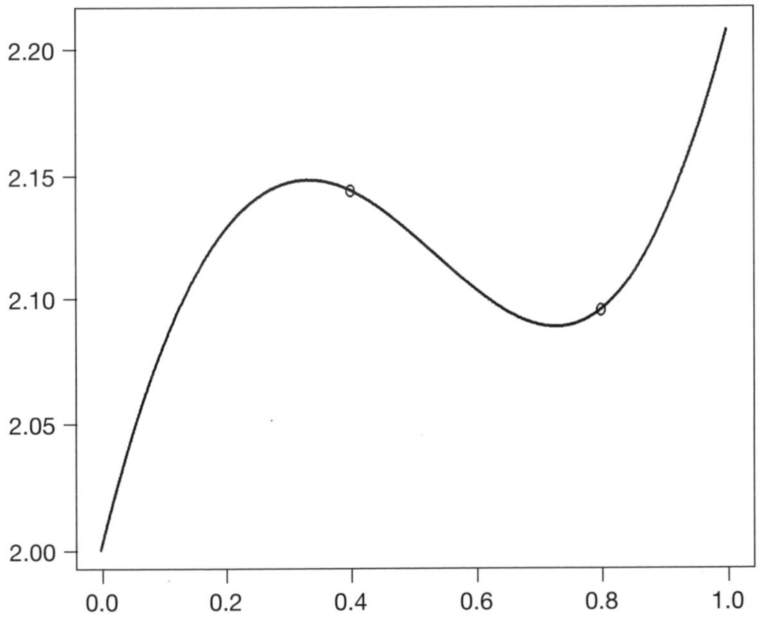

Figure 3.5: An example of estimation by cubic splines

However, the formulation of such a base is somewhat more complicated as it is defined recursively. To define a B-spline base of dimension $r + 1$:

$$B_0^p(x), B_1^p(x), \ldots, B_r^p(x), \tag{3.9}$$

allowing us to decompose in the spline base any curve that is locally similar to a polynomial of degree p at each of the points, we first have to choose $r + p + 2$ knots, denoted by $\kappa_0, \kappa_1, \ldots, \kappa_{r+p+1}$. The B_j^p components of the base are defined recursively as follows:

$$B_j^p(x) = \frac{(x - \kappa_j)}{(\kappa_{j+p} - \kappa_j)} B_j^{p-1}(x) + \frac{(\kappa_{j+p+1} - x)}{(\kappa_{j+p+1} - \kappa_{j+1})} B_{j+1}^{p-1}(x),$$

for $j = 0, \ldots, r$ and $p > 0$. For $p = 0$, the $B_j^0(x)$ component is equal to 1 if $\kappa_j \leq x < \kappa_{j+1}$ and to 0 otherwise. With the B-spline base defined as above, the regression model (3.1) can be rewritten as follows:

$$y = \sum_{j=0}^{r} \beta_j \, B_j^p(x). \tag{3.10}$$

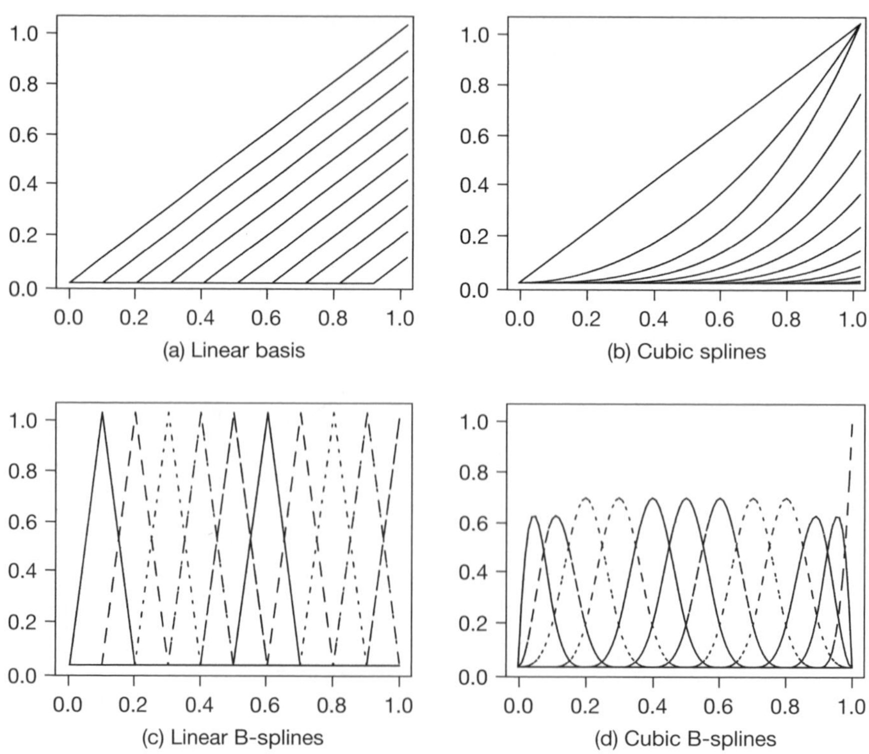

Figure 3.6: Spline bases

Note that the number of knots $(r + p + 2)$ is greater than the number of parameters to be estimated $(r + 1)$. For a given number of knots, a power function base (3.7) uses $2(p + 1)$ parameters more than does a B-spline base (3.9).[9]

Figure 3.6 presents a number of different bases, using knots of $\kappa = 0.1, 0.2, \ldots, 0.9$. Panel (a) depicts the power function base (3.7) with $p = 1$. The use of this base allows the estimation of piecewise linear models. Panel (b) shows the power function base (3.7) with $p = 3$; that is, with cubic splines. Panel (c) shows the B-spline base (3.9) with $p = 1$, and panel (d) represents the same base with $p = 3$; that is, the cubic B-spline base. We can see from this figure that the two B-spline bases have the following property: they are composed of functions which take values of zero outside of the $p + 2$ adjacent knots.

3.4 The Choice of the Parameters

The application of spline estimation requires prior choice of the knots, and of a smoothing parameter in the case of penalized splines. The choice of a set of knots raises two central questions: the number of knots and their position. In this section we consider the choice of the knots, and then turn to optimal smoothing.

3.4.1 *The Number and Position of Knots*

Comparing the two panels of Figure 3.4, we can see that the estimation results are sensitive to the number of knots. The greater the number of knots, the more the estimated function varies: more knots corresponds to a greater number of different regimes in the different segments of the estimation of the regression function. Knots can have an economic interpretation, if they are associated with a particular date or some observed change of regime. If we have information on all of the dates at which such regime changes took place, we can simply place the knots at these dates. In practice, our information is rarely complete enough for this to be a viable option.

The choice of the position of the knots can be carried out in two different ways. The first consists in positioning the knots at the various quantiles of the explanatory variable x (Ruppert et al., 2003). For example, if we fix the number of knots to be equal to three, then we place

[9] For $r + p + 2$ knots, the power function base uses $(r + p + 2) + p + 1$ parameters in the model (3.8), as against $r + 1$ parameters in the model (3.10).

them at the quartiles of x, such that each segment contains 25% of the observations. The second approach is to position the knots equidistantly, so that the segments are of the same width (Eilers and Marx, 1996). Eilers and Marx (2004) compare these two approaches.

Ruppert (2002) has developed an algorithm for the choice of the number of knots. He uses simulations to show that if the number of knots is small relative to a critical level, the estimated function will be biased and will contain relatively sizeable errors. If the number of knots is greater than this critical level, then the estimation results are globally satisfactory. In practice, we tend to favor a relatively large number of knots, in order to be above the critical value. It is, however, obvious that the choice of the number of knots may be limited by the sample size.

If the number of observations is relatively small, it is possible to choose as many knots as there are observations, by making each knot correspond to an observation. We refer to this as the special case of *smoothing by splines*. To control for the evenness of the function, only the smoothing parameter λ is used. One remarkable property is that when the number of knots rises with the number of observations at a suitable rate, the estimation of the regression function by penalized splines converges on the result from smoothing by splines (Faraway, 2006).

3.4.2 *The Smoothing Parameter*

To attenuate the effects of the number and position of the knots, a penalization parameter was introduced into the minimization criterion (3.6) describing the regression model. As we saw, this penalization parameter constrains the extent to which the estimated function fluctuates. The question which remains hanging is how the parameter associated with this term, λ, which plays the role of a smoothing parameter, should be chosen.

The optimal smoothing parameter is that which produces an estimation which is as close as possible to the true function. In other words, we want to select the value of λ which minimizes the distance between $\hat{m}(x)$ and $m(x)$. One solution consists in choosing the value of λ which minimizes the mean squared error:

$$\text{MSE}(\lambda) = \frac{1}{n}\sum_{i=1}^{n}[\hat{m}(x_i) - m(x_i)]^2.$$

But the function $m(x)$ is unknown, and it is not possible to actually calculate the MSE. We can get round this problem by appealing to cross-validation; that is, by choosing λ so as to minimize the following criterion:

$$\mathrm{CV}(\lambda) = \frac{1}{n}\sum_{i=1}^{n}[y_i - \hat{m}_{-i}(x_i)]^2,$$

where $\hat{m}_{-i}(.)$ is the estimated regression function from the sample of all observations apart from x_i. This criterion is similar to that used to choose the smoothing parameter in kernel (2.8). The drawback here is that we are required to estimate the same model n times, over n different samples of size $n - 1$. In practice, we often therefore use an approximation to this criterion, known as *generalized cross-validation*:

$$\mathrm{GCV}(\lambda) = \frac{n\sum_{i=1}^{n}[y_i - \hat{m}(x_i)]^2}{[tr(I - A)]^2},$$

where $A = X(X^TX + \lambda S)^{-1}X^T$ is the *hat matrix* of the regression, X is the column of the observed values $x_1, \ldots, x_n$, I is the identity matrix, and tr is the trace. The evaluation of GCV criterion requires only one estimation of the regression function, over the sample containing all of the observations. Moreover, for a sufficiently large number of observations, this criterion chooses a value of λ similar to that which pertains from the minimization of the MISE.

The application discussed in the introduction, regarding the Phillips curve (Figure 3.1), resulted from penalized spline estimation, with a cubic

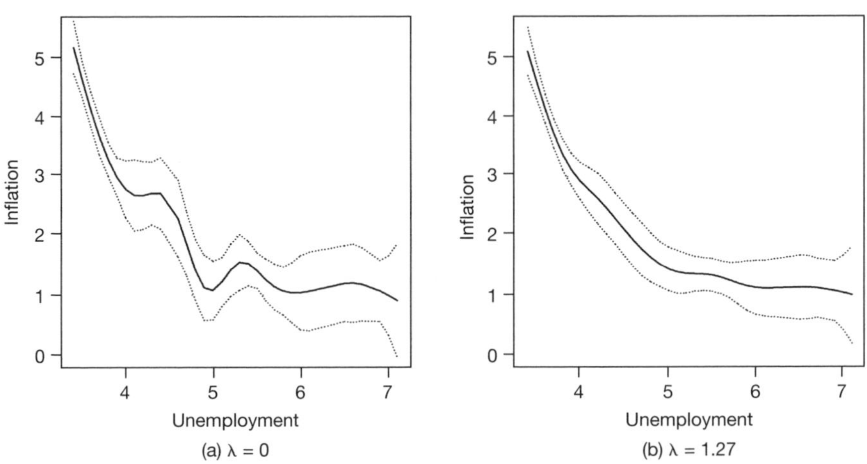

Figure 3.7: The smoothing parameter

base, ten knots, and bandwidth that was determined according to the GCV criterion ($\lambda = 2.19$).

Panel (a) of Figure 3.7 depicts the results from the estimation of the Phillips curve using the same data and with the same choices as in Figure 3.1, except for the smoothing parameter, which is here set so that λ equals 0. In other words, the estimation here comes from non-penalized splines. Compared to Figure 3.1, the estimated function is much more variable. A comparison of these two graphs emphasizes that the penalization of the estimation leads to a greater smoothing of the estimated function.

Panel (b) of Figure 3.7 presents the estimation of the Phillips curve using the same data and with the same choices as in Figure 3.1, except for the number of knots, which is here set equal to 9. The smoothing parameter, obtained from the GCV criterion, now produces $\lambda = 1.27$. The comparison to Figure 3.1, which has ten knots and $\lambda = 2.19$, reveals that the two figures are in fact very similar: different knot choices can make only little difference to the estimation results. Here it is the smoothing parameter which is adjusted, so as to penalize the estimation more severely when the number of knots is greater.

4

Wavelet Regression

4.1 Introduction

Regression estimation via wavelets and splines are both projective methods. The principle of the estimation of a function can be resumed as the estimation of a set of coordinates in a pre-determined base. Naturally, the choice of the base will influence the properties of the estimator and affect the ease with which the estimation can be carried out. For example, Fourier-type bases are orthogonal, a property which simplifies the estimation of the coordinates. However, this base has the drawback of not being a compact support, which means that the estimation of each coordinate requires the use of the entire database. As such, the estimator reflects the average characteristics of the function, rather than its local properties. Spline-type bases can have a compact support, but are not orthogonal. This chapter presents a new family of bases, the wavelets. These latter bring together a number of interesting properties. Not only are they orthogonal and with compact support, but they also have the property of multiresolution, which allows us to see the finest details of the estimated function without losing sight of its global characteristics.

The first illustration of non-parametric estimation by wavelets considers the estimation of inflation in the USA between December 1954 and December 2006. The data are monthly, and were obtained from the Federal Reserve Bank of St Louis.[1] Inflation rates are obtained from the first difference of the logarithm of the consumer price index, corrected for seasonal variation. Figure 4.1 presents the original series, as well as the results from wavelet and kernel estimation of the following regression:

$$y = m(x) + \varepsilon, \tag{4.1}$$

[1] The variable we use here is called CPIUFDSL (Consumer Price Index for All Urban Consumers: Food).

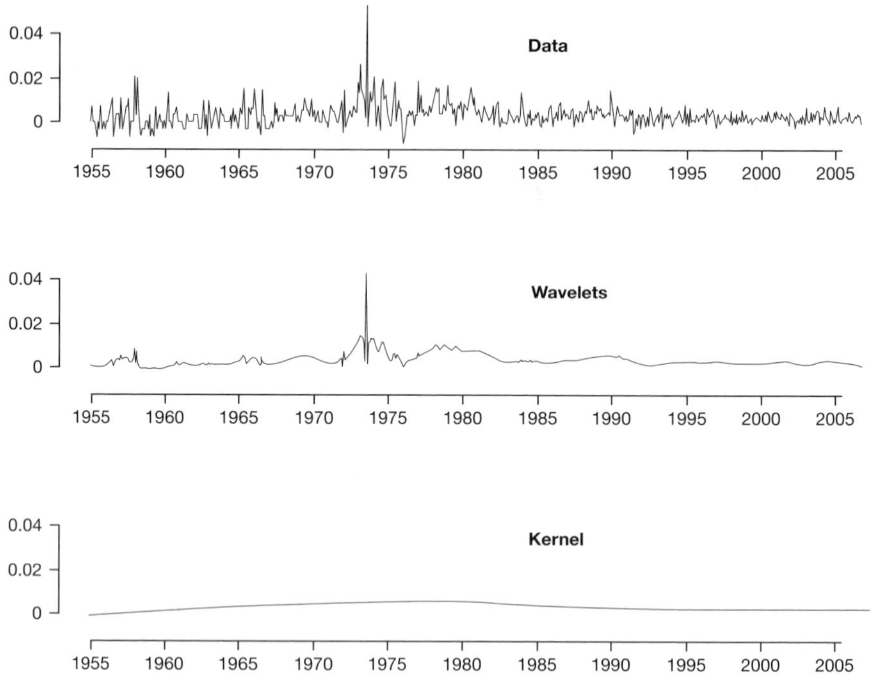

Figure 4.1: Inflation in the USA

where y is the series of inflation rates, x is time, and ε is white noise. Wavelet estimation clearly highlights certain notable events in the dynamics of inflation. For example, in the period between December 1954 and January 1959, we can see a certain irregularity in the inflation rate. This fluctuation can be explained by particular political economy events. In 1954 the USA was just coming out of a recession. The Federal Reserve, which feared the return of inflation, intensified its anti-inflation policy in 1957. The results of this policy seem to have been felt by the end of 1957, as we observe a small fall in inflation over this period. It is also of interest to note the peak of inflation in 1973. This corresponds to the period of the first oil-price shock, after OPEC quadrupled the price of oil in the fourth quarter of 1973, bringing about a rise in the price of energy of 47%. This explains part of the acceleration of inflation in this time-period. Last, we can see the effects of anti-inflation policies carried out at the beginning of the 1980s: a certain stability of the inflation rate begins in this period. The results described here have previously been discussed in Ahamada and Ben Aïssa (2005).

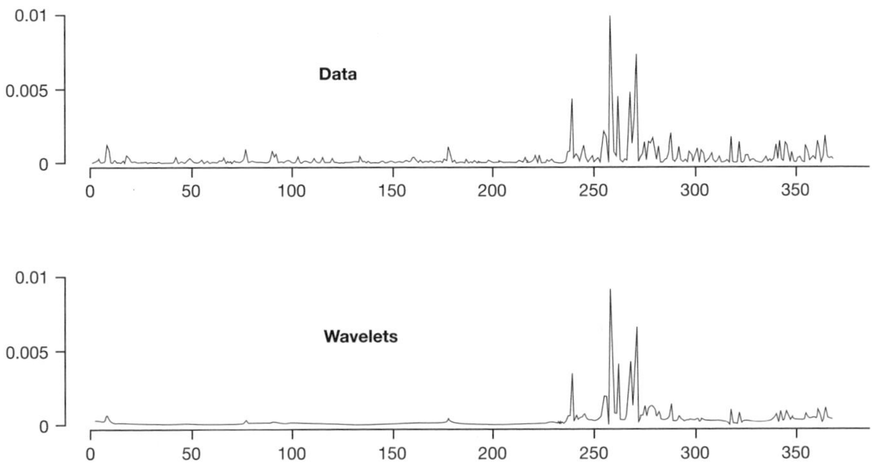

Figure 4.2: The volatility of returns on IBM shares

Estimations by wavelets and by kernel produce very different results. The kernel estimator suggests that there were no events of note during this period, with inflation estimated to be particularly stable. The kernel estimator at a point consists in calculating a weighted mean over all of the neighboring observations. This estimation principle tends to water down the impact of any one observation which is very different from those surrounding it. On the contrary, the wavelet estimator over the same period does suggest a number of distinct events and differences. We will set out in this chapter the principle of wavelet estimation which, as we will see, differs sharply from those of kernel and spline estimation.[2]

The second illustration relates to the volatility of returns in financial markets. The data used here are the daily returns on IBM shares between May 17, 1961 and November 2, 1962, producing 368 observations.[3] The returns are calculated as the difference in the log price of IBM shares between two consecutive dates. Figure 4.2 depicts the series of squared daily returns, as well as the results of wavelet estimation of the following regression:

$$y^2 = m(x) + \varepsilon,$$

where ε is white noise. The series of returns y has been centered. As such, the function $m(x)$ measures the unconditional variance of these

[2] The results from spline estimation of this same series are not shown here, but are very similar to those from kernel estimation.

[3] We use here the data which is supplied with the R program, from the `waveslim` library.

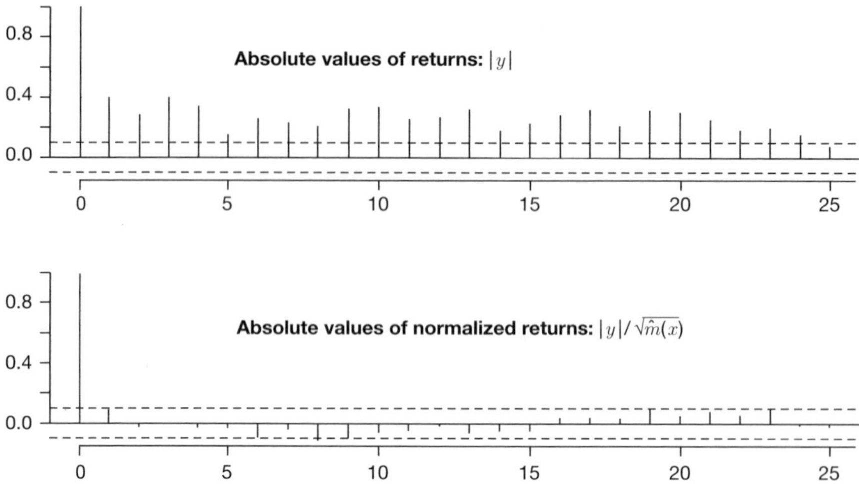

Figure 4.3: Autocorrelation functions

returns: $m(x) = E(y^2)$. Note that in estimating $m(x)$, we will be analyzing the stationarity of the second moment of y; that is, the hypothesis of constant unconditional variance of the series of returns. This hypothesis is required in a number of models, such as ARCH, GARCH, and FARIMA.[4]

In Figure 4.2, the wavelet estimation results suggest that the $\hat{m}(x)$ function is far from being constant. We chose to analyze IBM returns on purpose, in order to compare our results with those in Inclan and Tiao (1994), who highlighted the instability of the unconditional variance of this series. Our wavelet estimation confirms these previous results, revealing substantial instability in the second moment of the IBM returns series.

Figure 4.3 represents the sample autocorrelation functions (ACF), or correlograms, of the series $|y|$ and $|y|/\sqrt{\hat{m}(x)}$, where $\sqrt{\hat{m}(x)}$ is the estimated variance from the wavelet regression. There is considerable persistence in the ACF for $|y|$. This result suggests that we should use estimation methods that take such long-memory phenomena into account. On the other hand, the inspection of the results with respect to the normalized estimated variance $|y|/\sqrt{\hat{m}(x)}$ suggests that this series is a white noise. This result suggests that the persistence in $|y|$ is not in fact due to long memory but rather to non-stationarity in the variance (i.e. $\hat{m}(x)$ is not a constant function). As such, a more apt estimation technique would

[4] Autoregressive conditional heteroskedasticity, generalized autoregressive conditional heteroskedasticity, and fractional autoregressive integrated moving average, respectively.

be one that actually excludes long memory. This conclusion has been put forward by a number of authors, including Stărică and Granger (2005) and Loretan and Phillips (1994). However, the literature is not unanimous on this point. Faced with a persistent autocorrelation function, some authors adopt stationary long-memory types of models (ARFIMA), while others suspect instability of the unconditional variance and use non-stationary techniques.

The illustrations above underline the contrast in the results, depending on the estimation method used. Wavelet estimation would seem to be particularly appropriate in the case of data with substantial fluctuations. This estimation method has been extensively developed by Donoho and Johnstone (1994, 1995, 1998), Donoho et al. (1995), and Gao and Bruce (1997). Davidson et al. (1998) and Crowley (2007) provide brief summaries of the essential points of the associated theory in the context of a number of economic applications. The books by Chui (1992), Härdle et al. (1998), Percival and Walden (2000), Gençay et al. (2001), and Delouille (2002) are also useful.

The following section presents the principle of non-parametric estimation by wavelets, as well as their multiresolution property. To carry out wavelet estimation, a number of *a priori* choices need to be made. For example, the illustrations above resulted from estimations using a soft filter with a universal threshold. A dedicated section will discuss the choices of filter and threshold. The last section concerns the choice of the wavelet base, and illustrates the principle of the discrete wavelet transform by a numerical example.

4.2 Principles

In this section we will first set out the principle of wavelet estimation, and then the notion of multiresolution. Finally, we describe the methodological schema leading to non-parametric wavelet estimation.

The fundamental idea is to decompose the observed series of data into a pre-chosen base. One such wavelet base is a base of functions, typically written as $\{\phi_{j_0k}(x), \psi_{jk}(x)\}$, where j_0 is a fixed integer,[5] $j = j_0, j_0 + 1, \ldots$ and $k = 0, \ldots, 2^{j-1}$ for each j. A series of observations y can be rewritten in this base as follows:

[5] Some programs set j_0 equal to 4 by default. For a discussion of this choice of j_0, see, amongst others, Hall and Patil (1996) and Efromovich (1999).

$$y = \sum_{k=0}^{2^{j_0}-1} c_{j_0k}\phi_{j_0k}(x) + \sum_{j=j_0}^{P-1}\sum_{k=0}^{2^j-1} d_{jk}\psi_{jk}(x), \tag{4.2}$$

where $P = \ln(n)/\ln(2)$ and n is the number of observations.

The components of the wavelet base—$\phi_{j_0k}(x)$ and $\psi_{jk}(x)$—are respectively transformations of functions ϕ and ψ, chosen *a priori*. The ϕ function is called the father wavelet function, or scaling function: its role is to capture the general shape of the function. The function ψ is called the mother wavelet function: this serves to complement the scaling function by bringing local detail. The mother wavelet is scaled (or dilated) by a factor of j and translated (or shifted) by a factor of k. More precisely, j modifies the geometric characteristics (ranges and supports) of the function ψ in the vicinity of each observation. The index j provides different resolutions to the local analysis of the curve. This decomposition, which is known as the *multiresolution decomposition*, yields an analysis of a data series which is both global and local, which is the novelty of the wavelet estimation method.

The principle of wavelet estimation can thus be written as follows: (1) we calculate the coordinates c_{j_0k} and d_{jk} of the series y in the chosen wavelet base; (2) we filter these coordinates at the different levels of detail, that is, the coordinates d_{jk}, which are given by the mother wavelet; (3) we recompose the series with the filtered coordinates, $\hat{d}_{jk}$. The final results can be written as:

$$\hat{m}(x) = \sum_{k=0}^{2^{j_0}-1} c_{j_0k}\phi_{j_0k}(x) + \sum_{j=j_0}^{P-1}\sum_{k=0}^{2^j-1} \hat{d}_{jk}\psi_{jk}(x). \tag{4.3}$$

The difference between the original series y and the recomposed series $\hat{m}(x)$ corresponds to the noise that is removed by filtering the coordinates: $y - \hat{m}(x) = \hat{\varepsilon}$. In other words, the equation (4.3) is nothing other than the *wavelet estimator* of the function $m(x)$ in the regression model (4.1).

We suppose in this chapter that the sample size is a power of two, $n = 2^P$, and that the observations are regularly spaced, $x_i = i/n$ for $i = 1, \ldots, n$, such that the function $m(.)$ is defined over $[0, 1]$. For the extension to different-sized samples and to non-equidistant observations, as well as more sophisticated models, such as non-linear or autoregressive models, we recommend, amongst others, Gençay et al. (2001) and Delouille (2002).

4.2.1 *Multiresolution*

Equation (4.2) can be split up into a number of different components, which allows us to distinguish both the general shape of the series and a number of different levels of detail. This equation can be rewritten as:

$$y = S_{j_0} + \sum_{j=j_0}^{P-1} d_j, \tag{4.4}$$

where $S_{j_0} = \sum_{k=0}^{2^{j_0}-1} c_{j_0k}\phi_{j_0k}(x)$ and $d_j = \sum_{k=0}^{2^j-1} d_{jk}\psi_{jk}(x)$. Note that there are twice as many terms in d_j as in d_{j-1}: d_j contains 2^j terms, while d_{j-1} contains 2^{j-1}. Intuitively, this signifies that twice as many details will be captured at the level d_j than at d_{j-1}. The local resolution is thus twice as fine at level j as at level $j-1$. It is therefore the component S_{j_0} which supplies the general shape of $m(x)$, while the d_j provide different levels of detail. As such, the father wavelet function provides the general shape of the function, and the mother wavelet function the details.

This multiresolution feature is illustrated in the following example. Consider the value $y = 12.142$. We can decompose y as $y = S_{j_0} + \sum d_j$, with $S_{j_0} = 12$ and $d_{j_0} = 0.1$, $d_{j_0+1} = 0.04$, and $d_{j_0+2} = 0.002$. Hence $S_{j_0} = 12$ gives the general idea of the size of m, while the decomposition $\sum d_j = 0.1 + 0.04 + 0.002$ allows us to visualize the different values of y at one, two, and three decimal points.

Now consider a second example where y is a time-series. Figure 4.4 shows the decomposition of (monthly) American inflation between December 1954 and December 2006. The curves S_{j_0}, d_{j_0}, d_{j_0+1}, d_{j_0+2}, and d_{j_0+3} correspond to the different components of equation (4.4). The S_{j_0} curve provides the general shape of the $m(x)$ function produced by the wavelets from the father wavelet function (the scaling function). This exhibits a number of notable peaks, as for example in 1974, which indicate major structural changes in the evolution of American inflation (Ahamada and Ben Aïssa, 2005). Outside of these peaks, inflation seems pretty much stable over time. However, there may well be significant variation at the more detailed level. The d_{j_0}, d_{j_0+1}, d_{j_0+2}, and d_{j_0+3} curves show these details, as captured by the wavelets from the mother wavelet functions at different levels of resolution, j. The details at the d_{j_0+3} level are the finest and produce somewhat more variation over time than do those at intermediate levels of resolution, d_{j_0}, d_{j_0+1}, and d_{j_0+2}. Table 4.1 shows the decomposition of the variance of $m(x)$ as a function of these d_j, and confirms that the contribution of d_{j_0+3} to this variance is the largest:

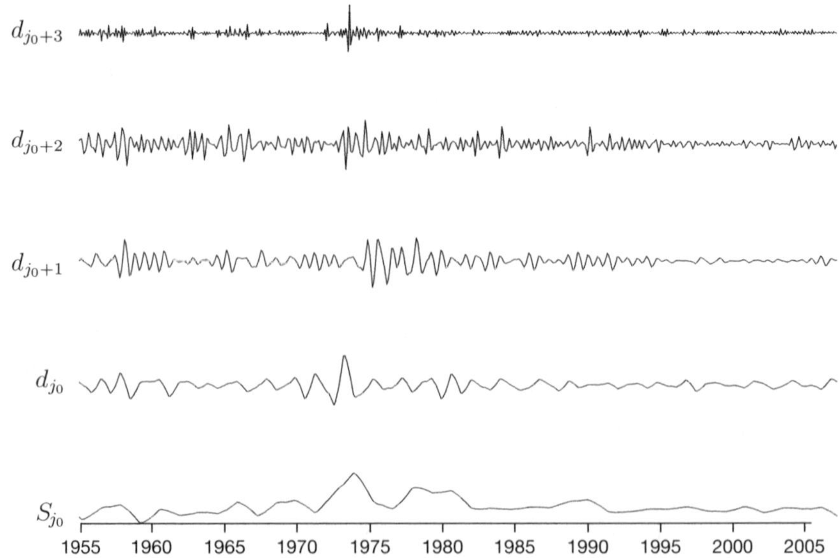

Figure 4.4: Multiresolution

Table 4.1: Variance decomposition

Level	S_{j_0}	d_{j_0}	d_{j_0+1}	d_{j_0+2}	d_{j_0+3}
	0.46	0.03	0.06	0.09	0.21

the d_{j_0+3} level explains 21% of the variance of $m(x)$, while the d_{j_0+2}, d_{j_0+1}, and d_{j_0} levels explain 9%, 6%, and 3%, respectively.[6] We therefore have a decomposition of movements in inflation at different levels of resolution.

The reconstitution of the y series is carried out by progressively adding the different levels of detail d_j to the general shape S_{j_0}.

4.2.2 *Estimation*

The principle of wavelet estimation is to filter the components $d_{j_0}, d_{j_0+1}, d_{j_0+2}$, and d_{j_0+3} of Figure 4.4 to eliminate any noise and leave only the significant aspects of the data. The wavelet estimator then results from the reconstitution of the series; that is, by adding successive levels

[6] The sum of these four percentages is not exactly equal to one. This is because the sample size is not equal to a power of two. Another method of calculating these coefficients has been used here.

of filtered detail, $\hat{d}_{j_0}, \hat{d}_{j_0+1}, \hat{d}_{j_0+2}$, and $\hat{d}_{j_0+3}$, to the general shape S_{j_0}. The wavelet estimator is then written as follows:

$$\hat{m}(x) = S_{j_0} + \sum_{j=j_0}^{P-1} \hat{d}_j. \tag{4.5}$$

The first stage in obtaining this estimator is to calculate the coordinates of the observed data in a previously defined wavelet base. The calculation of these coordinates, denoted by c_{j_0k} and d_{jk}, is generally carried out using the discrete wavelet transform (DWT), which will be presented at the end of this chapter. The second stage is to filter the data d_{jk}. The most popular current method is to apply a filter $\delta_\lambda(.)$, which depends on one threshold parameter λ:

$$\hat{d}_{jk} = \delta_\lambda\left(d_{jk}\right).$$

In the third stage, the wavelet estimator (4.5) is obtained by reconstituting the series with the filtered coordinates. The series can then be written as:

$$\hat{m}(x) = \sum_{k=0}^{2^{j_0}-1} c_{j_0k}\phi_{j_0k}(x) + \sum_{j=j_0}^{P-1}\sum_{k=0}^{2^j-1} \delta_\lambda\left(d_{jk}\right)\psi_{jk}(x). \tag{4.6}$$

The equations (4.3), (4.5), and (4.6), defining the wavelet estimator, are all equivalent to each other.

A number of comments can be usefully made here:

- The variable y and the estimator $\hat{m}(x)$ defined in (4.2) and (4.6) have identical coordinates in the father wavelet function (their first terms are identical). As was noted in the multiresolution presentation, the father wavelet function serves to describe the general shape of the series. As such, it is natural that y and $\hat{m}(x)$ share the same broad characteristics.
- The difference between y and $\hat{m}(x)$ comes from the presence of the filter $\delta_\lambda(.)$ in the second term. In other words, the distinction between y and $\hat{m}(x)$ is at the level of the details, and is linked to the properties of the filter.

To sum up, we can describe the various parts of $\hat{m}(x)$ as follows:

$$\{y\} \quad \xrightarrow{\text{DWT}} \quad \{c_{j_0k}, d_{jk}\} \quad \xrightarrow{\text{filter } \delta_\lambda(.)} \quad \{c_{j_0k}, \hat{d}_{jk}\} \quad \xrightarrow{\text{IDWT}} \quad \hat{m}(x)$$

We first calculate the coordinates of y via the discrete wavelet transform of y. We then apply the filter $\delta_\lambda(.)$ to the d_{jk} to produce the $\hat{d}_{jk}$. Finally, we construct the $\hat{m}(x)$ estimator by using c_{j_0k} and $\hat{d}_{jk}$: this is the inverse discrete wavelet transform (IDWT).

4.3 The Choice of Filter and Threshold*

The use of wavelet estimators requires the prior choice of a filter and a threshold. This section discusses these two choices.

4.3.1 *Hard and Soft Filters*

There are a number of different filters that can be used. This section presents two of them, *hard* and *soft* filters, which are the most commonly used in practice.

The *hard filter*, denoted by $\delta_\lambda^{(H)}(.)$, is defined as follows:

$$\delta_\lambda^{(H)}\left(d_{jk}\right) = d_{jk} I\left(\left|d_{jk}\right| > \lambda\right),$$

where λ is a threshold and $I(.)$ the indicator function, which equals one when the argument holds and zero otherwise. The properties of the filter naturally depend on the value of λ. The effect of the hard filter on each d_{jk} is binary, in the sense that there is no intermediate option: the value of d_{jk} remains unchanged if its absolute value is strictly greater than λ; otherwise, it is replaced by zero in the reconstruction of $\hat{m}$. There is thus a sharp discontinuity at the points $-\lambda$ and λ. The advantage of this filter is that it does not affect the information contained in d_{jk}: if the coefficient d_{jk} is retained by the filter, then it is used in its original state in the construction of $\hat{m}$, with no correction being made to it. This filter thus tends to keep in $\hat{m}$ the observed peaks in y, without modifying their amplitude. We thus expect that the estimation of m via a hard filter will be more variable and less smooth.

The *soft filter*, denoted by $\delta_\lambda^{(S)}(.)$, is defined as follows:

$$\delta_\lambda^{(S)}\left(d_{jk}\right) = sgn\left(d_{jk}\right) \max\left(0, \left|d_{jk}\right| - \lambda\right).$$

In contrast to the hard filter, soft functions are continuous at the points $-\lambda$ and λ. The coefficients d_{jk} retained by this filter are not kept at their original values, as was the case for the hard filter: they lose a term equal to λ. As a result, the peaks present in the data are mitigated in $\hat{m}$ by the soft filter. We therefore expect that the soft filter will yield a smoother and less variable estimator than that produced by the hard filter. On the other hand, the bias will be larger when the soft filter is used.

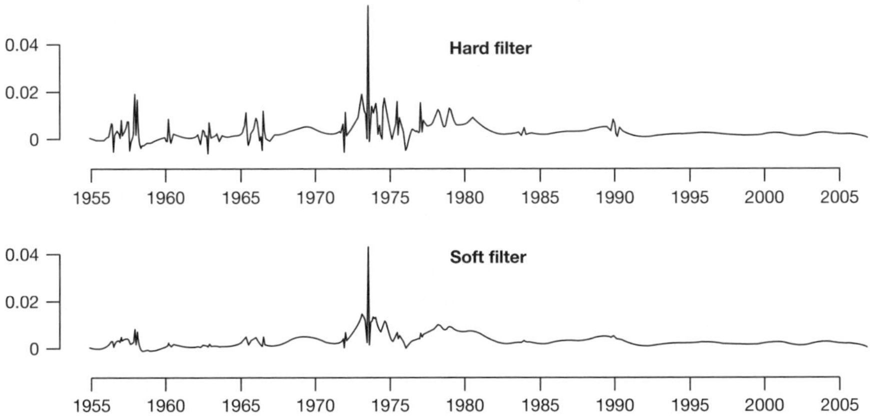

Figure 4.5: The choice of filter

To illustrate these various properties, Figure 4.5 presents the results from the estimation of the series of American inflation via hard and soft filters. The results from the soft filter do indeed seem to be less hilly and somewhat more even than those from the hard filter.

4.3.2 *Universal and SURE Thresholds*

The choice of the threshold λ is fundamental. If λ is too high, then the filter will tend to eliminate a large number of details, with the concomitant risk of throwing away important characteristics of the function to be estimated. On the contrary, a value of λ that is too small will keep too much information, and the filtered series will increasingly tend to look like the original series.

The filtering of the coordinates leads to a decomposition into two terms, which we can write as follows:

$$d_{jk} = \hat{d}_{jk} + d_\epsilon.$$

The term $\hat{d}_{jk}$ is the filtered coordinate and d_ϵ is the noise which is removed from d_{jk} by the filtering.[7] This equation produces a clearer picture of the role of the filter $\delta_\lambda(.)$. When d_{jk} is large relative to the fixed threshold λ, it suggests that d_{jk} is associated with a non-negligible value of $\hat{d}_{jk}$, which is partly concealed by the error d_ϵ. On the other hand, if d_{jk} is small compared to the threshold, it suggests that d_{jk} consists essentially of noise

[7] Bardet (2002) provides a statistical analysis of the d_ϵ terms when the error term in the regression is not white noise.

d_ϵ, with an insignificant value of $\hat{d}_{jk}$. The role of $\delta_\lambda(.)$ is then to keep the values d_{jk} which contain significant information about $m(.)$, while dampening the effects of the error, d_ϵ.

Donoho and Johnstone (1994) have proposed a *universal* threshold, defined as follows:

$$\lambda_{un} = \sigma\sqrt{2\log(n)}/\sqrt{n},$$

where $\sigma = \sqrt{var(\varepsilon)}$. As the standard deviation σ is in general unknown, it is replaced by an estimate. The following estimator is often used in the literature:

$$\hat{\sigma} = \frac{med\left\{\left|d_{j^*k}\right|,\ j^* = P-1,\ k = 0, ..., 2^{j^*}-1\right\}}{0.6745},$$

where *med* is the median and $P = \ln(n)/\ln(2)$. The set $\{|d_{j^*k}|\}_{k=0}^{k=2^{j^*}-1}$, $j^* = P-1$, commonly called level d_{P-1}, is the layer which contains the most d_{jk} terms. It is exactly at the level d_{P-1} where the most variation will be observed amongst all of the d_j levels. This fact justifies the use of this level d_{P-1} to estimate the variance of the white-noise error term ε. The use of the median here is supposed to provide a robust estimate of σ which will not be affected by the variation in $\hat{m}(x)$. The constant 0.6745 allows us to characterize $\hat{\sigma}$ as the standard deviation of a white noise error from a Normal distribution. We can show that, for all values of j and $k = 0, ..., 2^{j-1}$, the probability $P[max(|d_\epsilon|) \leq \lambda_{un}]$ converges towards 1 as the sample size n grows to infinity. This indicates that the universal threshold has a very good chance of eliminating any noise that comes from a white-noise error (this result holds asymptotically). However, there is a risk that the resulting estimator will be over-smoothed. The probability of wrongly excluding smaller components, which do not necessarily represent white noise ε, remains considerable even in large samples.

An alternative, proposed by Donoho and Johnstone (1995), is to calculate *adaptive* thresholds. This consists of the calculation of a threshold λ_j, for each set $\{d_{jk}, k = 0, \ldots, 2^j - 1\}$, $j = j_0, ..., P-1$. Each λ_j comes from the minimization of the following function:

$$\lambda_j = \arg\min_{\lambda\geq 0}\left[2^j - 2\sum_{k=0}^{2^j-1} I\left(\left|d_{jk}\right| \leq \lambda\right) + \sum_{k=0}^{2^j-1}\min\left(\left|d_{jk}\right|^2, \lambda^2\right)\right].$$

This approach is known in the literature as the *SURE* threshold (Stein's Unbiased Risk Estimate). It can be shown that the above expression corresponds to the minimization of a mean squared error; that is, the

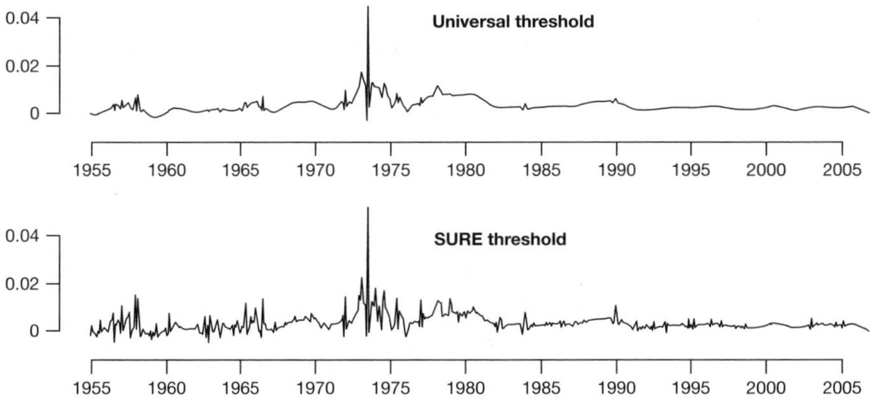

Figure 4.6: The choice of threshold

minimization of a variance for unbiased estimators. The variance is often associated with measures of risk in finance, which explains the link with Stein's unbiased estimator.

Figure 4.6 shows the results from two estimations of American inflation using the universal threshold and SURE. We note that the universal threshold produces estimation results that are smoother than those from SURE. This comes from the fact that SURE takes into account the stochastic properties of each separate level j, while the universal threshold is the same at every level. The universal threshold thus excludes a lot of coefficients, especially the smallest ones, and leads to a smoother estimator.

4.4 The Choice of the Wavelet Base*

In this section, we will discuss the bases of Haar and Daubechies, and evaluate the effect of their use on the construction of the wavelet estimator. We will then present the principle of the wavelet discrete transform, which allows us to calculate the coordinates of a series in a pre-defined base.

4.4.1 *The Haar and Daubechies Bases*

The construction of a base $\{\phi_{j_0k}(x), \psi_{jk}(x)\}$ requires the prior choice of the pair of parent functions $\{\phi, \psi\}$, where ϕ is the scaling function (father wavelet function) and ψ is the mother wavelet function. The elements of the base are then constructed by reiterating the formulae $\phi_{j_0k}(x) = 2^{j_0/2}\phi(2^{j_0}x - k)$ and $\psi_{jk}(x) = 2^{j/2}\psi(2^j x - k)$, for $k = 0, \ldots, 2^{j-1}$ and $j = j_0$, $j_0 + 1, \ldots, P - 1$.

The oldest base is that of Haar. This is characterized by the following father wavelet function:

$$\phi^{(Haar)}(x) = \begin{cases} 1 & \text{if} \quad x \in [0, 1) \\ 0 & \text{if} \quad x \notin [0, 1) \end{cases}$$

and the mother wavelet function:

$$\psi^{(Haar)}(x) = \begin{cases} 1 & \text{if} \quad x \in [0, 0.5) \\ -1 & \text{if} \quad x \in [0.5, 1). \end{cases}$$

The following technical remarks are worth making:

- The mother wavelet function has the following properties: $\int_R \psi^{(Haar)} dx = 0$, and $\int_R \psi^{(Haar)} x^p dx \neq 0$ for $p \neq 0$. The Haar base possesses only one zero moment, that of order one. In general, we say that a base ψ has N zero moments if $\int_R \psi(x) x^p dx = 0$, for $p = 0, \ldots, N - 1$. In the case of the Haar base, for example, $N = 1$. This intuitively signifies that any polynomial of degree $p \leq N - 1$ can be located in a wavelet base with N zero moments. In the other direction, a wavelet with N zero moments absorbs polynomials of degree $N - 1$ or less.
- Figure 4.7 depicts the wavelet $\psi_{jk}^{(Haar)}(x)$ produced by the Haar mother wavelet function, for $j = 0$ and different values of k. As k increases, the supports move to the right. This demonstrates that the index k acts to shift the base along the time axis. In a classic kind of base, such as the Fourier base, the coordinates of a function are supposed not to vary with time. On the contrary, in a wavelet base, the k index allows us to reflect any time variation in the coordinates of a function.
- Figure 4.7 also shows the wavelet function $\psi_{jk}^{(Haar)}(x)$ associated with the Haar mother wavelet function, for $k = 0$ and a variety of values of j. As j increases, the supports become increasingly narrow. In the same way, sinusoidal functions become increasingly tight for higher frequencies. Equally, they are increasingly spread out at lower frequencies. In other words, the j parameters affect the wavelets in the same way that the frequency affects sinusoidal functions. The j index can thus be compared to a frequency, even if this equivalence is not exact. Higher values of j are associated with higher frequencies, and conversely smaller values of j are associated with lower frequencies.

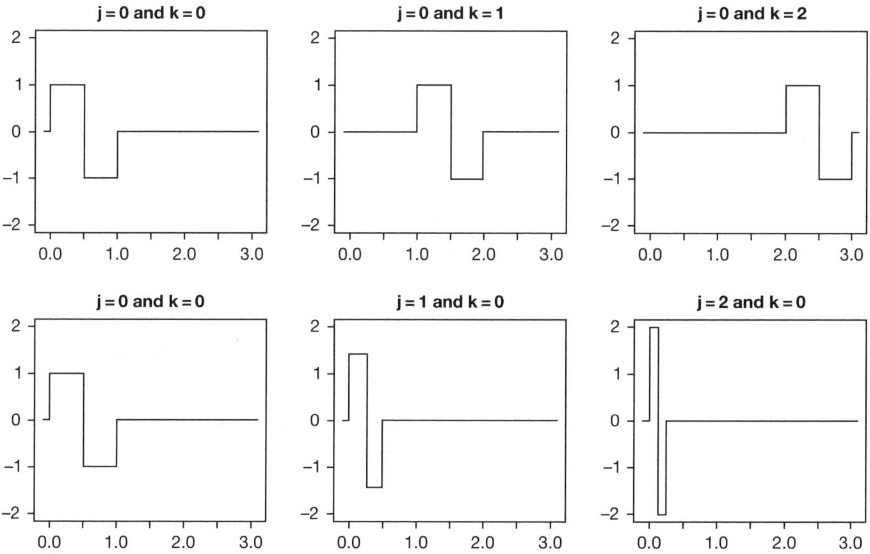

Figure 4.7: The Haar mother wavelet function, for various choices of j and k

More formally, at any time k, the wavelet $\psi_{jk}^{(Haar)}(x)$ is only significant within the interval $I_j = [k2^{-j}, (1+k)2^{-j}]$. The width of I_j thus varies inversely with j. In the same way, the length of the periods of sinusoidal functions are negatively correlated with the frequencies. Larger values of j generate wavelets $\psi_{jk}^{(Haar)}(x)$ characterized by supports I_j that are narrower: these are *thin wavelets*. Conversely, the wavelet supports I_j are wider for smaller values of j: these are *coarse wavelets*. At any given instant k, the set $\{\psi_{jk}^{(Haar)}(x), j = j_0, j_0 + 1, \ldots, P - 1\}$ yields the coordinates of the function in question at different levels of resolutions (different window sizes), depending on the value of j. Higher values of j, which produce finer wavelets, will allow us to pick up finer details of the distribution. Conversely, smaller values of j will describe the broader details of the distribution. A wavelet base thus allows us to measure both the coordinates of a function in time, via k, as well as varying degrees of resolution, via j.

- We can check that $\int_R \psi_{jk}^{(Haar)}(x)\psi_{lm}^{(Haar)}(x)dx = 0$ if $(j, k) \neq (l, m)$. In addition, $\int_R (\psi_{jk}^{(Haar)})^2 = 1$ for any pair (j,k). The Haar wavelet base thus has an *orthonormal* structure in the space of *integrable square* functions, denoted by $L^2(R) = \{g \text{ such that } \int_R g^2(x)dx < \infty\}$. Orthogonality is an interesting and often-prized property. It facilitates the calculation of the coordinates of a function in the base, as well as the analysis of the variance. The function $m(.)$ that we estimate in the regression model is supposed to be in $L^2(R)$.

The Haar mother wavelet function $\psi^{(Haar)}$ is piecewise constant; the same holds for the wavelets $\psi_{jk}^{(Haar)}$. As such, the Haar base is particularly suitable for the decomposition of *locally constant functions*. However, due to this discontinuity, it is not optimal for the estimation of continuous differentiable functions. To estimate these latter, we turn to other kinds of bases. For example, Daubechies (1988, 1992) proposes two families of regular bases, with a finite number N of zero moments, and which bring together the properties of orthogonality and a compact support. However, the Daubechies wavelets do not have an analytical expression, and are constructed by exploiting the principle of multiresolution (see, e.g., Gençay et al. 2001).

Intuitively, if the function $m(.)$ in the regression models reflects the local behavior of a polynomial of degree r, we can construct a wavelet base that is sufficiently regular which will allow us to capture the regularity of $m(.)$. The degree of regularity r of the wavelets is positively correlated with the width of their support and the number N of zero moments. There is hence a trade-off between the regularity of the wavelets and their compactness. The more regular the wavelets (a higher value of r), the smoother is the estimator. The more compact the wavelets (a lower value of r), the less smooth is the estimator, but the better is its local precision. We here come across again the classic trade-off between the bias and the variance of a non-parametric estimator. In reality, the optimal value of r depends on unknown characteristics of the $m(.)$ function that we wish to estimate.

Figure 4.8 illustrates the use of two types of wavelet base to estimate American inflation: the Haar wavelet base and one of the Daubechies family of bases. We can see that the Haar base produces piecewise estimates (a step function), while that from the Daubechies family produces smoother estimation. This example underlines the drawbacks of using the Haar base to estimate continuous functions.

4.4.2 *The Discrete Wavelet Transform*

The first stage of the calculation of the wavelet estimator consists in calculating the coordinates of y in the chosen base. We now show via a simple example how these coordinates are determined.

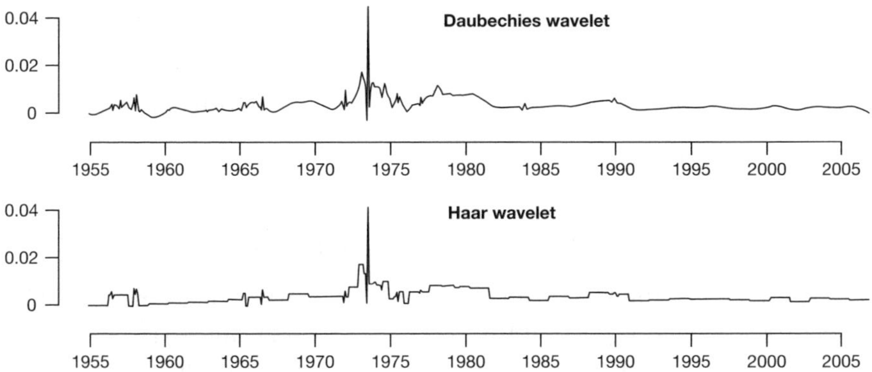

Figure 4.8: Wavelet bases

In a wavelet base $\{\phi_{j_0k}(x), \psi_{jk}(x)\}$ we can decompose y as follows:

$$y = \sum_{k=0}^{2^{j_0}-1} c_{j_0k}\phi_{j_0k}(x) + \sum_{j=j_0}^{P-1}\sum_{k=0}^{2^j-1} d_{jk}\psi_{jk}(x),$$

where $j_0 < P - 1$, $P = \ln(n)/\ln(2)$, and n is the sample size. This equation can be rewritten more simply as:

$$y = Wd,$$

where d is the vector bringing together the coefficients c_{j_0k} and d_{jk}. The matrix W is composed of $\phi_{j_0k}(x)$ and $\psi_{jk}(x)$, and is orthogonal, as the wavelet base used is orthogonal. The discrete wavelet transform of the vector y is given by:

$$d = W^{-1}y.$$

The inverse matrix W^{-1} is easy to calculate due to the orthogonality of W.[8] We can thus determine the required coordinates of the d vector.

To illustrate, consider the vector $y = [y_0, y_1, y_2, y_3]^T = [2, 5, 2, 7]^T$ of size $n = 2^2$; that is, $P = 2$. Now calculate the discrete wavelet transform of $y = [2, 5, 2, 7]^T$ in the Haar base. We set $j_0 = 0$, which means that we consider the representation: $y_i = c_{00}\phi_{00}(x_i) + \sum_{j=0}^{1}\sum_{k=0}^{2^j-1} d_{jk}\psi_{jk}(x_i)$ for $i = 0, 1, 2, 3$,

[8] The inverse of a real orthogonal matrix A of dimension $n \times n$ is given by $[\det(A)]^{-2/n}A^T$, where A^T is the transpose of A.

and $x_i = i/4$. The vector d is thus $d = [c_{00}, d_{00}, d_{10}, d_{11}]^T$ and the matrix W is given by:

$$W = \begin{pmatrix} \phi_{00}(0) & \psi_{00}(0) & \psi_{10}(0) & \psi_{11}(0) \\ \phi_{00}(1/4) & \psi_{00}(1/4) & \psi_{10}(1/4) & \psi_{11}(1/4) \\ \phi_{00}(2/4) & \psi_{00}(2/4) & \psi_{10}(2/4) & \psi_{11}(2/4) \\ \phi_{00}(3/4) & \psi_{00}(3/4) & \psi_{10}(3/4) & \psi_{11}(3/4) \end{pmatrix}.$$

The simplicity of the Haar base allows us to calculate the elements of the Wmatrix. We have: $\phi_{jk}(x_i) = 1$ if $x_i \in [2^{-j}k, 2^{-j}(k+1)]$ and $\phi_{jk}(x_i) = 0$ if $x_i \notin [2^{-j}k, 2^{-j}(k+1)]$. For the mother wavelet functions, we have: $\psi_{jk}(x_i) = 1$ if $x_i \in [2^{-j}k, 2^{-j}(k+1/2)]$ and $\psi_{jk}(x_i) = -1$ if $x_i \in [2^{-j}(k+1/2), 2^{-j}(k+1)]$. Hence:

$$W = \begin{pmatrix} 1 & 1 & \sqrt{2} & 0 \\ 1 & 1 & -\sqrt{2} & 0 \\ 1 & -1 & 0 & \sqrt{2} \\ 1 & -1 & 0 & -\sqrt{2} \end{pmatrix}.$$

We can see that the matrix $W$is orthogonal, as the scalar product of each pair of column or line vectors is zero. The inverse of Wequals:

$$W^{-1} = \frac{1}{4}\begin{pmatrix} 1 & 1 & 1 & 1 \\ 1 & 1 & -1 & -1 \\ \sqrt{2} & -\sqrt{2} & 0 & 0 \\ 0 & 0 & \sqrt{2} & -\sqrt{2} \end{pmatrix}.$$

Finally, we obtain the discrete wavelet transform of y:

$$W^{-1}y = d = \begin{pmatrix} 4 \\ -1/2 \\ \frac{-3}{2\sqrt{2}} \\ \frac{-5}{2\sqrt{2}} \end{pmatrix} = \begin{pmatrix} c_{00} \\ d_{00} \\ d_{10} \\ d_{11} \end{pmatrix}.$$

This shows that, for $i = 0, 1, 2, 3$, we have $y_i = 4\phi_{00}(x_i) - (1/2)\psi_{00}(x_i) - (3/2\sqrt{2})\psi_{10}(x_i) - (5/2\sqrt{2})\psi_{11}(x_i) = S(x_i) + \sum d_j(x_i)$ with $S(x_i) = 4\phi_{00}(x_i)$. This example emphasizes the respective roles of the mother and father wavelet functions. If we calculate the average of the elements of $y = [2, 5, 2, 7]^T$, we find $\overline{y} = 4$, which is exactly equal to $S(x_i) = c_{00}\phi_{00}(x_i) = 4 * 1 = 4$, since $\phi_{00}(x_i) = 1$ for $i = 0, 1, 2, 3$ (see the matrix W). As such, $S(x_i)$ provides the general shape of the y_i, as is normal in general in wavelet decomposition. The results of the scaling function—that is, $S(x_i) = \sum_{k=0}^{2^{j_0}-1} c_{j_0k}\phi_{j_0k}(x_i)$—determine the general shape of y_i. The $d_j(x_i)$ then bring the additional details which are required to identify the series completely.

When y is a vector of size 2^n, the W matrix is of dimension $2^n \times 2^n$. The calculation of the wavelet transform of y ($W^{-1}y$) and of the inverse transform (Wd) are simple to carry out via a pyramidal algorithm developed by Mallat (1989), which requires a number of operations of the order of 2^n. When the size of y is not a power of two, alternative methods can be used; see, for example, Gençay et al. (2001).

5

Semi-parametric Regression Models

5.1 Introduction

The preceding chapters considered the estimation of a regression model with one explanatory variable. We now move on to the case of multivariate regressions, containing a number of explanatory variables. The extension of non-parametric estimation to multivariate regression does not present any particular theoretical difficulties. For example, consider the following regression model:

$$y = m(x_1, x_2, \ldots, x_k) + \varepsilon. \tag{5.1}$$

The Nadaraya-Watson estimator, defined by (2.4), can be used, replacing the univariate kernel by its multivariate counterpart (Section 1.6). In practice, the *curse of dimensionality* can easily render such estimations unreliable: the number of observations required to yield reliable estimation results can be extremely large when there are a number of explanatory variables (Section 1.6.2). To overcome this problem, *semi-parametric models* can be used. These models mix parametric and non-parametric elements. For example, a *partial linear model* can be written as follows:

$$y = X\beta + m(z) + \varepsilon,$$

where X is a matrix of $k-1$ variables and z is a vector. The relationship between y and X is parametric, while that between y and z is non-parametric. This kind of specification has the advantage of containing β parameters which can be given an economic interpretation, while being robust to other aspects of the model which are difficult to express in a parametric way.

The non-parametric component of partial linear models can be a function of a number of different variables, which can be decomposed additively. For example, a function of three variables can be decomposed as follows: $m(z_1, z_2, z_3) = m_1(z_1) + m_2(z_2, z_3)$, which yields the following *additive model*:

$$y = X\beta + m_1(z_1) + m_2(z_2, z_3) + \varepsilon, \qquad (5.2)$$

where m_1 and m_2 are two distinct non-parametric functions. The estimation of this model yields two non-parametric estimators of m_1 and m_2, which are of dimensions one and two, respectively. It is also possible to decompose the m_2 function additively so that all of the functions are of order one: $m(z_1, z_2, z_3) = m_1(z_1) + m_2(z_2) + m_3(z_3)$. Many different specifications are possible, with the principle of this type of decomposition being to mitigate the problems related to the curse of dimensionality.

To illustrate the estimation of the semi-parametric model (5.2), we consider 1,135 observations of the sales price of housing in Brest in 1995, as used in Ahamada et al. (2007) The explanatory variables in the matrix X here are all dummies: the type of housing (studio, one, two, three, four, or five rooms, where these latter are referred to as T1, T2, T3, T4, and T5), being a house rather than a flat, and if a parking space was included. The z_1 variable is the distance of the accommodation from the nearest green space (DistG) and the z_2 and z_3 variables correspond to the geographical coordinates of the dwelling (Coord1 and Coord2). These coordinates allow us to take into account any price effect from the location of the housing, which is typically taken into account by the use of spatial autocorrelation models (Anselin, 1988). The semi-parametric model is as follows:

$$\log(\text{Price}) = X\beta + m_1(\text{DistG}) + m_2(\text{Coord1}, \text{Coord2}) + \varepsilon.$$

The estimation results are presented in panel (a) of Figure 5.1 (the standard errors are shown in italics). These estimated coefficients have an economic interpretation, analogous to that in a parametric model. The reference category for housing type here is "studio". As such, the coefficients on the other housing types show the estimated gap in the average price, expressed as a percentage, between a studio and T1, T2, T3, T4, and T5, holding everything else constant. For example, the sales price of a T2 in Brest in 1995 was on average 38.6% higher than that of a studio with the same characteristics. Equally, the results suggest that houses cost on average 24.1% more than did flats, and that a parking space increased the sales price by 24.2%, holding all other characteristics constant.

X	coef	s.e.
Const.	4.775	*(0.052)*
T1	0.079	*(0.056)*
T2	0.386	*(0.051)*
T3	0.763	*(0.049)*
T4	0.992	*(0.050)*
T5	1.139	*(0.055)*
House	0.241	*(0.032)*
Parking	0.242	*(0.024)*

(a)

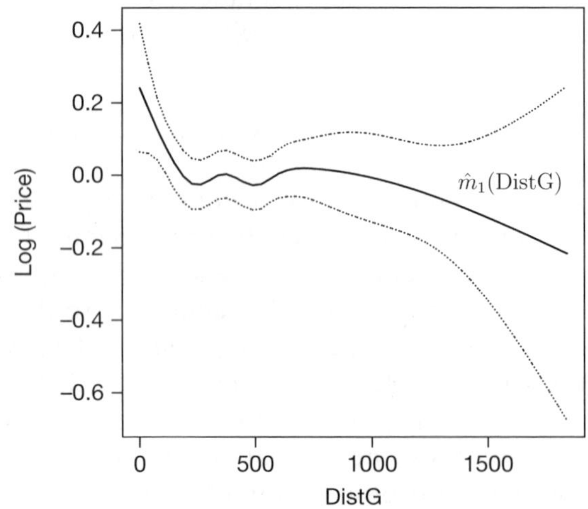

(b) Green space effect

Figure 5.1: The determinants of housing prices

The estimation of semi-parametric models also yields estimates of the m_1 and m_2 functions. Panel (b) of Figure 5.1 depicts the estimate of the m_1 function, with the sales price (in log) of housing on the Y-axis and the distance to the nearest green space on the X-axis. The 95% confidence intervals appear as dotted lines. This figure suggests that the price of housing falls as the distance to the nearest green space rises, at least up to a distance of around 200 meters; over 200 meters, the effect becomes negligible.[1] Figure 5.2 shows the estimated m_2 function, which measures the impact of geographical localization on housing prices. This figure reveals strong non-linearity in the estimated relationship. The two axes in this figure are the geographical coordinates, which means that we can superimpose the estimated relationship on a map of the city. We can thus ascertain that the non-linearity in the estimated function actually reflects the geographical characteristics of the city, with two peaks that are situated either side of the Penfeld river, areas where observed prices are the highest.

While the goal of this analysis is to determine exactly how green space affects the price of housing, it is also of use to consider a parametric

[1] Beyond 200 meters, a straight line at level zero can be drawn between the confidence intervals.

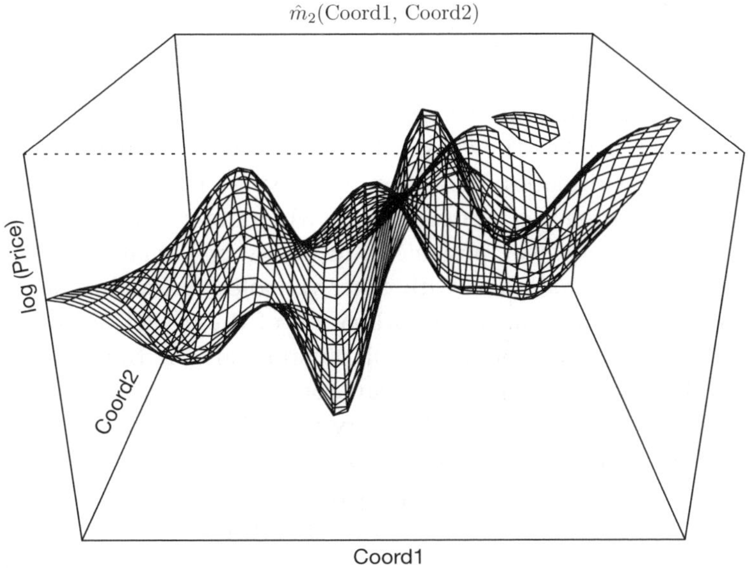

Figure 5.2: Localization effects on housing prices

formulation, justified by a prior non-parametric estimation. In the example presented here, the relationship suggested by panel (b) of Figure 5.1 is piecewise linear:

$$m_1(\text{DistG}) = \gamma\,\text{DistG} + \delta(\text{DistG} - 200)_+, \tag{5.3}$$

where $(\text{DistG} - 200)_+$ is equal to $(\text{DistG} - 200)$ when the expression is positive and zero otherwise. The estimated relationship is thus linear and negative up to 200 meters if $\gamma < 0$, with there being no relationship beyond 200 meters if $\gamma = -\delta$. The estimation of the model (5.2) with the specification (5.3) produces numerical results which are similar to those in the table in Figure 5.1 and in Figure 5.2, with estimated coefficients of $\hat{\gamma} = -0.00130$ and $\hat{\delta} = 0.00133$, and standard errors close to 0.0004. This parametric estimation of the effect of green spaces on housing prices thus does indeed suggest a negative relationship up to 200 meters, and no relationship beyond that point.[2] The advantage of this approach is the replacement of the graph in Figure 5.1 by one sole parameter, $\hat{\gamma}$, which has an economic interpretation: if we consider two identical dwellings

[2] The estimated coefficient γ is negative and significant, and γ is not significantly different from $-\delta$.

situated less than 200 meters from a green space, that which is 100 meters further away from the green space will have, on average, a sales price that is lower by about 13%.

In this application, dummy variables are not part of the non-parametric element of the model. They instead appear in the parametric part. The non-linear transformation of a dummy variable, which only takes the values of 0 and 1, has no particular sense when the variable is considered on its own. It is, however, possible to include such variables in the non-parametric part of the model with other variables, in order to take interaction effects into account. The estimation of the model can be carried out via kernels or appropriate local polynomials. In this chapter, we consider the case of continuous explanatory variables. The joint presence of continuous and discrete explanatory variables is discussed in Racine and Li (2004) and Li and Racine (2006).

Semi-parametric models thus represent a kind of compromise between parametric models, the results of which are sensitive to the model being correctly specified, and non-parametric models, which are subject to the curse of dimensionality. A wide variety of specifications exist which can be qualified as semi-parametric, and it will not be possible here to draw up an exhaustive list of them. The non-parametric formulation can apply to different parts of the regression model: to the functional form, as before, but also to the variance or to the distribution of the error terms. In many cases, the estimation of a semi-parametric model is a useful tool to determine the form of an adequate parametric model.

The following sections present the partial linear model (Section 5.2), before moving on to additive models (Section 5.3). The errors in these models are considered to be independent and identically distributed (*i.i.d.*) and the regressors non-stochastic. In later sections, both of these hypotheses will be relaxed, to introduce heteroskedasticity (Section 5.4) and autocorrelation (Section 5.5). Finally, the endogeneity of explanatory variables (Section 5.6) and discrete-choice models (Section 5.7) will briefly be summarized. More detailed information is available in Horowitz (1998), Pagan and Ullah (1999), Yatchew (2003), Ruppert et al. (2003), Härdle et al. (2004), Li and Racine (2006), and Gao (2007).

5.2 Partial Linear Models

In practice, econometricians often have to choose between robustness and precision. On the one hand, the choice of a parametric model produces information that is in general finer, allowing the model to be successfully estimated, if it is correctly specified. On the other hand, non-parametric models produce consistent estimation results whatever model specification is chosen, although the result is less efficient.

In general, the *partial linear* model can be written as follows:

$$y = X\beta + m(Z) + \varepsilon, \tag{5.4}$$

where X and Z are two matrices of explanatory variables. The parameter vector β and the function m are the unknown elements of the model. The advantage of this model is its robustness to any form whatsoever of the function m. Robinson (1988) shows that this model can produce an estimation of β that is of equal quality to that obtained from a correctly specified parametric model (where m is known).[3] This is an important result, as it demonstrates that greater model robustness can be gained without any loss of efficiency in the estimation of β.

5.2.1 *Double-residual Estimator*

The estimation of the partial linear model (5.4) can be carried out in several stages. The error terms are supposed to be *i.i.d.*, so that $E(\varepsilon|X, Z) = 0$ and $V(\varepsilon|X, Z) = \sigma_\varepsilon^2$. Calculating the conditional expectation over Z of both sides of (5.4), we have:

$$E(y|Z) = E(X|Z)\,\beta + m(Z).$$

The subtraction of this equation from (5.4), then yields:

$$y - E(y|Z) = [X - E(X|Z)]\,\beta + \varepsilon.$$

Robinson (1988) proposes replacing the conditional expectations in this equation by non-parametric estimations, and then estimating the resulting model by Ordinary Least Squares (OLS) to obtain an estimate of β. Consider the model

$$y = m_y(Z) + \varepsilon_1, \tag{5.5}$$

where ε_1 is a vector of *i.i.d.* error terms, with zero mean and variance of $\sigma_{\varepsilon_1}^2$. The non-parametric estimation of this model yields consistent estimates of the conditional expectation $E(y|Z)$. Analogously, we have the model

$$X = m_x(Z) + \varepsilon_2, \tag{5.6}$$

[3] It is shown that the speed of convergence of the estimator of β, as the sample size tends towards infinity, is of the order of $\sqrt{n}$, which is the same property as that found for parametric estimators.

where ε_2 is a matrix of *i.i.d.* error terms, with zero mean and variance of $\sigma^2_{\varepsilon_2}$. The non-parametric estimation of this model yields consistent estimates of the conditional expectation $E(X|Z)$.

The *double-residual estimator* of the partial linear model then corresponds to the OLS estimation of the following model:

$$y - \hat{m}_y = (X - \hat{m}_x)\,\beta + \varepsilon, \tag{5.7}$$

where $\hat{m}_y$ and $\hat{m}_x$ are the non-parametric estimates from the models (5.5) and (5.6). The estimated coefficients are then given by:

$$\hat{\beta}_{res} = [(X - \hat{m}_x)^\top (X - \hat{m}_x)]^{-1}(X - \hat{m}_x)^\top (y - \hat{m}_y).$$

The estimator's name comes from the fact that the model (5.7) corresponds to the regression of the residuals of the model (5.5) on those of model (5.6). In other words, the double-residual estimator can be rewritten as: $\hat{\beta}_{res} = (\hat{\varepsilon}_2^\top \hat{\varepsilon}_2)^{-1}\hat{\varepsilon}_2^\top \hat{\varepsilon}_1$. This estimator has an asymptotic Normal distribution, with variance of $\sigma^2_\varepsilon/(n\sigma^2_{\varepsilon_2})$, where n is the sample size. The estimator of the m function comes from the non-parametric estimation of the following model:

$$y - X\hat{\beta}_{res} = m(Z) + \varepsilon.$$

Confidence intervals can be obtained directly via bootstrap methods, as described in Section 2.5.

The double-residual estimator $\hat{\beta}_{res}$ is thus based on the prior estimation of two non-parametric regressions, which estimation can be carried out via kernel, splines, or wavelets. The preceding chapters have underlined the extent to which these different estimators are sensitive to the choice of certain parameters (bandwidth, knots, filters, and thresholds). This is therefore also implicitly the case for the double-residual estimator. The remainder of this chapter will not explicitly spell out how the resulting estimates are sensitive to the choices made for the non-parametric estimations, and instead refers the reader to the relevant sections of the preceding chapters.

5.2.2 *Differencing Estimator*

Yatchew (1998) shows that an estimate of the parameters of the partial linear model (5.4) can be obtained from the simple OLS estimation of a first-differenced model, without any prior non-parametric estimation.

First, consider the matrix Z, composed of a single continuous variable z. To calculate the parameter estimates, we first need to sort the sample

(y, X, z) with respect to z. This allows us to write the model using first differences as below:

$$y_s - y_{s-1} = (X_s - X_{s-1})\,\beta + [m(z_s) - m(z_{s-1})] + \varepsilon_s - \varepsilon_{s-1}. \tag{5.8}$$

As the sample size tends to infinity, $n \to +\infty$, the element between square brackets tends to zero, $m(z_s) - m(z_{s-1}) \to 0$. This comes from the fact that, for a large enough sample size, two successive observations will be very close to each other after having been sorted, $z_s - z_{s-1} \to 0$. The estimate of the function will thus also be very similar at these two successive points. Consequently, for a large enough sample size, the above model is approximately equal to the model

$$y_s - y_{s-1} \approx (X_s - X_{s-1})\,\beta + \varepsilon_s - \varepsilon_{s-1}. \tag{5.9}$$

The OLS estimation of this produces asymptotically consistent estimates of the parameters β of the partial linear model.

The *differencing estimator* of the partial linear model (5.4) corresponds to the OLS estimation of the parameters of the following model:

$$\Delta y = \Delta X \beta + \eta, \tag{5.10}$$

where Δy and ΔX are two matrices, of which the rows s are equal to $y_s - y_{s-1}$ and $X_s - X_{s-1}$, respectively. The estimator is thus:

$$\hat{\beta}_{diff} = (\Delta X^\top \Delta X)^{-1} \Delta X^\top \Delta y. \tag{5.11}$$

This estimator is asymptotically normal, with a variance of $1.5\,\sigma_\varepsilon^2/(n\sigma_{\varepsilon_2}^2)$. It is relatively efficient, as the coefficient 1.5 on the variance makes the latter larger than that in the case of double-residual estimation. No non-parametric estimation is required to calculate $\hat{\beta}_{diff}$. Nonetheless, we do need non-parametric estimation to estimate $\sigma_{\varepsilon_2}^2$, and thus the variance of $\hat{\beta}_{diff}$, unless we appeal to percentile bootstrap techniques (Section 2.5). The estimator of the m function is obtained from the non-parametric estimation of the following model:

$$y - X\hat{\beta}_{diff} = m(z) + \varepsilon.$$

Confidence intervals can be obtained either directly or by using bootstrap techniques (Section 2.5). Yatchew (2003) extends the principle of differencing to the case of a Z matrix including a number of different variables.

5.2.3 *The Significance of the Coefficients*

In the classic linear regression model, the Frisch-Waugh-Lovell theorem shows that the estimated coefficient on an explanatory variable is to be interpreted as the *net* effect of a change of one unit of that variable on the dependent variable, *net* of any influence that the other explanatory variables might have on the mean of the dependent variable. We will show here that this interpretation continues to hold for the estimates of the β parameters of the partial linear model (5.4).

From the Frisch-Waugh-Lovell theorem, under the classic conditions of linear regression, the OLS estimator of the parameters $\hat{\beta}$ and the residuals $\hat{\varepsilon}$ of the model $y = X\beta + Z\gamma + \varepsilon$ are numerically equivalent to those from the model

$$\hat{\varepsilon}_1' = \hat{\varepsilon}_2' \beta + \varepsilon',$$

where $\hat{\varepsilon}_1'$ and $\hat{\varepsilon}_2'$ are the residuals from the models $y = Z\delta_1 + \varepsilon_1$ and $X = Z\delta_2 + \varepsilon_2$ (Davidson and MacKinnon 2003, Section 2.4). The vector $\hat{\varepsilon}_1'$ represents the "residual" part of y which is not explained by Z, and the vector $\hat{\varepsilon}_2'$ represents the part of X which is not explained by Z. As a result, as the estimate of β comes from the regression of $\hat{\varepsilon}_1'$ on $\hat{\varepsilon}_2'$, it measures the effect of X on y, *net* of any direct or indirect effect of Z on these variables. The double-residual estimate of β in the partial linear model is equally calculated from the regression of the residuals of y on Z and of X on Z, but where these residuals have been calculated from non-parametric regressions (cf. equations (5.5), (5.6), and (5.7)). The principle is thus the same and identical reasoning can be applied to the significance of the $\hat{\beta}_{res}$ estimator.

A different kind of reasoning is necessary to ensure that the estimates from the differencing estimator can be interpreted in the same way. Suppose that the X and z variables are not independent, so that we can write $X = g(z) + u$. In other words, X can be decomposed into a part that is explained by z, and another part, u, that is not explained by z. The differencing model (5.8) can then be rewritten as:

$$y_s - y_{s-1} = [g(z_s) - g(z_{s-1})]\,\beta + (u_s - u_{s-1})\,\beta + [m(z_s) - m(z_{s-1})] + \varepsilon_s - \varepsilon_{s-1}.$$

The two terms in square brackets tend towards zero as the sample size increases. If the sample size is sufficiently large, then this model is equivalent to:

$$y_s - y_{s-1} \approx (u_s - u_{s-1})\,\beta + \varepsilon_s - \varepsilon_{s-1}.$$

The OLS estimation of this model measures the influence of u (the part of X which is not explained by z) on the dependent variable. Since the sample is ranked according to z, we have $X_s - X_{s-1} \approx u_s - u_{s-1}$ in large samples. As such, the above model is equal to (5.9) and its estimator is exactly the differencing estimator $\hat{\beta}_{diff}$ of the partial linear model.

5.3 Additive Models

The partial linear model allows us to sidestep the problem of the curse of dimensionality, as long as the part of the model that is difficult to express parametrically is reduced to one or two dimensions. If the non-parametric element contains a number of different dimensions, we often turn to the hypothesis of additive separability, the simplest version of which is $m(z_1, z_2) = m_1(z_1) + m_2(z_2)$. More generally, the part of the model expressed non-parametrically is decomposed into the sum of a number of distinct functions of one or two dimensions:

$$y = m_1(Z_1) + m_2(Z_2) + \cdots + m_k(Z_k) + \varepsilon,$$

where $Z_1, Z_2, \ldots, Z_k$ are matrices of one or two variables and $m_1, m_2, \ldots, m_k$ are k unknown functions. This hypothesis includes a wide variety of specifications, including the additive model (5.2) presented in the introduction. In this section, we set out the estimation principles of this kind of model, which is iterative, and then consider the consequences of such a decomposition.

5.3.1 *Iterative Estimation*

The necessity of an iterative algorithm to estimate additively separable models can be seen clearly by consideration of the following model:

$$y = m_1(z_1) + m_2(z_2) + \varepsilon,$$

where z_1 and z_2 are two vectors. Calculating the conditional expectation over z_1 for both sides of this equation, as well as the conditional expectation over z_2, yields:

$$E[y - m_2(z_2)|z_1] = m_1(z_1),$$
$$E[y - m_1(z_1)|z_2] = m_2(z_2).$$

The first equation suggests that, if we have an estimate of m_2, then m_1 can be estimated non-parametrically by regressing $y - \hat{m}_2$ on z_1. Analogously, the second equation suggests that m_2 can be estimated non-parametrically by regressing $y - \hat{m}_1$ on z_2. In other words, to estimate m_1 we need to have already estimated m_2, and vice versa. This then leads us to think of the following algorithm:

1. Choose the initial estimates $m_1^{(0)}$ and $m_2^{(0)}$.
2. Obtain an estimate $\hat{m}_1^{(i)}$ by regressing $y - \hat{m}_2^{(i-1)}$ on z_1.
3. Obtain an estimate $\hat{m}_2^{(i)}$ by regressing $y - \hat{m}_1^{(i-1)}$ on z_2.
4. Repeat stages 2 and 3 until convergence is attained.

The initial values $m_1^{(0)}$ and $m_2^{(0)}$ may be set to zero, or estimated via a parametric model.

This algorithm can be generalized without difficulty to additively separable models with more than two additive terms, composed of one or more variables each, and where one term may be parametric, as in the model in the introduction (5.4).

5.3.2 *The Separability Hypothesis*

The hypothesis of additive separability allows us to decompose a function of a number of variables into the sum of a number of different functions of lower dimensions, thus avoiding the curse of dimensionality. However, this hypothesis does restrict the form of the relationship between the variables.

To illustrate the consequences of the hypothesis of additive separability, we come back to the application discussed in the introduction. In this example, which referred to the price of housing, one element of the partial linear model is a non-linear function of the geographical coordinates, m_2(Coord1,Coord2). The estimated form of this function was presented in Figure 5.2: this underlines the considerable non-linearity in this relationship. If we now posit additive separability with respect to this function, we can estimate the same regression model, but now replacing the function by a sum of two non-linear functions, and then by the sum of two linear functions.

The left-hand panel of Figure 5.3 shows the estimation results for the function m_2, decomposed into two separate functions:

$$m_2(\text{Coord1,Coord2}) = m_{21}(\text{Coord1}) + m_{22}(\text{Coord2}).$$

The comparison with Figure 5.2, where the m_2 function was not decomposed in this way, underlines the consequences of the hypothesis of additive separability for the nature of the relationship between the two variables. In Figure 5.3, we can see that the relationship between y and Coord1 always has the same shape, independently of the value of Coord2.

By considering this figure with the Coord1 and Coord2 axes inverted, we note that the relationship between y and Coord2 is equally always the same, independently of the value of Coord1. This figure again identifies two peaks, along the Coord1 axis. However, contrary to Figure 5.2, which identified peaks associated with specific local areas in Coord1 and Coord2, here the peaks are of the same height for all values of Coord2. They therefore cannot be associated with specific local areas according to Coord2. Overall, the difference between the two figures is substantial. Figure 5.3, which is estimated under the hypothesis of separability, identifies much less non-linearity than does Figure 5.2.

The right-hand side of Figure 5.3 shows the estimate of the m_2 function, decomposed into two linear functions:

$$m_2(\text{Coord1},\text{Coord2}) = \text{Coord1}\,\delta_1 + \text{Coord2}\,\delta_2.$$

The relationship between the two variables is now restricted to be a straight line in each of the Coord1 and Coord2 directions. There is thus no non-linearity in the graph, which depicts a "plain" in two dimensions. While the analysis summarized in Figure 5.2 brought out the specificities of certain geographical locations in Brest, no such information is captured by this decomposition into two linear functions.

Non-parametric models allow a great deal of flexibility in terms of the nature of the relationship between a number of variables. Figure 5.3 shows that the separability hypothesis restricts these relationships, and the linear parametric hypothesis does so severely. The final choice of a particular modeling strategy is a difficult one in practice. Statistical tests are not always the best solution to this problem, as the estimation results are often sensitive to a number of different factors and the tests are not

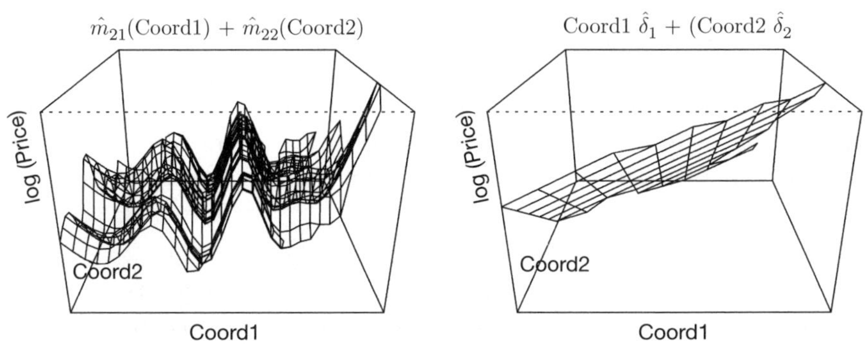

Figure 5.3: Consequences of the additive separability hypothesis

always very reliable in finite samples. As such, detailed knowledge of the question at hand and the data used to analyze it is often the best tool for the identification of a suitable modeling strategy.

5.4 Heteroskedasticity

So far we have considered the errors in the regression model to be *i.i.d.* We relax this hypothesis in this section, and discuss the case of heteroskedastic errors; that is, errors that remain independent but which do not all have the same variance. In the classic linear model:

$$y = X\beta + \varepsilon, \tag{5.12}$$

this hypothesis is captured by the following conditions: $E(\varepsilon|X) = 0$ and $V(\varepsilon|X) = \Omega$, where Ω is a diagonal matrix, $\Omega = \text{diag}\{\sigma_1^2, \sigma_2^2, \ldots, \sigma_n^2\}$. The presence of heteroskedasticity in this model calls for the use of efficient or robust estimators, according to the information we have about the nature of the heteroskedasticity in question. We here present two scenarios in the context of semi-parametric models.

5.4.1 *Efficient Estimators*

When the errors in the classic linear model (5.12) are heteroskedastic, the OLS estimator of the parameters remains consistent, but is not the best linear unbiased estimator. This latter is the Generalized Least Squares (GLS) estimator which has minimum variance:

$$\hat{\beta}_{gls} = (X^\top \Omega^{-1} X)^{-1} X^\top \Omega^{-1} y \quad \text{and} \qquad V(\hat{\beta}_{gls}) = (X^\top \Omega^{-1} X)^{-1}. \tag{5.13}$$

The main practical problem is that the variances of the error terms σ_i^2 are unknown. To use the GLS estimator, we thus require a consistent estimate of the matrix Ω. We commonly appeal to a parametric model of the variance of the errors, of the form $\sigma_i^2 = W_i\gamma$, where W_i contains one or more variables. The predicted values from the OLS estimation of

$$\hat{\varepsilon}^2 = W\gamma + \eta, \tag{5.14}$$

are consistent estimators of the variances of the error terms, $\hat{\sigma}_i^2 = W_i\hat{\gamma}$, where $\hat{\varepsilon}$ is the vector of the residuals from (5.12) and η is an *i.i.d.* error term. These estimates are used to calculate the GLS estimates, replacing Ω by $\hat{\Omega} = \text{diag}\{\hat{\sigma}_1^2, \hat{\sigma}_2^2, \ldots, \hat{\sigma}_n^2\}$.

Now consider the partial linear model (5.4), where the double-residual estimator $\hat{\beta}_{res}$ corresponds to the OLS estimator in the following model:

$$y - \hat{m}_y = (X - \hat{m}_x)\,\beta + \varepsilon, \tag{5.15}$$

where $\hat{m}_y$ and $\hat{m}_x$ are the non-parametric estimates of the models (5.5) and (5.6). The estimates $\hat{m}_y$ and $\hat{m}_x$ are consistent in the presence of heteroskedasticity. As a result, the above model can be estimated directly by GLS to obtain parameter estimates and standard errors which remain valid when there is heteroskedasticity. The parameter estimates are given by:

$$\hat{\beta}_{gres} = [(X - \hat{m}_x)^\top \hat{\Omega}^{-1}(X - \hat{m}_x)]^{-1}(X - \hat{m}_x)^\top \hat{\Omega}^{-1}(y - \hat{m}_y). \tag{5.16}$$

The variance of this estimator is:

$$V(\hat{\beta}_{gres}) = [(X - \hat{m}_x)^\top \hat{\Omega}^{-1}(X - \hat{m}_x)]^{-1}, \tag{5.17}$$

where $\hat{\Omega}$ is a diagonal matrix, the diagonal elements of which are the predicted values of the model (5.14), and where $\hat{\varepsilon}$ is the vector of residuals from the model (5.15).

The differencing estimator $\hat{\beta}_{diff}$ of the partial linear model corresponds to the OLS estimation of the model (5.10), when the sample is ranked. This model can be estimated directly by GLS to produce estimated parameters and standard errors which remain valid under heteroskedasticity.

In the above estimators, the model (5.14) is estimated to obtain consistent estimators of the elements of the variance–covariance matrix of the errors Ω. This model is parametric, however, and may not be best suited. Note that we can replace this parametric formulation by a non-parametric or semi-parametric formulation, according to the dimension of the matrix W. The predicted values from the estimation of these kinds of models are used to obtain a consistent estimator of Ω which is more robust to the specification of heteroskedasticity.

5.4.2 *Robust Estimators*

When we do not have sufficient information about the form of the heteroskedasticity, in the sense that we do not have a consistent estimator of the variance of the error terms, GLS estimation is not possible. In the presence of heteroskedastic errors in the linear model (5.12), the OLS estimator of the parameters $\hat{\beta}$ is consistent but its variance is no longer so. Any tests based on these estimates will thus no longer be valid. It is nonetheless possible to calculate an estimate of the variance which is robust to heteroskedasticity, as proposed by White (1980):

$$\tilde{V}(\hat{\beta}_{ols}) = (X^\top X)^{-1} X^\top \tilde{\Omega} X (X^\top X)^{-1},$$

where $\tilde{\Omega}$ is a diagonal matrix, the diagonal elements of which are the squared residuals, $\tilde{\Omega} = \text{diag}\{\tilde{\varepsilon}_1^2, \tilde{\varepsilon}_2^2, \ldots, \tilde{\varepsilon}_n^2\}$. It is clear that $\tilde{\Omega}$ is not a consistent estimator of Ω. Nonetheless, White shows that the matrix $X^\top \tilde{\Omega} X$ is a consistent estimator of $X^\top \Omega X$.[4] This variance estimator is thus consistent and any tests based on it will be valid. While often used in practice, the tests based on this estimator are actually not very reliable in finite samples, unless the sample size is very large or appropriate bootstrap techniques are used (Flachaire, 2005b; Davidson and Flachaire, 2008).

When we introduce heteroskedasticity of unknown form into the errors of the partial linear model (5.4), the parameter estimates from double-residual estimation correspond to the OLS estimator in the model (5.15), and thus remain consistent. An estimator of the variance which is robust to heteroskedasticity can be obtained by the direct calculation of the robust White estimator in this model. The heteroskedasticity-robust estimator of the variance of $\hat{\beta}_{res}$ is thus given by:

$$\tilde{V}(\hat{\beta}_{res}) = [(X - \hat{m}_x)^\top (X - \hat{m}_x)]^{-1} (X - \hat{m}_x)^\top \tilde{\Omega} (X - \hat{m}_x) [(X - \hat{m}_x)^\top (X - \hat{m}_x)]^{-1},$$

where $\tilde{\Omega}$ is a diagonal matrix composed of the squared residuals of the model (5.15).

The same holds for the differencing estimator of the parameters (5.11). This estimator remains consistent when we introduce heteroskedasticity of unknown form into the errors of the partial linear model (5.4). A heteroskedasticity-robust estimator of the variance can be obtained by the direct calculation of the robust White estimator in the model (5.10).

5.5 Autocorrelation

Time-series data are often characterized by temporal correlation. To take this into account, regression models relax the hypothesis of the independence of the error terms or introduce lagged values of the dependent variable as additional right-hand-side variables. Semi-parametric methods can be useful in both scenarios. In this section, we limit our attention to models where the underlying process is stationary. Under this hypothesis,

[4] As the dimension of the matrix $X^\top \tilde{\Omega} X$ is fixed as the sample size increases, the Central Limit Theorem applies.

the kernel estimator of the density is valid with autocorrelated data, as are the properties of the parameter estimators from semi-parametric models obtained under the *i.i.d.* assumption. Further reading is available in the literature reviews of Härdle et al. (1997) and Heiler (1999), as well as the books by Fan and Yao (2005) and Gao (2007).

5.5.1 *Models with Autocorrelated Errors*

Autocorrelated errors in the classic linear model (5.12) will not affect the consistency of the OLS estimator of the parameters, but will ensure that this former is no longer the best linear unbiased estimator. The GLS estimator (5.13) is that which has minimum variance, where Ω is a non-diagonal covariance matrix of the errors. To use GLS estimation, we require a consistent estimate of the Ω matrix. One way of addressing this problem is to specify the temporal correlation in a parametric manner. For example, the first-order autoregressive model, AR(1), is written as follows:

$$y_t = X_t\beta + \varepsilon_t, \qquad \text{where} \qquad \varepsilon_t = \rho\,\varepsilon_{t-1} + \eta_t,$$

where η_t is an *i.i.d.* error. The covariance matrix of the errors $V(\varepsilon|X)$ is then given by:

$$\Omega = \frac{\sigma_\eta^2}{1-\rho^2}\begin{pmatrix} 1 & \rho & \rho^2 & \dots & \rho^{n-1} \\ \rho & 1 & \rho & \dots & \rho^{n-2} \\ \vdots & \vdots & \vdots & \vdots & \vdots \\ \rho^{n-1} & \rho^{n-2} & \rho^{n-3} & \dots & 1 \end{pmatrix}, \tag{5.18}$$

where σ_η^2 is the variance of η. With consistent estimators of σ_η and ρ, we can obtain a consistent estimator of Ω. This latter is then used in the place of Ω in (5.13) to obtain efficient estimates of the β parameters. Note that this principle also applies to other parametric formulations of temporal correlation, such as MA, ARMA, or ARCH models.[5]

If we now turn to the partial linear model (5.4), the double-residual estimator $\hat{\beta}_{res}$ corresponds to the OLS estimation of the model:

$$y - \hat{m}_y = (X - \hat{m}_x)\,\beta + \varepsilon, \tag{5.19}$$

where $\hat{m}_y$ and $\hat{m}_x$ are the non-parametric estimates from the models (5.5) and (5.6). The $\hat{m}_y$ and $\hat{m}_x$ estimators remain consistent when there is

[5] Moving Average, Autoregressive Moving Average, and Autoregressive Conditional Heteroskedasticity, respectively.

autocorrelation. As a result, the above model can be estimated directly by GLS in order to obtain estimates of the parameters and standard errors which are valid in the presence of autocorrelation. These latter estimates are identical to those defined in (5.16) and (5.17), with $\hat{\Omega}$ being a consistent estimator of the covariance matrix of the errors Ω, of the form (5.18) in the case of AR(1) errors.

While the above estimation strategy is valid, its behavior in finite samples can be affected by the presence of temporal correlation in the errors, and in particular by the fact that the estimates $\hat{m}_y$ and $\hat{m}_x$ come from non-parametric regressions where the errors may be autocorrelated. The results of kernel estimation are sensitive to the choice of bandwidth. When errors are independent, cross-validation is a satisfactory method for the automatic selection of this parameter (Section 2.4). However, if the errors are autocorrelated, cross-validation can produce much less satisfactory results, according to the strength of the autocorrelation. A number of different methods have been proposed to address this problem—notably cross-validation by blocks and the block bootstrap (Chu and Marron, 1991; Hall et al., 1995). Even so, the results of the automatic selection procedures remain in general less satisfactory than in the case of independent errors. A discussion of the consequences of autocorrelated errors in non-parametric regression models, with the kernel, spline, and wavelet estimation methods, can be found in Opsomer et al. (2001).

If it is not possible to obtain a consistent estimator $\hat{\Omega}$ of the covariance matrix of the errors, Ω, then we cannot use the GLS estimator. On the contrary, the double-residual estimator of the parameters remains consistent, and it is possible to calculate a robust estimate of its variance. By generalizing the estimator of White (1980), Newey and West (1987) propose a variance estimator that is robust to heteroskedasticity and autocorrelation. This estimator can be calculated directly from the model (5.19) to yield the robust standard errors of the double-residual estimator. However, this estimator does not possess particularly good properties in finite samples, and is not reliable unless we have a huge sample at our disposal. As such, it is less widely used in practice.

5.5.2 *Dynamic Models*

To take temporal correlation into account, dynamic models include lagged values of the dependent variable amongst the right-hand-side variables. In the partial linear model, these lagged values can appear in either the parametric or the non-parametric part of the model.

Non-linear autoregressive models have been developed to overcome the weaknesses of linear models, which do not capture certain aspects of time-series (Bera and Higgins, 1993). Semi-parametric models can be used here, such as the *partial linear autoregressive model*, the simplest form of which is:

$$y_t = \beta\, y_{t-1} + m(y_{t-2}) + \varepsilon_t, \tag{5.20}$$

where y_t, $t = 1, \ldots, n$ is a stationary series and ε_t an *i.i.d.* error such that $E(\varepsilon_t | y_{t-1}, y_{t-2}) = 0$ and $V(\varepsilon_t | y_{t-1}, y_{t-2}) = \sigma_\varepsilon^2$. This model contains a first linear autoregressive term, and a second non-linear autoregressive term. Applying the principle of double residuals, if we subtract the conditional expectation relative to y_{t-2} from this model, we obtain:

$$y_t - E(y_t | y_{t-2}) = \beta\, [y_{t-1} - E(y_{t-1} | y_{t-2})] + \varepsilon_t.$$

The double-residual estimator corresponds to the OLS estimation of this model. It is consistent if we replace the conditional expectations by consistent estimates. These latter are obtained from the non-parametric estimation of y_t on y_{t-2}, and of y_{t-1} on y_{t-2}. Gao and Lee (2000) show that, under certain conditions, this estimator is asymptotically Normal, with variance equal to $\sigma_\varepsilon^2 / (n\sigma_{\varepsilon_2}^2)$, where $\sigma_{\varepsilon_2}^2$ is the variance of the errors in the regression of y_{t-1} on y_{t-2}.

Other autoregressive specifications are also possible. For example, one practical pertinent question is to ask whether the model (5.20) is more appropriate than a model of the form $y_t = m(y_{t-1}) + \beta y_{t-2} + \varepsilon$. To answer this question, Wong and Kohn (2000) estimate an *additive autoregressive model*:

$$y_t = m_1(y_{t-1}) + m_2(y_{t-2}) + \varepsilon_t.$$

In their application, they choose the model (5.20) as being the most appropriate. For more details on semi-parametric models in the context of non-linear time-series, see Gao (2007).

5.6 Endogenous Variables

The hypothesis of no correlation between the error terms and the explanatory variables is a crucial one. If this hypothesis does not hold, then all of the estimators discussed up to this point are not valid. In practice, this problem is particularly salient in the presence of measurement errors in the variables and when two or more variables (endogenous) are jointly determined by a system of simultaneous equations. In the classic linear model:

$$y = X\beta + \varepsilon,$$

this problem is characterized by $E(\varepsilon|X) \neq 0$. OLS estimation is thus no longer valid, and we need to turn to instrumental variable (IV) estimation. The principle of instrumental variable estimation consists in appealing to W variables which are strongly correlated with regressors X, but which are not correlated with the errors in the model. This allows us to decompose the regressors into two parts: one explained by these "instrumental" variables, denoted by $P_W X$, and the other, which is a residual. The IV estimator corresponds to the OLS estimator in the regression of y on $P_W X$:

$$\hat{\beta}_{vi} = (X^\top P_W X)^{-1} X^\top P_W y \qquad \text{and} \qquad V(\hat{\beta}_{vi}) = \sigma^2 (X^\top P_W X)^{-1},$$

where σ^2 is the variance of the errors in the linear model. The matrix $P_W X$ corresponds to the predicted values from the regressions of each of the explanatory variables on the matrix of the instruments:

$$X = W\pi + \nu,$$

where ν is a vector of *i.i.d.* errors, which are not correlated with the instruments, $E(\nu|W) = 0$. It then follows that $P_W X = W(W^\top W)^{-1} W^\top X$. A necessary condition is that the number of instruments be greater than or equal to the number of explanatory variables.

Now consider the partial linear model,

$$y = X\beta + m(Z) + \varepsilon. \tag{5.21}$$

The correlation between the errors ε and the explanatory variables can occur: (1) with the X variables, which appear in the parametric part; or (2) with the Z variables, which appear in the non-parametric part of the model. In this section, we consider both types of endogenous variables.

5.6.1 *Endogeneity in the Parametric Part*

In the partial linear model (5.21), if the X variables are endogenous, but the Z variables are not, we have $E(\varepsilon|X) \neq 0$ and $E(\varepsilon|Z) = 0$. The double-residual estimator $\hat{\beta}_{res}$ corresponds to the OLS estimator in the following model:

$$y - \hat{m}_y = (X - \hat{m}_x)\,\beta + \varepsilon,$$

where $\hat{m}_y$ and $\hat{m}_x$ are non-parametric estimators in the models (5.5) and (5.6). The $\hat{m}_y$ and $\hat{m}_x$ estimators will be consistent as long as the Z variables are not endogenous. As a result, the model above can be estimated directly by IV to obtain valid parameter estimates:

$$\hat{\beta}_{ivres} = [(X - \hat{m}_x)^\top P_W (X - \hat{m}_x)]^{-1} (X - \hat{m}_x)^\top P_W (y - \hat{m}_y).$$

The variance of this parameter estimator is given by:

$$V(\hat{\beta}_{ivres}) = \sigma_\varepsilon^2 [(X - \hat{m}_x)^\top P_W (X - \hat{m}_x)]^{-1},$$

where σ_ε^2 is the variance of the errors in model (5.21).

5.6.2 *Endogeneity in the Non-parametric Part*

If the Z variables, but not the X variables, are endogenous in the partial linear model (5.21), we have $E(\varepsilon|X) = 0$ and $E(\varepsilon|Z) \neq 0$. Whenever the Z variables are endogenous in the non-parametric models (5.5) and (5.6), then the estimators $\hat{m}_y$ and $\hat{m}_x$ are no longer consistent. Two different approaches to this problem are possible.

INSTRUMENTAL VARIABLES

A first approach, presented by Florens (2003) and Newey and Powell (2003), consists in extending the principle of instrumental variables to the non-parametric case. If we apply the conditional expectation over the instruments W, rather than over the regressors Z, to the partial linear model, we obtain:

$$E(y|W) = E(X|W)\beta + E[m(Z)|W].$$

The problem that arises here is that when we subtract this equation from the partial linear model, the non-parametric term does not disappear. The solution to this problem, which boils down to the ill-posed inverse problem, is not simple and requires the use of particular methods (the regularizations of Tykhonov and Landweber-Fridman). This kind of analysis goes beyond the scope of the current book. More details on this subject can be found in, amongst others, Blundell and Powell (2003), Park (2003), Darolles et al. (2003), Florens et al. (2005), Hall and Horowitz (2005), Florens and Lestringant (2007), and Carrasco et al. (2007).

CONTROL FUNCTIONS

A second approach, presented by Newey et al. (1999), calls for an additional hypothesis. Let W be a matrix of instruments, strongly correlated with the endogenous variables Z, but uncorrelated with the errors of the partial linear model, $E(\varepsilon|W) = 0$, such that:

$$Z = W\pi + \nu, \tag{5.22}$$

where ν is a vector of *i.i.d.* errors, which are not correlated with the instruments, $E(\nu|W) = 0$. We now make the additional hypothesis: $E(\varepsilon|Z, \nu) = \rho\nu$, such that we can write $\varepsilon = \rho\nu + \eta$. The partial linear model (5.4) can then be rewritten as:

$$y = X\beta + m(Z) + \nu\rho + \eta, \tag{5.23}$$

where there is now no problem of endogeneity, as $E(\eta|X, Z, \nu) = 0$. It is therefore possible to appeal to the double-residual estimator (or the differencing estimator) to obtain consistent estimates of the β parameters. The application of a conditional expectation over Z to the above model, which we then subtract from the partial linear model, allows us to eliminate the non-parametric term:

$$y - E(y|Z) = [X - E(X|Z)]\beta + [\nu - E(\nu|Z)]\rho + \eta.$$

We use the OLS residuals $\hat{\nu}$ from the model (5.22) instead of the unobserved values of ν, and replace the conditional expectations by non-parametric estimations $\hat{m}_y$, $\hat{m}_X$, and $\hat{m}_\nu$, from the regressions of y, X, and $\hat{\nu}$, respectively on the Z variables. The OLS estimation of the model:

$$y - \hat{m}_y = (X - \hat{m}_X)\beta + (\hat{\nu} - \hat{m}_\nu)\rho + \eta$$

yields consistent estimators of both the β and ρ parameters and their variances. Note that a simple test of exogeneity can be carried out using this model, by considering the null hypothesis $H_0 : \rho = 0$. In addition, a non-parametric estimation of the model:

$$y - X\hat{\beta} - \hat{\nu}\hat{\rho} = m(Z) + \eta$$

provides an estimate of the function m of the partial linear model.

5.7 Discrete-choice Models

When the dependent variable only takes a small number of discrete values, standard linear regression is not appropriate, and other models should be applied instead. In this section, we limit the analysis to binary choice models, in which the dependent variable takes on only two distinct values. The extension to other regression models, for example Multinomial or Poisson, is discussed in Hastie and Tibshirani (1990) and Wood (2006), who present them in the context of generalized additive models.

In the parametric case, a binary choice model can be characterized by an underlying model of the form:

$$y^{\circ} = X\beta + \varepsilon \qquad \varepsilon \sim G(0, 1),$$

where X is a matrix consisting of k explanatory variables, β is a vector of k unknown parameters, and the errors ε are considered to be *i.i.d*, with a distribution of G and variance of 1.[6] The dependent variable y° is unobserved, and as such is a latent variable. What we do observe is a binary variable y, which takes on the values of 1 or 0. In this case, the conditional expectation of y over X can be written as follows:[7]

$$E(y|X) = P(y = 1|X) = G(X\beta).$$

In other words, y has a Bernoulli distribution, with parameter $P(y = 1|X) = G(X\beta)$. Let y_i and X_i be the i elements of the vector y and the matrix X, then the estimated Maximum Likelihood (ML) parameters are obtained from the maximization of:

$$\ell(y, \beta) = \sum_{i=1}^{n} \Big(y_i \log G(X_i\beta) + (1 - y_i) \log \big(1 - G(X_i\beta)\big) \Big). \tag{5.24}$$

In practice, a parametric distribution of the errors G is determined *a priori*. The Logistic or Normal distribution functions are often used, producing the logit and probit models, respectively.

Semi-parametric methods can be used here in two different ways: (1) by considering a semi-parametric specification of the underlying model, such as partial linear or additive; and (2) by considering an underlying linear model and an unknown distribution, G, which is estimated non-parametrically.

5.7.1 *Partial Linear Models*

A first semi-parametric approach consists in applying the principle of partial linear models to discrete-choice models (Section 5.2). This implies

[6] If the standard deviation of the errors is not equal to 1, we can always divide y°, β, and ε by this value to get back to the above latent model.

[7] We have $P(y = 1|X) = P(y^{\circ} > 0|X) = P(X\beta + \varepsilon > 0) = P(\varepsilon \leq X\beta) = G(X\beta)$.

specifying the model in a partial linear way:

$$E(y|X, Z) = G[X\beta + m(Z)],$$

where G is a cumulative distribution function chosen *a priori*. The unknown parts of the model are the parameters β and the m function, which can be estimated iteratively. For a given estimator of the non-parametric function, $\hat{m}^{(d)}$, an estimator of the β parameters can be obtained from the maximization of the log-likelihood function:

$$\ell(y, \beta) = \sum_{i=1}^{n} \left(y_i \log G[X_i\beta + \hat{m}^{(d)}] + (1 - y_i) \log \left(1 - G[X_i\beta + \hat{m}^{(d)}]\right)\right).$$

This estimate, denoted by $\hat{\beta}^{(d)}$, can then itself be used to obtain a new estimate of m via the maximization of the log-likelihood function:

$$\ell(y, m) = \sum_{t=1}^{n} \left(y_t \log G[X_t\hat{\beta}^{(d)} + m(Z)] + (1 - y_t) \log \left(1 - G[X_t\hat{\beta}^{(d)} + m(Z)]\right)\right).$$

This procedure is iterated up to the point where the difference between the iterated values is negligible. An initial set of estimation values can be obtained from a completely parametric linear model, $\hat{m}^{(0)} = Z\hat{\gamma}$. The maximization of these log-likelihoods requires the resolution of non-linear optimization problems which can be very complicated. Further technical details are available in Hastie and Tibshirani (1986, 1987) and Abe (1999), who consider the more general framework of generalized additive models.

5.7.2 *Index Models*

In a linear regression model with *i.i.d.* error terms, exogenous explanatory variables, and a continuous dependent variable, the OLS estimates of the parameters are consistent even if the distribution of the error terms is not Normal. In a linear regression model with a binary dependent variable, the *a priori* choice of the distribution of the errors is decisive: if this is not correctly specified, the maximum likelihood parameter estimates will in general no longer be consistent. It is for this reason that much work has been carried out on the semi-parametric estimation of discrete-choice models, in which no *a priori* specification of the distribution G of the errors is required. In the following discussion, we consider that the model is specified linearly:

$$E(y|X) = G(X\beta),$$

where β is a vector of unknown parameters and G is an unknown function. This type of model is called an *Index Model*, as the argument $X\beta$ is of dimension 1, while the X matrix is composed of k explanatory variables. The specification of Index models thus allows us to avoid the curse of dimensionality.

A certain number of conditions need to be respected for us to be able to estimate this kind of model. In particular, the G function has to be differentiable and non-constant, and the explanatory variables X have to contain at least one continuous variable and no constant. For a discussion of these identification conditions of index models, see Manski (1988), Ichimura (1993), and Horowitz (1998). A number of different estimation methods have been put forward in the literature. These consist of the following steps:

1. Obtain an initial estimate of the parameters $\hat{\beta}$.
2. Calculate the value of the index $z = X\hat{\beta}$.
3. Estimate the G function from the simple regression of y on z.

The main difficulty comes in obtaining an initial estimate of the parameters.

In the case of a discrete-choice model with a binary dependent variable, if the G function is known, then we are back to the case of a standard model and parameter estimation poses no particular problem, by maximizing the log-likelihood. However, if the G function is not known, then estimation is more difficult, as this is not the only unknown quantity (the vector of parameters β is unknown as well). Klein and Spady (1993) propose to estimate the parameters by maximizing the following log-likelihood function:

$$\ell(y, \beta, h) = \sum_{i=1}^{n} \left(y_i \log \hat{G}(X_i\beta) + (1 - y_i) \log \left(1 - \hat{G}(X_i\beta)\right)\right),$$

where $\hat{G}(X_i\beta)$ is a non-parametric estimator of $G(X_i\beta)$. For example, with the Nadaraya-Watson estimator:

$$\hat{G}(X_i\beta) = \frac{\sum_{j\neq i} K\left(\frac{X_j\beta - X_i\beta}{h}\right) y_j}{\sum_{j\neq i} K\left(\frac{X_j\beta - X_i\beta}{h}\right)}.$$

They thus propose replacing the parametric expression for the G function (the Normal or Logistic distribution) in the standard model (5.24) by a non-parametric estimator. The resulting log-likelihood can be multimodal and strongly non-linear, which renders its maximization difficult and requires the use of a numerical optimization algorithm. After the initial estimation of the $\hat{\beta}$ parameters, the G function can be estimated by the maximization of the log-likelihood below:

$$\ell(y, G) = \sum_{i=1}^{n} \left(y_i \log G(z) + (1 - y_i) \log \left(1 - G(z)\right)\right), \qquad \text{where} \qquad z = X\hat{\beta}.$$

This is the *Pseudo Maximum Likelihood* method.

Index models are not limited to the discrete case; they can also be used when the dependent variable y is continuous. If the G function is known, the model is reduced to a standard non-linear model, and the parameters can be estimated without any particular difficulty by non-linear least squares. If the G function is unknown, however, estimation poses far greater problems, as again both G and the parameter vector β are unknown. Ichimura (1993) proposes replacing the parametric expression $G(X_i\beta)$ by its non-parametric counterpart $\hat{G}(X_i\beta)$ in the expression for the sum of squares of the residuals. The estimated parameters are obtained from the minimization of this sum of squares via a numerical optimization algorithm. A non-parametric estimate of G can then be obtained from the simple regression of y on the index values $z = X\hat{\beta}$. Other estimators have also been proposed in the literature, which do not involve the use of costly numerical calculation (Powell et al., 1989; Horowitz and Härdle, 1996); however, these do not have satisfactory properties in finite samples. A prior test of the suitability of a given parametric function G can also be carried out (Horowitz and Härdle, 1994). Further details on estimation and inference in the case of index models can be found in Pagan and Ullah (1999), Horowitz (1998, 2004), and Li and Racine (2006).

6

Mixture Models

6.1 Introduction

Finite mixture models are *semi-parametric* methods, and are particularly useful for the modeling of population heterogeneity in the estimation of a density or a regression model. The interpretation of these models is the clearest if we consider that the population is not homogeneous, but rather divided up into a number of distinct groups. The observed population can then clearly be thought of as the outcome of a mixture of these different groups:

- in the context of a density, this interpretation implies that the population density is a mixture of the densities associated with each of the different groups. Mixture models allow us not only to estimate any type of density function, but also to decompose the population into groups. The analysis of the density and the way in which it varies within and between groups is simple to carry out;
- in the regression context, the mixture approach allows the identification of homogeneous groups with respect to the relationship between the dependent and explanatory variables. This approach allows us to take into account some heterogeneity which is not picked up by the explanatory variables in the initial regression.

In mixture models, the group to which each individual belongs is not observed. They thus allow us to capture the effect of *unobserved heterogeneity*.

To estimate a probability density, a *mixture model* defines the population density as a combination of parametric densities:

$$f(y, \Theta) = \sum_{k=1}^{K} \pi_k f_k(y; \theta_k), \tag{6.1}$$

where Θ is the set of all of the parameters, K is the number of distinct groups, called the number of mixture components, π_k is the proportion of the population belonging to group k, and $f_k(y; \theta_k)$ is a probability distribution characterized by the set of parameters contained in the vector θ_k. The π_k parameters have the following properties:

$$0 \leq \pi_k \leq 1 \quad \text{and} \quad \sum_{k=1}^{K} \pi_k = 1.$$

In our sample, we do not know to which group any of the observations belong. It is then standard to consider mixture models as presenting a problem of missing data. The role of estimation here is to identify the unknown parameters, by taking into account the likelihood that each of the observations belongs to each of the different groups.

The estimation of a density by a mixture model allows us to bring out the link between parametric and non-parametric estimation. If we consider one single group ($K = 1$), then the mixture models amount to just one parametric function. Adding additional groups allows us to estimate more complicated densities, which cannot be modeled with one sole group; adding more groups allows us to reflect the heterogeneity of the population. Mixture models thus permit much greater modeling flexibility. In the extreme case, where we have as many groups as we do observations ($K = n$), the mixture is equivalent to the estimation of a density by kernel methods (Chapter 1).[1] For values of K between 1 and the size of the sample n, the mixture model can thus be seen as a *semi-parametric* compromise between parametric estimation and non-parametric kernel estimation. The parametric aspect is reflected in the fact that the density is expressed as a sum of parametric density functions; the non-parametric aspect is captured by the presence of a number of different groups.

The extension to a *mixture regression model* is carried out by introducing explanatory variables into either the mixture proportions π_k or the distributions $f_k(.)$, and can be written as follows:

$$f(y|x, z, \Theta) = \sum_{k=1}^{K} \pi_k(z, \alpha_k) f_k(y|x; \beta_k, \theta_k),$$

[1] We also have to have groups of equal size: $\pi_1 = \pi_2 = \cdots = \pi_K = 1/n$. Equation (6.1) is then equivalent to equation (1.5), where the $f_i(.)$ function is the kernel function $K(.)$.

where α_k and β_k are parameter vectors associated with the complete set of variables, z and x. The same variables may appear in both vectors x and z, or they may be completely independent. To distinguish between them, the z variables that appear in the mixture proportions are called *concomitant variables*, and those in x are called *explanatory variables*, as they play the same role here as the regressors in a regression model. If we consider one group only, and a parametric distribution belonging to the exponential family, then under the hypothesis of independent errors, the mixture model is equivalent to a generalized linear regression, including, amongst others, linear regression, and the discrete-choice, count-data, and duration models (Dobson, 2001; McCullagh and Nelder, 2001). The mixture approach with more than one group allows us to model population heterogeneity, and is widespread in the analysis of duration models (Heckman and Singer, 1984). It is also common in Marketing, in classification analysis and market segmentation (Wedel and Kamakura, 1999). With respect to discrete-choice models, the mixture approach has introduced greater model flexibility, and notably allows the analyst to approximate any random utility model (McFadden and Train, 2000; Train, 2003). The extension of mixture models to the case of correlated errors has been developed via *Hidden Markov* models. These are useful in particular for the analysis of non-linear time-series (Hamilton, 1989; Le et al., 1996).

Section 6.2 below discusses the estimation of a univariate density by a finite mixture of Normal distributions. Mixture models with concomitant variables are then presented in Section 6.3, and mixture regression models in Section 6.4. Finally, the extension of mixture models to correlated data is considered via Hidden Markov models in Section 6.5. For further reading on this subject, we recommend Titterington et al. (1985), Everitt (1993), Lindsay (1995), Wedel and Kamakura (1999), McLachlan and Peel (2000), and Frühwirth-Schnatter (2006).

6.2 Density Estimation

The theory of mixture models tells us that, under certain regularity conditions, any probability density can be consistently estimated as a mixture of Normal distributions.[2] The empirical results on this topic suggest that a *finite* mixture of Normal distributions produces a satisfactory estimate

[2] See Ghosal and van der Vaart (2001) for recent results regarding the speed of this convergence.

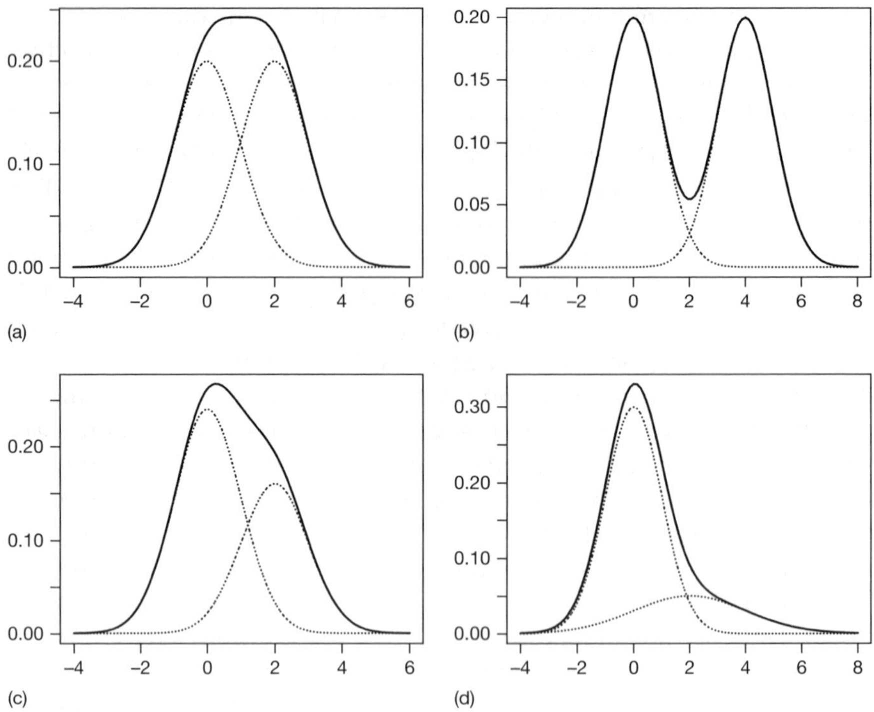

Figure 6.1: Mixtures of two Normal distributions

of any density.[3] In this section, we limit the discussion to mixtures of Normal distributions. We first show that a wide variety of densities can be represented by a mixture of only two Normal distributions; we then consider the problem of estimation, and introduce multivariate densities.

6.2.1 *Finite Mixtures of Normal Distributions*

Figure 6.1 depicts a number of different mixtures of two Normal distributions, of which the density can be written as $\pi_1\phi(y;\mu_1,\sigma_1)+\pi_2\phi(y;\mu_2,\sigma_2)$, where $\phi(.)$ is the density of the Normal distribution, with mean μ_k and variance σ_k, for $k=1,2$. The global density and the two individual components are represented in the same figure. The individual components of

[3] Other distributions can also be used. Paap and van Dijk (1998) consider mixtures of two different types of distribution (Normal, Log-Normal, Gamma, Weibull), Davidson and Flachaire (2007) and Cowell and Flachaire (2007) appeal to the mixture of a non-parametric estimator together with a Pareto distribution to produce an estimator of the distribution function which is less sensitive to extreme values in the sample.

the densities shown in panels (a) and (b) have the same weight $\pi_1 = \pi_2 = 0.5$, and the same variance $\sigma_1 = \sigma_2 = 1$. The difference between the two panels comes from the distance separating the two means, which is equal to twice the standard deviation in panel (a), $\mu_1 = 0, \mu_2 = 2$, but twice as large in panel (b), $\mu_1 = 0, \mu_2 = 4$. The two groups are thus closer together in panel (a) than they are in panel (b), which produces a unimodal distribution in the first case, but a bimodal distribution in the second. If we wanted to construct a classification rule, the best one would be to place in the first group all of the observations which are below the population mean, and in the second those which are above this mean. In panel (b), the mean equals 2 and the classification will correctly identify which observations belong to which group. However, in panel (a), the mean is 1 and there will be a greater number of classification errors due to the closeness of the two groups.

If the means of the two groups are relatively similar, any difference in the proportions of the observations that are found in each group will produce asymmetric distributions. This is depicted in panel (c), which presents two Normal distributions which have similar parameters to those shown in panel (a) of the same figure, but different proportions of the observations: $\pi_1 = 0.6$ and $\pi_2 = 0.4$. Panel (d) shows the case where both proportions and variances are different: $\pi_1 = 0.75$, $\pi_2 = 0.25$, $\sigma_1 = 1$, and $\sigma_2 = 2$. This mixture allows us to produce a strongly asymmetric distribution, where the right-hand-side tail is much thicker than that of a standard Normal distribution. These four panels demonstrate how a considerable number of densities can be well approximated by a mixture of two Normal distributions. Many further examples can be provided to illustrate the very wide variety of distributions that can be characterized by a mixture of K Normal distributions: see, amongst others, Marron and Wand (1992). All of these examples reveal the great flexibility of mixture models in estimating densities.

6.2.2 *Estimation*

A *mixture model of Normal distributions* can be written as the sum of a number of different Normal distributions:

$$f(y, \Theta) = \sum_{k=1}^{K} \pi_k \, \phi(y\,; \mu_k, \sigma_k).$$

For a given number of K groups, we thus wish to estimate the unknown parameters of this model. In general, there is no analytic representation of the solution, and we turn to iterative estimation methods. A number of different approaches can be used in this respect. Maximum likelihood estimation is often used via the application of the EM algorithm of Dempster et al. (1977).[4] There are no major obstacles in the estimation of mixtures, but it is wise to take a number of precautions. First, as the log-likelihood of a mixture of Normal distributions with unequal variances is not bounded, global maxima do not exist.[5] Maximization over a restricted parameter space produces solutions which have attractive properties. This involves constraining the algorithm so that the variances in the different groups are not too dissimilar to each other. To avoid identification problems, we also need to impose the constraint that $\mu_1 < \mu_2 < \cdots < \mu_K$ or $\sigma_1 < \sigma_2 < \cdots < \sigma_K$ at the end of each iteration (Redner and Walker, 1984). Finally, as the log-likelihood is multi-modal, the algorithm may well converge to a local maximum. This phenomenon is more likely to occur when the two groups are not clearly separate from each other. The problem can be avoided by estimating the mixture a number of times, with different initial values. Bayesian methods are also increasingly popular for the estimation of mixture models, with the recent development of Markov Chain Monte Carlo (MCMC) techniques (Gilks et al., 1995; Robert and Casella, 2005). These were relatively limited in scope until the article by Gelfand and Smith (1990) demonstrated the potential of Gibbs sampling for the resolution of the associated statistical problems. Introductions to Bayesian econometrics are provided in Bauwens et al. (2000) and Koop (2003).

Once we have obtained the parameter estimates, Bayes' theorem allows us to deduce the *a posteriori* probability that an observation *i* belongs to the group *k*:

$$\pi_{ik} = \frac{\pi_k \phi(y_i; \mu_k, \sigma_k)}{\sum_{k=1}^{K} \pi_k \phi(y_i; \mu_k, \sigma_k)}. \tag{6.2}$$

These individual probabilities can be used to classify the observations into the different groups.

The choice of the number of components K can be made in a number of different ways, according to the relative importance that we attach to the quality of the fit of the density and the detection of distinct groups. There is a vast literature on this topic, which remains very active (see McLachlan

[4] The simplicity of this approach explains why it is more often used than the iterative method of Newton-Raphson, for which latter convergence is not guaranteed (McLachlan and Basford, 1988).

[5] The log-likelihood is infinite if one of the groups contains only one observation (as its variance is zero).

and Peel, 2000). If the main concern is the best fit of the estimation of a density, a particularly simple and viable method consists in choosing the value of K which minimizes the Bayesian Information Criterion, or BIC (Schwarz, 1978),

$$\mathrm{BIC} = -2\,\hat{\ell} + (3K - 1)\log n,$$

where $\hat{\ell}$ is the estimated log-likelihood, n is the number of observations, and the term $3K - 1$ corresponds to the number of parameters to be estimated.[6] This criterion produces a consistent estimate of K in mixture models (Leroux, 1992; Keribin, 2000). An alternative approach is to test the hypothesis H_0: $K = K_0$ against the alternative hypothesis H_1: $K = K_1$ or $K_1 > K_0$ via the likelihood-ratio statistic:

$$\mathrm{LR} = 2\left[\hat{\ell}(\Theta_1) - \hat{\ell}(\Theta_0)\right],$$

where $\hat{\ell}(\Theta_1)$ is the estimated log-likelihood in the mixture model with K_1 groups and $\hat{\ell}(\Theta_0)$ is that from the model with K_0 groups. However, in the context of mixture models, the asymptotic distribution of this statistic is not chi-squared. Bootstrap methods can be used to calculate the critical value or P-values (McLachlan and Peel, 2000). Whichever selection rule for K is used, the visual inspection of the sensitivity of the results to small changes in K is very often useful. In some cases, the graphical representation of the mixture estimator varies little across different values of K, while in others it is very sensitive to it.

If the main concern is the detection of distinct groups, the choice of K is much less simple. First, there is no automatic correspondence between the choice of K and the number of distinct groups. For example, we saw above that one additional component is required for a good fit of the upper tail of a strongly asymmetric distribution (Figure 6.1, panel d). Thus, it may be difficult to know if the role of an additional component is to better fit the density or to identify a distinct group in the population. In addition, the choice of K depends on the choice of the parametric mixture distribution. Up to this point, we have considered mixtures of Normal distributions, but mixtures of different distributions (Log-Normal, Gamma, Weibull, etc.) can lead to the selection of a different value for K. One way of resolving these problems consists in identifying the number of groups via the number of modes of the distribution (Ray and Lindsay,

[6] As the log-likelihood increases with the number of parameters, we need to find a criterion which penalizes the likelihood so as to be able to usefully compare specifications with different numbers of parameters.

2005). The definition of what constitutes a distinct group will always be arbitrary, and is at the heart of an active debate in the current literature.

We now illustrate the estimation of a density via an empirical application. Marron and Schmitz (1992) showed that the non-parametric estimation of the income distribution in the United Kingdom produced a bimodal distribution, which was not taken into account in preceding work that had used parametric techniques to estimate this same density. Analyzing the same data, Figure 6.2 presents the results from the estimation of the income distribution by a kernel method (on the left) and by a mixture of Log-Normal distributions (on the right). The value of the bandwidth ($h = 0.08559$) in the kernel estimation comes from Silverman's empirical rule, defined by (1.11), which allows us to reproduce the results in Marron and Schmitz (1992). We know that this rule tends to select values of h that are too large in the case of distributions that are multi-modal and significantly asymmetric, which produces over-smoothing of the estimated function (see Section 1.4). Income distributions are indeed typically multi-modal and strongly asymmetric, and a better estimation of the distribution would result from a smaller value of h. As such, the results from kernel estimation with a smaller value of h (0.01) are overlaid in the same figure. The comparison of the two estimators reveals that the results differ significantly. In the first case ($h = 0.08559$), the first mode is smaller than the second, while in the second case ($h = 0.01$) the

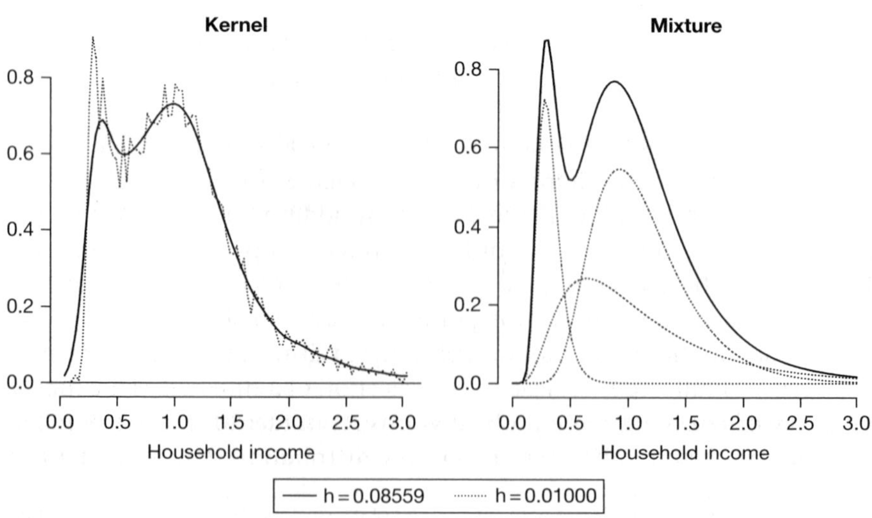

Figure 6.2: Income distribution in the United Kingdom (1973)

reverse holds. This confirms that the kernel estimator with an automatic choice of h does indeed tend to over-smooth the function, and to flatten out considerably the first mode in the example above relative to the second.

The right-hand side of Figure 6.2 depicts the estimator of the income distribution from a mixture of three Log-Normal distributions. This results from the estimation of the log transformation of income via a mixture of three Normal distributions. The number of separate densities which make up the mixture (here three) was chosen via the BIC criterion. The results from this estimation of the income distribution are not the same as those in Marron and Schmitz (1992) in the left-hand panel ($h = 0.08559$): the main difference is that the first mode is now higher than the second mode. A comparison of the mixture estimator to the kernel estimator with $h = 0.01$ reveals that the two curves are actually fairly similar, to the extent that the mixture estimator can be seen as a smoothed representation of the kernel estimator with $h = 0.01$. In addition to providing an approximation of the distribution of income, the mixture estimator yields a decomposition of the population into groups. In the current case, three components are identified, as shown by the three densities drawn with dotted lines. The numerical results are as follows:

$$\hat{f}(y; \Theta) = 0.162\,\Lambda(-1.20, 0.30) + 0.326\,\Lambda(-0.11, 0.66) + 0.512\,\Lambda(0.06, 0.38),$$

where $\Lambda(.)$ is the Log-Normal density function with parameters representing the mean and the variance of the Normal distribution. Both the figure and the numerical results suggest that the first and the third components are distinctly separate from each other.[7] The first component is estimated to cover 16.2% of the sample and the third component 52.2%. As the data are normalized by the mean, these results suggest that 16.2% of households constitute a distinct group, with income of less than half of the population mean. The fact that two modes are visible in the overall distribution underlines the distinct separation of this group, which is composed of poorer households, from other households. The estimator identifies three separate components. The second component overlaps to a considerable extent with the third, and to a lesser extent with the first. The presence of this second component allows a better fit of the right-hand-side tail of the distribution, but cannot be clearly associated with a distinct group.

[7] The means of these two groups are very different (−1.20 vs 0.06) relative to the standard deviations (0.30 and 0.38).

6.2.3 *The Multivariate Case*

The extension of a mixture of Normal distributions to the multivariate case is simple, and involves the use of multivariate Normal distributions. Let y be a vector in p dimensions, then the mixture model can be written as:

$$f(y, \Theta) = \sum_{k=1}^{K} \pi_k \, \phi(y\,; \mu_k, \Sigma_k),$$

where μ_k is the vector of means and Σ_k is the covariance matrix of a multivariate Normal distribution of dimension p.[8] The elements of this model are ellipsoids, centered around the means μ_k. The covariance matrix determines the geographical characteristics of these ellipsoids (i.e. their orientation, volume, and form), which can differ between groups or be constrained to be identical across groups. If this matrix is diagonal, then the ellipsoids are oriented parallel to one of the axes. The BIC criterion can be used to determine the number of groups:

$$\text{BIC} = -2\,\hat{\ell} + (\#\text{params}) \log n,$$

where $\hat{\ell}$ is the estimate of the log-likelihood, n is the number of observations, and (#params) is the number of parameters estimated by the model.

To illustrate, consider the convergence of economies to the same level of wealth, which can be tested by regressing the growth rate between two periods on the initial level of wealth:[9]

$$\log \text{GDP}_1 - \log \text{GDP}_0 = \alpha + \beta \log \text{GDP}_0 + \varepsilon, \tag{6.3}$$

where GDP_0 is the Gross Domestic Product per capita in the first period and GDP_1 is that in the second period. We have unconditional convergence, also called absolute β-convergence, if the parameter β is negative and significantly different from zero ($\beta < 0$). This indicates that there is a catching-up effect: a country with an initial level of per capita income which is lower than the average will also have, on average, a growth rate that is faster than the average. The empirical results in the literature from the estimation of this regression are mixed. Some work finds convergence, and others not, according to the countries that are included in the sample (Mankiw et al., 1992; Durlauf and Johnson, 1995). More light can be shed

[8] This density is written as $\phi(y\,; \mu, \Sigma) = (2\pi)^{-p/2}|\Sigma|^{-1/2} \exp\{-0.5(y-\mu)^\top \Sigma^{-1}(y-\mu)\}$.

[9] See, e.g., the work of Jones (2001), Barro and Sala-i-Martin (2003), and Aghion and Howitt (2009).

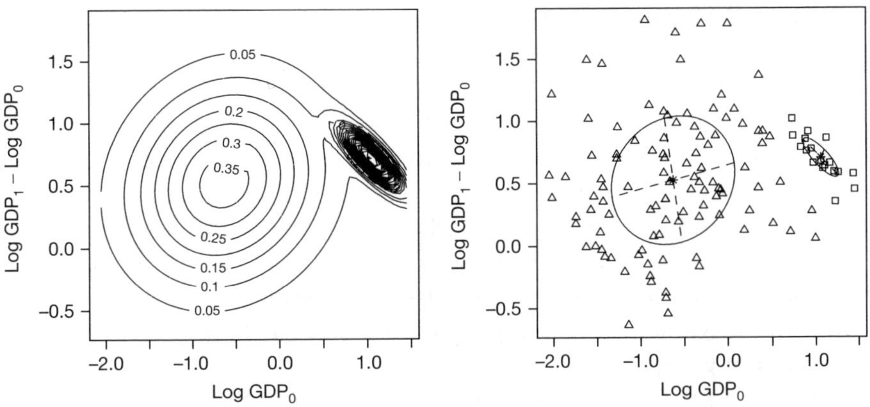

Figure 6.3: The convergence of economies between 1961 and 1988

on this question by a non-parametric approach, such as kernel (Desdoigts, 1994) or mixture-model methods.

The left-hand panel of Figure 6.3 represents the results of the estimation of the joint density of initial wealth and the growth rate, in the form of contour lines,[10] via a mixture of bivariate Normal distributions, over the 1961–1988 period. The right-hand panel shows each one of the observations as well as the classification produced by the estimator (as represented by squares and triangles, respectively). Over all of the observations, the slope which best fits the data is not easy to identify, and we might be tempted to think that a zero slope is the most appropriate. As the Y-axis here represents the dependent variable of the model (6.3) and the X-axis the explanatory variable, this zero slope is consistent with the non-convergence of economies over time to the same level of wealth. However, the mixture model identifies two distinct groups (via the BIC criterion). The group of the "richest" countries (as shown by the squares) corresponds to OECD countries, and yields a cloud of points for which a negative regression line seems to produce the best fit. Indeed, the estimation of (6.3) for these countries only produces results which suggest the convergence of economies towards the same wealth level. The second group (the triangles), on the other hand, is in no way consistent with this convergence conclusion.

[10] That is, the joint density of $(\log PIB_{1988} - \log PIB_{1961})$ and $(\log PIB_{1961})$, which are the variables in (6.3).

6.3 Density Estimation with Concomitant Variables

The particularity of the mixture model is that it can be written as the sum of a number of parametric distributions. This allows us to introduce explanatory variables and thus to construct a model which explains the dependent variable. The estimation of the density at any point thus becomes conditional on the observed values of the explanatory variables. There are a number of different ways of doing this. In this section, we present that which adds regressors to the mixture probabilities, called concomitant variables. This approach allows us to specify the profiles of the different groups.

Let z be a set of individual characteristics, then the *Mixture Model of Normal Distributions with Concomitant Variables* can be written as follows:

$$f(y\,|z;\Theta) = \sum_{k=1}^{K} \pi_k\,(z, \alpha_k)\,\phi(y\,;\mu_k, \sigma_k)\,, \tag{6.4}$$

where $z = \{z_1, \ldots, z_l\}$ is a vector of l observed variables and $\alpha_k = \{\alpha_{1k}, \ldots, \alpha_{lk}\}$ is a vector of l unknown parameters. This model defines a *conditional density* function, which takes into account directly the fact that the probability of group membership may be a function of individual characteristics. For example, if we consider the distribution of income, larger families where no-one works have a greater probability of belonging to the group of the poorest households than do households consisting of two adults without children who both work. Household characteristics thus help to explain the probability that households belong to the different groups identified in the population. As well as the non-parametric estimation of the density and the decomposition into different groups, concomitant variables also explain the variability between groups.

A first approach is to use an ordered probit model to specify the relationship between π_k and the concomitant variables. This model, developed by Flachaire and Nuñez (2007), takes into account the ordered nature of the different groups, with the parameter vector associated with the concomitant variables being the same for each group: $\alpha = \{\alpha_1, \ldots, \alpha_l\}$. In this model, α provides information about the relative position of an observation in the distribution, as a function of the associated individual characteristics. If α_l is positive (negative), then the position of this observation moves to the right (left) of the distribution as the variable z_l increases. On the other hand, a value of α_l which is not significantly different from zero indicates that the characteristic z_l does not help us to explain the decomposition of the sample into the different groups. The unconditional (marginal) density can be written as follows:

$$f(y;\Theta) = \sum_{k=1}^{K} \bar{\pi}_k\, \phi(y\,;\mu_k,\sigma_k) \qquad \text{with} \qquad \bar{\pi}_k = \frac{1}{n}\sum_{i=1}^{n} \pi_k(z_i, \alpha),$$

where z_i represents the vector of characteristics of the ith observation and n is the number of observations. In other words, $\pi_k(z_i, \alpha)$ is the probability that the individual i with characteristics z_i belong to the group k.

Figure 6.4 shows the results of the estimation of the distribution of household income in the United Kingdom in 1979 and 1988, obtained in Flachaire and Nuñez (2007).[11] The comparison of these two unconditional densities does not tell any particularly clear story regarding the evolution over time in the UK income distribution. However, the decomposition into groups of the mixture estimator does indeed emphasize clear changes over time. The analysis by groups shows that, in 1988, a small separate group had formed to the extreme left of the distribution, while that situated to the far right of the distribution had grown in size. This indicates that a small group of extremely poor households had appeared, while the number of households in the richest group had increased. The widening of the gap between the two groups situated at the opposite ends of the income distribution helps to explain the measured increase in income inequality in the UK between 1979 and 1988.

The use of mixture models with concomitant variables allows us to deepen the analysis by explaining the allocation of different observations between the groups. Flachaire and Nuñez (2007) analyze the following variables: z_1 for a retired household, z_2 for single-parent families, z_3 for households where all of the adults work, z_4 if no adult works in the household (in a non-retired household), and z_5 for the number of children. The estimation results are displayed in Table 6.1 (with standard errors in parentheses).

The dummy variables z_1, z_3, and z_4 are mutually exclusive (a household consisting only of retired people cannot also be a household where all of the adults work or no adults work), so that we can directly compare the size of the estimated coefficients. Retired and non-working households are more likely to be found towards the bottom of the income distribution, as the associated estimated coefficients α_1 and α_4 are significantly negative.

[11] The analysis here uses the same data as Marron and Schmitz (1992), with the exception that the incomes here are normalized via an equivalence scale in order to account for differences in household size.

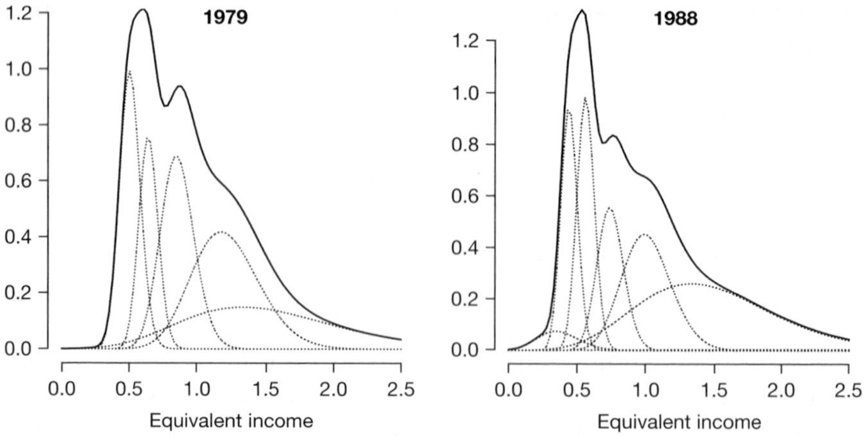

Figure 6.4: The distribution of income

Households where all adults work, on the contrary, are more likely to be found towards the right of the distribution, as the estimated value of α_3 is large and positive. A comparison of the estimated coefficients over the two periods indicates that the gap between households where all adults work and households where no adults work has grown sharply ($\alpha_3 - \alpha_4$ equals 1.771 in 1979, but 2.221 in 1988). In addition, the position of retired households has improved over this period, while that of households where no-one works has deteriorated. The interpretation of the estimated coefficients in this model is particularly simple and provides more detailed information about the evolution of income inequality. These results emphasize the usefulness of mixture models with concomitant variables, which yield an overall picture of the distribution of income and how this has changed over time, with richer results than those obtained from other commonly employed techniques.

A second possibility is the use of a multinomial model (logit or probit) to specify the relationship between π_k and the concomitant variables z. The parameter vector associated with the concomitant variables is

Table 6.1: Coefficient estimates for concomitant variables

	α_1	α_2	α_3	α_4	α_5
1979	−1.770 (0.059)	−0.672 (0.106)	0.611 (0.050)	−1.160 (0.086)	−0.439 (0.020)
1988	−1.329 (0.058)	−0.694 (0.106)	0.781 (0.053)	−1.440 (0.068)	−0.352 (0.022)

then no longer identical across the different groups: $\alpha_k = \{\alpha_{1k}, \ldots, \alpha_{lk}\}$ for $k = 1, \ldots, K$. As such, while there were l parameters associated with the concomitant variables in the preceding model, there are now $l \times (K - 1)$ parameters in the multinomial specification. The interpretation of the parameters and the resulting inference is exactly the same as in discrete-choice multinomial regression models. The α_{lk} parameter picks up the impact of variable l on the probability that the observation belongs to the group k. A positive coefficient indicates that higher values of the variable l increase the probability of belonging to group k, relative to the reference group.

6.4 Regression Models

In the preceding section, the regressors played a role in assigning observations to different groups; in this section, regressors are introduced into the modeling of the densities in each of the groups. This approach allows us to simultaneously assign observations to the groups and to estimate a regression model within each group. We thus identify groups that are homogeneous in terms of the relationship between the dependent and explanatory variables, but also capture a certain heterogeneity within each group via the explanatory variables included in the regression model.

6.4.1 *Mixture of Standard Regressions*

The simple linear regression model consists in specifying the conditional expectation of the dependent variable y as a linear function of a number of explanatory variables: $E(y|X) = x\beta$, where x is a matrix of explanatory variables and β a vector of parameters. One obvious approach is to specify the means of the density functions in each of the mixture groups in the same way. If we consider a mixture of Normal distributions with variance σ_k^2, we can re-write equation (6.1) so as to obtain a *mixture of linear regression models*, as follows:

$$f(y|x; \Theta) = \sum_{k=1}^{K} \pi_k \, \phi\,(y|x; \beta_k, \sigma_k)\,. \tag{6.5}$$

The means of the densities are no longer parameters to be estimated directly. They are conditional on the values of the explanatory variables

x, and are obtained from the estimation of the model: $\mu_k = x\beta_k$. If there are two groups ($K = 2$), then we have the following model:

$$\begin{aligned} &\text{Group 1:} \quad y = x\beta_1 + \varepsilon_1, \qquad \varepsilon_1 \sim N(0, \sigma_1^2), \\ &\text{Group 2:} \quad y = x\beta_2 + \varepsilon_2, \qquad \varepsilon_2 \sim N(0, \sigma_2^2), \end{aligned}$$

where ε_1 and ε_2 are independent and identical Normally distributed error terms within each group, with variances of σ_1^2 and σ_2^2, respectively. In this model, we consider that the population is composed of two different groups, for which the relationship between the dependent and explanatory variables is different. This type of model is frequently used in econometric analysis, specifying the different groups *a priori* and then carrying out a Chow test to see whether $\beta_1 = \beta_2$, for example to test whether there is wage discrimination between women and men. The main difference is that, in a mixture model, the observations come from the different groups in the population in unknown proportions. The groups are thus not defined *a priori*, but are estimated so as to consist of observations that are homogeneous in terms of the relationship between y and x. Moreover, the number of groups is not fixed, but determined according to a criterion (BIC) or a test (LR).

Other types of regression models can be considered by appealing to mixtures of distributions which are other than Normal. For example, a mixture of binomial distributions allows us to consider discrete-choice models such as the logit or probit models:

$$f(y|x;\Theta) = \sum_{k=1}^{K} \pi_k \binom{n}{y} p_k^y (1 - p_k)^{1-y}. \tag{6.6}$$

In a mixture of logistic regressions, p_k is assumed to depend on the explanatory variables in the following way:

$$p_k = \frac{\exp(x\beta_k)}{1 + \exp(x\beta_k)},$$

while, for a mixture of probit regressions, the relationship is expressed as by the cumulative Normal distribution: $p_k = \Phi(x\beta_k)$. These models allow the restrictive hypotheses of the simple logit model, such as the hypothesis of the independence of irrelevant alternatives (IIA), to be relaxed, and provide an approximation to any kind of random utility model (McFadden and Train, 2000; Train, 2003). The extension to other types of regression models results from the consideration of distributions that are exponential rather than Normal and binomial (McLachlan and Peel,

2000; Dobson, 2001; McCullagh and Nelder, 2001). This latter allows us to analyze, amongst others, duration models, which appeal to mixture models to reflect the presence of any unobserved individual heterogeneity (Heckman and Singer, 1984).

These kinds of models are widely used in Marketing (Wedel and Kamakura, 1999). For example, Kamakura, et al. (1996) used a mixture of nested logit regression models in order to evaluate the effect of special offers on consumers' purchasing decisions. The empirical results suggested the presence of three consumer groups, who exhibited similar preferences regarding alternative choices (different products of the same brand, or similar products from rival brands) and the same kind of behavioral responses to special offers. The first group was characterized by an initial choice of a brand, and then the choice of a product within the brand range. On the contrary, the second group chose the product first, and the brand second. Finally, the third group seemed to have no particular hierarchy in their purchase decisions, and thus could be specified as a multinomial logit model with the IIA hypothesis. Their results provide a characterization of consumer preferences with respect to brands and products, a hierarchy of decision-making, and the impact of special offers on consumer purchases in each of the different groups.

The mixture model allows us to capture heterogeneity which is not reflected in the explanatory variables of the regression model. Taking this unobserved heterogeneity into account is particularly important in the case of discrete-choice models, where omitted variables have non-negligible consequences. The omission of a variable in a linear model has no effect on the other estimated parameters as long as this omitted variable is not correlated with the model's explanatory variables. This no longer holds in logit/probit models or duration models: the parameter estimates can be significantly biased even if the omitted variable is not correlated with the explanatory variables (Yatchew and Griliches, 1984).

6.4.2 *Discrete and Continuous Heterogeneity Distributions*

In general, we can write a mixture regression model as follows:

$$f(y\,|x;\Theta) = \int f\,(y|x\,;\theta)\,h(\theta)d\theta, \tag{6.7}$$

where $h(.)$ is a density function, called the mixture density. If we suppose that θ takes K distinct values, $\theta_1, \ldots, \theta_K$, with respective probabilities $\pi_1, \ldots, \pi_K$, the $h(.)$ function will be discrete and we have the case of the mixture regression models discussed above.[12] Rather than a discrete distribution for $h(.)$, we can also consider a continuous distribution. There is no reliable rule to determine whether we should use discrete or continuous mixture densities. As we will see below, the two approaches are conceptually very different. It is rather the underlying theory or the particular problem to hand which may guide us in the choice of the different mixture densities.

Consider a mixture of Normal densities. Equation (6.7) can then be rewritten as a mixture of linear regression models as below:

$$f(y\,|x;\Theta) = \int \phi\,(y|x\,;\beta,\sigma)\,h(\beta)d\beta.$$

This is a generalization of equation (6.5) to the continuous case. This mixture model is equivalent to the following regression model:

$$y_i = x_i\beta_i + \varepsilon_i \qquad \varepsilon_i \sim N(0,\sigma^2),$$

where the vector β_i is random with a probability distribution of $h(.)$. Considering $h(.)$ as a continuous distribution, each individual i has their own regression model with parameters β_i, which are commonly referred to as *random parameters*. This model thus reflects heterogeneity between individuals. However, if we consider that $h(.)$ is a discrete distribution, then we return to (6.5), where the heterogeneity is modeled at the group level rather than the individual level.

The choice between continuous and discrete mixture densities thus implies different types of unobserved heterogeneity. For a finite mixture, the underlying hypothesis is that the population is composed of a limited number of homogeneous groups. This hypothesis is relaxed when we turn to continuous mixture functions. It is evident that, in the presence of unobserved heterogeneity between individuals that is sufficiently strong that homogeneous groups cannot be identified, a finite mixture approach that partitions the population artificially into a number of groups is inappropriate. In this case, a better estimation will likely result from the use of an appropriate continuous mixture density. The choice of this latter density needs to be made *a priori*. In practice, unimodal continuous distributions are often used (Normal, Log-Normal, Gamma, etc.). The drawback of this estimation approach is that the results are often sensitive to the correct specification of this continuous mixture function (Heckman and Singer, 1984). In the case of a finite mixture, any

[12] The equation (6.7) is then equivalent to equation (6.5) if $f(.)$ is a Normal distribution, and to equation (6.6) if it is a binomial distribution.

continuous distribution can be well approximated by a discrete mixture as the number of groups increases (Section 6.2). Further, there is no unimodal restriction, as this result continues to hold for multi-modal continuous functions. From a statistical point of view, finite mixture models are thus robust to the specification of the mixture density, at the price of a certain efficiency loss in the estimation of the parameters.

Recent developments have combined the two approaches, proposing both inter-group and intra-group heterogeneity (Allenby and Rossi, 1999; Lenk and DeSarbo, 2000; Frühwirth-Schnatter and Kaufmann, 2008). This work uses a finite mixture of regression models, and unobserved heterogeneity, which is reflected in a continuous function in each of the discrete groups. The results suggest that taking intra-group heterogeneity into account leads to a reduction in the number of groups that are identified. This work is still in its early stages, and more research is required to better understand and take into account the different types of heterogeneity within each distinct group, as well as the relationship between this heterogeneity and that which is found between the different groups.

6.4.3 *Mixture Regressions with Concomitant Variables*

In the case of a finite mixture of regressions, the heterogeneity between groups can be explained by the use of concomitant variables. These latter are introduced into the mixture probabilities and describe the characteristics of each of the groups (Section 6.3). From equations (6.4) and (6.5), we can write a *mixture of regressions with concomitant variables* as follows:

$$f(y|x, z; \Theta) = \sum_{i=1}^{K} \pi_k(z, \alpha_k)\, \phi\,(y|x; \beta_k, \sigma_k)\,,$$

where $z = \{z_1, \ldots, z_l\}$ is a vector consisting of l observed concomitant variables and $\alpha_k = \{\alpha_{1k}, \ldots, \alpha_{lk}\}$ is a vector of l unknown parameters. The relationship between π_k and the concomitant variables z is specified via a multinomial model (logit).[13] The interpretation of the parameters here is exactly analogous to that in multinomial discrete-choice models. The parameter α_{lk} describes the impact of variable l on the probability that the observation belongs to group k. A positive estimated value for this parameter indicates that a greater value of z_l increases the probability of belonging to the group k. Note that, as in the classic multinomial model,

[13] In contrast to the case of density estimation in Section (6.3), where the means of the different components can be ranked, the use of an ordered model (such as ordered probit) is not appropriate here as the regression models have no rank structure.

the coefficients on the variables cannot be identified for the entirety of the K groups. To resolve this problem, the coefficients for one of the groups are not estimated, and the coefficients for all of the other groups are thus interpreted relative to this reference group.

A first question to ask is the extent to which this model is different from one in three stages, where: (1) we estimate a mixture of linear regressions *without* concomitant variables; (2) we make classification by assigning each observation to a group (see equation (6.2)); and (3) we then estimate a multinomial model to explain the characteristics of the observations that are found in each of the groups. This three-stage procedure has a number of drawbacks. To start with, the first stage is carried out independently of all of the others, using different criteria. The information provided by the concomitant variables is thus not used to identify the groups. Further, the multinomial model used to characterize the observations in the different groups does not take into account the intrinsic estimation error of the classification; that is, the standard errors of the first-stage estimation. The mixture regression with concomitant variables can thus be seen as a simultaneous estimation of these three stages, but one which does not have the drawbacks of a procedure which is carried out in separate stages. The inclusion of a richer information set, provided by the concomitant variables, produces a better separation and identification of the different groups.

A second important question is which concomitant variables z to include in the analysis. How does this differ from using the z variables directly in the model, like the explanatory variables x? Concomitant and explanatory variables play different roles in this analysis. The concomitant variables z serve to explain the heterogeneity between the groups; explanatory variables play the same role as the regressors in a standard regression model, and help to explain the heterogeneity within each group. The theory behind the phenomenon under consideration should help us in our choice of concomitant variables.

To illustrate, consider a simple Mincer earnings equation, which explains the logarithm of an individual's earnings by number of years of education and number of years of labor-market experience. One way of testing for earnings discrimination between men and women is to test whether the parameters of the earnings equation are statistically significantly different between the two groups of individuals, via a Chow test (Berndt, 1990). We thus define *a priori* two groups of individuals—men and women—and assume that those groups are homogeneous. We then test the hypothesis that the coefficients in the two regressions are

Table 6.2: Mincer earnings equations

Variables	Group 1 ($\pi_1 = 0.406$)	Group 2 ($\pi_2 = 0.594$)
Explanatory Variables		
Constant	0.67517*	0.34909*
Education	0.08202*	0.09844*
Experience	0.05147*	0.02590*
(Experience)^2	−0.00078*	−0.00040*
Concomitant Variables		
Constant	—	−0.49423*
Female	—	9.03215*
Union member	—	−8.16128†

Note: * $p < 0.05$, † $p = 0.057$.

different. There is no particular reason, however, to assume that the group of men and the group of women are homogeneous. Mixture models with concomitant variables are a useful device to avoid this hypothesis. These allow us to identify homogeneous groups with respect to the relationship between the dependent and explanatory variables, without making any *a priori* hypotheses regarding these groups. Moreover, the inclusion of concomitant variables allows us to characterize these different groups. In terms of the question that we are analyzing here, a male/female dummy variable would seem appropriate in this role.

Table 6.2 presents the results from the estimation of a mixture of Mincer earnings equations, using data from a household survey carried out by the US Census Bureau in May 1985.[14] Education and labor-market experience appear as explanatory variables. Two dummy variables are taken into account as concomitant variables: the first is for the individual being a woman, and the second for the individual being a union member. The BIC criterion suggests that there are two groups: $K = 2$. The mixture identified in these two groups corresponds to two regressions with different estimated coefficients.

As the dependent variable is the log of earnings, the results show that one additional year of education increases earnings by around 8.2% for individuals in the first group, and 9.8% for individuals in the second. The earnings profiles as a function of labor-market experience are very different between the two groups. These are traced out in Figure 6.5 for eight

[14] These data come from Chapter 5 of Berndt (1990).

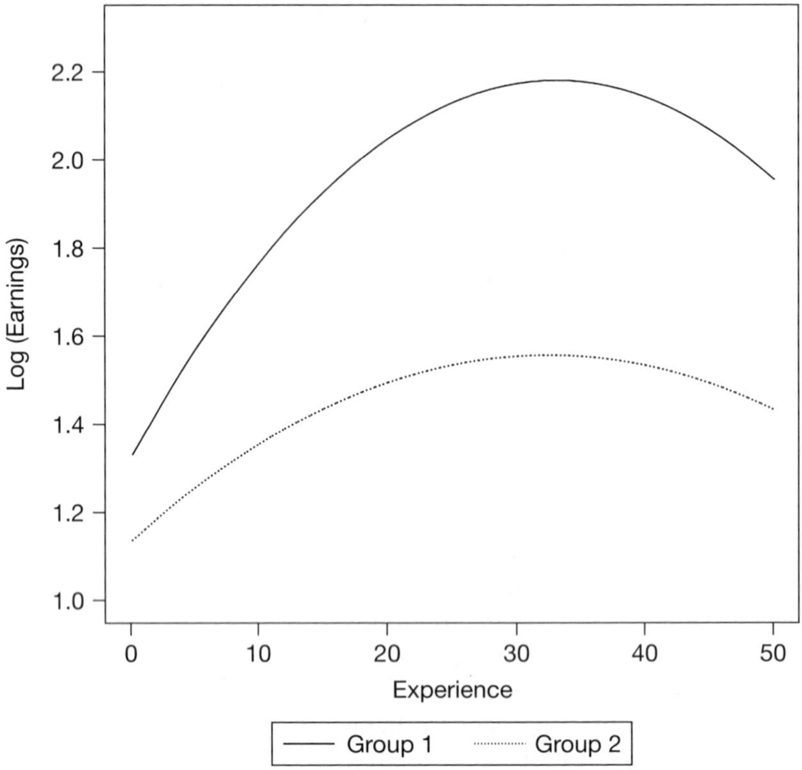

Figure 6.5: The relationship between earnings and labor-market experience

years of education.[15] From this figure, the increase in expected earnings from labor-market experience is sharply higher for individuals in the first group: the gap between the two curves widens with experience at first, before narrowing again after around 30 years of labor-market experience.

The estimated coefficients on the concomitant variables allow us to identify the characteristics that are associated with each of these two groups. The positive and significant estimated coefficient on the "Female" variable indicates that women are more likely to belong to the second group than to the first group. The negative significant coefficient on union membership[16] shows that unionized workers are less likely to belong to the second than to the first group. The percentage of women

[15] The curve for the first group corresponds to the polynomial $y = 0.67517 + 8 * 0.08202 + 0.05147 * x - 0.00078 * x^2$, and that for the second to $y = 0.34909 + 8 * 0.09844 + 0.02590 * x - 0.0004 * x^2$.

[16] This coefficient is significant at the 1% level according to an LR test.

who are classified in group 2 from the estimation of the mixture model is 96.3%, while the analogous percentage of men is only 19%. Equally, the percentage of union members classified in group 1 is 80.2%. Last, the results of this analysis suggest that, for the vast majority of women, the relationship between earnings and experience is much flatter than that for most men and union members, holding everything else equal. The initial earnings gap widens with the number of years of experience. However, this does not hold for all women.

6.5 Dynamic Regression Models

The way in which we have interpreted mixture models up to this point, based on the population consisting of a number of distinct groups, is intuitive if we have individual-level data to hand. When we have time-series data, we can still suppose that, at a given date, the series is in one group, while at another date it is in a different group. The interpretation in terms of unobserved groups is in general replaced by that of hidden states or regimes, which is more natural in the case of time-series data. The movement from one state to another is interpreted as a switch of regime at an unknown date. This section presents the extension of mixture models to the dynamic case, first for time-series and then for panels.

6.5.1 *Regime-switching Models*

The previous section showed that a mixture of linear regressions can be written as:

$$f(y|x;\Theta) = \sum_{k=1}^{K} \pi_k \, \phi\,(y|x;\beta_k,\sigma_k)\,,$$

where y is the dependent variable, x is a matrix of explanatory variables, and K is the number of components or groups in the model. The particularity of this model is that the group to which each observation belongs is not observed. Up to now, we considered that the observations were independent: the fact that an observation i belongs to a certain group does not depend on the fact that the observation j belongs to the same or a different group, for $j \neq i$. With time-series data, the idea of an unobserved group is replaced by that of a hidden state. The extension of the previous model to the dynamic case is then effected: (1) by considering that x might include lagged values of the dependent variable; and (2) by modeling the fact that the (hidden) state in which we are found at a certain date depends on the (hidden) states in which we were at previous dates.

Hamilton (1989) suggests the use of an Autoregressive Regime-switching Model to specify the data on American GDP growth. The underlying idea is that economic growth is characterized by periods of growth and of recession, and that the dynamic process is different according to the regime in which we are found. An autoregressive model with two states can be written as follows:

$$\begin{aligned} &\text{Regime 1:} \quad y_t = \beta_1 y_{t-1} + \alpha_1 + \varepsilon_1, \qquad \varepsilon_1 \sim N(0, \sigma_1^2),\\ &\text{Regime 2:} \quad y_t = \beta_2 y_{t-1} + \alpha_2 + \varepsilon_2, \qquad \varepsilon_2 \sim N(0, \sigma_2^2). \end{aligned}$$

Two similar regressions are considered, with unknown parameters which need not be the same. The estimated values of these parameters describe the dynamic process in each of the two regimes.

In the mixture model, the regime in which we are found at a given date is not observed. In other words, regime changes can occur over time, but the dates at which these changes take place are unknown. The dynamic aspect of this model results from the hypothesis that the current regime at a given date is not independent of the regimes which pertained at past dates. This temporal dependence of hidden states is typically modeled via Markov chains. Let s_t be a random variable which takes on only integer values $\{1, 2, \ldots, N\}$. The probability that s_t equals j depends on the recent past only:

$$P(s_t = j | s_{t-1} = i, s_{t-2} = l, \ldots) = P(s_t = j | s_{t-1} = i) = p_{ij}.$$

This process is described by a Markov chain with transition probabilities $\{p_{ij}\}_{i,j=1,2,\ldots,N}$, where p_{ij} is the probability that state i is followed by state j. For a Markov chain with two states, the *transition matrix* is:

$$P = \begin{bmatrix} p_{11} & 1 - p_{22} \\ 1 - p_{11} & p_{22} \end{bmatrix}.$$

This kind of dynamic model is particularly useful for describing processes which alternate over time.

The extension of mixture models to the dynamic case then leads us to include lagged values of the dependent variable in the regressors and to model the dynamic relationship via a Markov chain. For a mixture of AR(1) models with two hidden states, there are four possible combinations at date t: $(s_t = 0, s_{t-1} = 0)$, $(s_t = 0, s_{t-1} = 1)$, $(s_t = 1, s_{t-1} = 0)$, and

$(s_t = 1, s_{t-1} = 1)$. This leads us to a Autoregressive Markov-switching Model as follows:

$$f(y_t|y_{t-1};\Theta) = \sum_{i=0}^{1}\sum_{j=0}^{1} f(y_t|s_t = j, s_{t-1} = i, y_{t-1};\theta_j)\, p_{ij}\, p_i,$$

where $p_i = P(s_{t-1} = i|y_{t-1})$.[17] The joint estimation of the parameters and the transition probabilities is carried out via maximum likelihood techniques using the EM algorithm (Hamilton, 1994), or Bayesian MCMC methods (Frühwirth-Schnatter, 2001).

Filardo (1994) and Diebold et al. (1994) have developed the inclusion of concomitant variables in the transition probabilities. In Hamilton's model, the transition probabilities are constant over time. The introduction of concomitant variables allows these transition probabilities to vary over time:

$$P_t = \begin{bmatrix} p_{11}(z_t) & 1 - p_{22}(z_t) \\ 1 - p_{11}(z_t) & p_{22}(z_t) \end{bmatrix}.$$

Filardo shows that data on macroeconomic indicators and the interest rate help to predict the dates at which regime-switching occur (from a recessionary to an expansionary regime, or vice versa). A variety of other topics have been studied using the same approach. Amongst others, Dolado and María-Dolores (2006) analyzed the impact of monetary policy on regime changes in the Euro zone, and Bauwens et al. (2006) considered the dynamics of financial returns. More information on this type of analysis is available in Hamilton and Raj (2002), Fan and Yao (2005), Frühwirth-Schnatter (2006), and Geweke and Keane (2007).

6.5.2 *Panel Data*

Panel data refer to data on the same individuals who are observed over a number of successive points in time: these data describe individual dynamic trajectories. If the number of points in time is small, the estimation of each individual's separate trajectory will be very imprecise. One way of improving this precision, is to consider that the individual observations all follow a "similar" trajectory, which latter can be estimated using information from the whole sample. The obvious problem is that if the trajectories are in fact different between some individuals, the

[17] This comes from the fact that $f(y_t|y_{t-1};\Theta) = \sum_i \sum_j f(y_t, s_t = j, s_{t-1} = i|y_{t-1};\theta_j) = \sum_i \sum_j f(y_t|s_t = j, s_{t-1} = i, y_{t-1};\theta_j)P(s_t = j, s_{t-1} = i)$ and $P(s_t = j, s_{t-1} = i) = p_{ij}\,p_i$.

parameter estimates will be biased. Regression models with panel data resolve this difficulty by taking unobserved individual heterogeneity into account via individual fixed or random effects (Baltagi, 2005).

If we apply mixture regression model techniques to panel data, then the unobserved heterogeneity is of a group, rather than an individual, nature. The underlying idea of the mixture is to detect and group together the individual observations that have "similar" trajectories, while at the same time evaluating the profile of the trajectories in the different groups that are identified. For a mixture of linear regressions with K groups, the trajectory of individual i who belongs to the group k is described by the regression model below:

$$\text{Group } k: \quad y_{it} = X_{it}\beta_k + \varepsilon_{it},$$

where ε_{it} is an error term, and the subscript i refers to the individual and t to the time-period. The group-level heterogeneity could affect only some of the parameters: $y_{it} = X^1_{it}\alpha + X^2_{it}\beta_k + \varepsilon_{it}$, where X^1_{it} and X^2_{it} are made up of different explanatory variables. In this model, then, we consider that only the X^2_{it} variables have a different effect on the dependent variable across the different groups.

Concomitant variables can be introduced in the case of mixture regressions with panel data. Frühwirth-Schnatter and Kaufmann (2008) appeal to just such an approach to analyze economic convergence across 144 European regions over the 1980–1992 period. Their empirical results identify two convergence clubs, with different adjustment speeds. The use of the initial level of income per capita as a concomitant variable brings additional precision to the model, and yields a clearer classification of each region into one of the two groups.

Hamilton's Autoregressive Regime-switching Model can be extended to panel data, by considering both the individual and the temporal dimension at the same time. For an AR(1) model with two regimes and a mixture of K groups, the dynamics of a time-series which belongs to group k can be described by the following regression model:

$$\text{Group } k \begin{cases} \text{Regime 1:} & y_{it} = \beta_{1k}\, y_{i,t-1} + \alpha_{1k} + \varepsilon_{it}, \\ \text{Regime 2:} & y_{it} = \beta_{2k}\, y_{i,t-1} + \alpha_{2k} + \varepsilon_{it}, \end{cases}$$

where ε_{it} is an independent error term. The idea behind this kind of estimation is that we can group together the time-series which have "similar" dynamics in the same group, while evaluating at the same time the dynamic processes within each of the identified groups. This approach was used by Frühwirth-Schnatter and Kaufmann (2008) to reveal the different dynamic processes of business cycles across countries, as well as differences in behavior between regimes—expansion and recession—in each of the groups of countries. Their analysis shows that countries in the Euro zone exhibit dynamics which are similar to each other, while Great Britain and Luxembourg are closer to the second group, which consists of the USA, Australia, Canada, and Japan. In addition, Bauwens and Rombouts (2007) appeal to the same approach with GARCH models to analyze the dynamics of the volatility of a number of financial returns. The extension of this model to the multivariate case has led to the development of vector autoregression (VAR) models with regime changes; see Krolzig (1997) and Sims and Zha (2006), amongst others.

In the models above, the individual observations were considered to belong to the same group in each period. In other words, the composition of the different groups is constant over time, and it is not possible for an individual to change from one group to another. A different approach, which is currently less widespread, consists in allowing such switching of groups over time, which means that the size of the different groups will also change over time. Going back to work by Poulsen (1990) on repeated choices by consumers, this approach was used in marketing by Ramaswamy (1997) to analyze the change in preferences before and after the introduction of a new product on the market. More details on these models and their extension to the case of concomitant variables can be found in Böckenholt (1996) and Wedel and Kamakura (1999).

APPENDIX A

IMPLEMENTATION IN R

A number of statistical software packages exist which allow the application of the non-parametric and semi-parametric methods described in this book. However, not all of the estimation methods presented here have been implemented in a standard way in the major statistical packages.[1] In this book we chose the R program to carry out the analytical applications described in each of the chapters. This program supports all of the estimation procedures that are presented here. It also has the advantage of being freeware,[2] freely available to anyone under the conditions of the GNU licence. It can be freely downloaded and installed under Windows, MacOS X, and Linux systems. Hundreds of regularly updated packages are available in R, and the number of such packages is growing steadily. Introductions to R are available in Fox (2002) and Venables and Smith (2009). The program itself and a great deal of information about it can be found on the R software's home page (<http://www.r-project.org>).

We will limit ourselves in this Appendix to the functions and packages that we used in the empirical applications presented in the preceding chapters. It is entirely possible that updating of the packages and the continual development of new functions in R will render some of the functions that we present here obsolete. This Appendix is therefore not an R user's guide. It may, however, be of use for a first implementation of the different empirical techniques that have been set out here.

The R programming language is based on the S and S-plus languages, developed by John Chambers in Bell Laboratories. A number of packages are loaded automatically when the program starts up. To use the non-parametric and semi-parametric methods we will need to use other packages, which are not part of the basic installation of the software, but which are available from the list of contributions on the CRAN file server Comprehensive R Archive Network (<http://cran.r-project.org>).

[1] Stata, SAS, Matlab, and Xplore include a number of functionalities, already implemented or in the process of development, which allow some of the techniques in the previous chapters to be applied.

[2] A program is called "free" if users can redistribute copies of it, either with or without changes, freely or otherwise, to anyone they wish. The source code has to remain accessible.

A new package, for example "mgcv", can be installed on a computer that is connected to the internet by executing the command:

```
> install.packages("mgcv")
```

For a computer that is not connected to the internet, the necessary file has to be picked up from the file server, and then installed manually on the hard drive. In this case, some care is needed due to interdependencies, as the package that we wish to install may depend on other packages which have not yet been installed, which will thus need to be taken from the file server and installed beforehand. To be able to use these new functions, the relevant package has to be loaded:

```
> library(mgcv)
```

In the following sections, we consider that all of the data that we need is contained in the text file called `data.txt`, with the variables being in columns and the first line containing the variable names. To read this data file in `R`, the following command line is executed:

```
> tutu <- read.table("C:/data.txt", header=T)
```

The content of the data table can be displayed by typing its name: `tutu`. Consider that this data file contains variables that are called `y`, `x1`, `x2`, `z1`, and `z2`. These variables are not directly accessible via their names. To activate the names of the variables, we use the following command:

```
> attach(tutu)
```

A help file can be displayed at any time for each of the functions. For the function used above, we would type `help(attach)`. The command `help.start()` opens a web navigator which simplifies access to relevant documentation.

A.1 Kernel Density Estimation

The kernel estimation method of a density in `R` is presented in chapter 7 of Everitt and Torsten (2006). To estimate the density of a variable `y`, the relevant function is `density`. This function is directly accessible in `R`. The graphical depiction of the estimation of the density of `y` using kernel methods is given by the following command:

```
> plot(density(y))
```

Some options of the `density` function allow the value of the bandwidth to be set and the choice of the kernel. More information on the use of this function and the associated options that are available can be obtained using the on-line search facility by typing `help(density)`.

The adaptive estimation method is not available by default. The relevant function, `akj`, is found in the package `quantreg`, which needs to be installed and loaded beforehand. The following commands define a vector x of 100 equidistant points, and then evaluate the density of y over these points using the adaptive kernel method, before producing a graphical representation of the results:

```
> library(quantreg)
> toto <- seq(min(y),max(y),length=100)
> titi <- akj(y,toto)
> plot(toto,titi$dens)
```

For the kernel estimation of a bivariate density, we use the `kde2d` function, which is found in the package `MASS`. Three-dimensional graphical representations in the form of contour lines can then be drawn:

```
> library(MASS)
> titi <- kde2d(x1,x2)
> persp(titi)
> contour(titi)
```

A wide variety of options is available here, which are described in the help file for each function.

A.2 Kernel Regression

The function `loess` is directly available in `R` for the estimation of the simple regression $y = m(x) + \varepsilon$ by kernel method. The estimation of m by local polynomials of degree 2 and the graphical representation of the results are obtained from the following commands:

```
> titi <- loess(y~x, degree=2)
> plot(titi$x,titi$fit)
```

Confidence intervals can be calculated and depicted on the same figure as above by typing:

```
> tata <- seq(min(x),max(x))
> toto <- predict(titi,tata,se=TRUE)
> plot(tata,toto$fit)
> lines(tata,toto$fit+196*toto$se.fit)
> lines(tata,toto$fit-1.96*toto$se.fit)
```

The function `predict` is generic, and calculates the predicted values of the model over the desired range (`tata`).

A.3 Spline Regression

The penalized spline estimation of the simple regression $y = m(x) + \varepsilon$ is carried out by the function `gam` in the package `mgcv`. The estimation and the graphical representation of the estimated function m are obtained as follows:

```
> library(mgcv)
> toto<-gam(y~s(x, bs="cr"), data=tutu)
> plot(toto)
```

The option "cr" allows us to select a cubic base for the estimation of the model.

A.4 Wavelet Regression

To estimate the regression $y = m(t) + \varepsilon$ using wavelets, we use the wavelet decomposition function `dwt` and its inverse `idwt` in the package `waveslim`. The choice of the threshold is made via the function `universal.thresh` for a universal threshold, and via the function `sure.thresh` for a SURE threshold. The wavelet estimation of m with a Daubechies base, a soft filter, and a universal threshold is carried out as follows:

```
> library(waveslim)
> toto<-dwt(y)
> titi<-universal.thresh(toto, hard=F)
> tata<-idwt(titi)
> plot(tata)
```

A similar estimation with a Haar base, a hard filter, and a SURE threshold would require the following code:

```
> toto<-dwt(y, wf="haar")
> titi<-sure.thresh(toto)
```

A.5 Semi-parametric Regression Models

The estimation of the partial linear model $y = \alpha + x_1\beta + m(x_2) + \varepsilon$ is carried out using the `gam` function, which is available in `R` in the package `mgcv`, which thus needs to be loaded beforehand. This function uses the penalized spline method. The estimation of m and the graphic representation of the results are obtained from:

```
library(mgcv)
toto<-gam(y~x1+s(x2), data=tutu)
plot(toto)
```

An additive model, $y = \alpha + x_1\beta + m_1(x_2) + m_2(z_1, z_2) + \varepsilon$, can be estimated using:

```
library(mgcv)
titi<-gam(y~x1+s(x2)+s(z1,z2), data=tutu)
summary(titi)
plot(titi)
```

The `summary` function displays the estimation results regarding the unknown parameters of the model, α and β. Executing the function `plot` yields successive graphical representations of the estimates of the m_1 and m_2 functions. The different graphs can be obtained separately using the function `vis.gam`. A three-dimensional depiction of the results, and then a representation via contour lines of the m_2 function, are obtained from the following lines of code:

```
vis.gam(titi,view=c("z1","z2"),plot.type="persp")
vis.gam(titi,view=c("z1","z2"),plot.type="contour")
```

Simon N. Wood, who developed this package, presents semi-parametric models with their application in `R` in detail in Wood (2006).

Another package, developed by Jeff S. Racine and called `np`, also allows semi-parametric estimation, based on kernel and local polynomial methods. The estimation here allows in particular for the joint presence of continuous and discrete explanatory variables in non-parametric estimation. This package is presented in Hayfield and Racine (2008).

A.6 Mixture Models

Mixture models were estimated using two different packages. The package `Mclust`, developed by Fraley and Raftery (2006) in order to estimate mixtures of Normal distributions, was used to estimate bivariate densities:

```
library(mclust)
toto=data.frame(x1,x2)
titi <- Mclust(toto)
surfacePlot(toto,parameters=titi$parameters)
```

In addition, the package `flexmix` enables the estimation of mixtures of densities or regressions (linear, logit, Poisson) with or without concomitant variables (Leisch, 2004; Grün and Leisch, 2006; 2007). For a mixture of linear regressions with $k = 2$ elements, and explanatory variables x_1 and x_2, we write:

```
library(flexmix)
tata <- flexmix(y~x1+x2,k=2)
summary(tata)
summary(refit(tata))
```

In practice, we can reiterate the estimation for different values of k and keep that which minimizes the BIC criterion. It is also possible to introduce concomitant variables. For example, for a mixture of linear regressions with $k = 2$ elements, with explanatory variables x_1 and x_2, and concomitant variables z_1 and z_2, we have:

```
tata <- flexmix(y~x1+x2,k=2,concomitant=FLXmultinom(~z1+z2))
summary(refit(tata), which="concomitant")
```

If we replace `y~x1+x2` by `y~1`, we then estimate the density of `y` by a mixture of Normal distributions, with concomitant variables z_1 and z_2 in the form of a multinomial model.

Bibliography

Abe, M. (1999). "A generalized additive model for discrete-choice data". *Journal of Business & Economic Statistics* 17, 271–84.

Abramson, I. S. (1982). "On bandwidth variation in kernel estimates—a square root law". *Annals of Statistics* 10, 1217–23.

Aghion, P. and P. Howitt (2009). *The Economics of Growth*. The MIT Press.

Ahamada, I. and M. S. Ben Aïssa (2005). "Changements structurels dans la dynamique de l'inflation aux USA". *Annales d'Economie et Statistique* 77, 187–99.

Ahamada, I., E. Flachaire, and M. Lubat (2007). "Prix des logements et coordonnées spatiales: une approche semi-paramétrique". *Économie Publique* 20, 131–45.

Allenby, G. M. and P. E. Rossi (1999). "Marketing models of consumer heterogeneity". *Journal of Econometrics* 89, 57–78.

Anselin, L. (1988). *Spatial Econometrics: Methods and Models*. Springer.

Baltagi, B. H. (2005). *Econometric Analysis of Panel Data*. Wiley.

Bardet, J.-M. (2002). "Statistical study of the wavelet analysis of fractional Brownian motion". *IEEE Transactions on Information Theory* 48, 991–99.

Barro, R. J. and X. Sala-i-Martin (2003). *Economic Growth*. MIT Press.

Bauwens, L., M. Lubrano, and J. F. Richard (2000). *Bayesian Inference in Dynamic Econometric Models*. Oxford University Press.

Bauwens, L., A. Preminger, and J. V. K. Rombouts (2006). "Regime switching GARCH models". CORE DP 2006/11.

Bauwens, L. and J. V. K. Rombouts (2007). "Bayesian clustering of many GARCH models". *Econometric Reviews* 26, 365–86.

Bera, A. K. and M. L. Higgins (1993). "A survey of ARCH models: properties, estimation and testing". *Journal of Economic Surveys* 7, 305–66.

Beran, R. (1986). Discussion of "Jackknife bootstrap and other resampling methods in regression analysis" by C. F. J. Wu. *Annals of Statistics* 14, 1295–98.

Berndt, E. R. (1990). *The Practice of Econometrics: Classic and Contemporary*. Addison Wesley.

Blundell, R. W. and J. L. Powell (2003). "Endogeneity in nonparametric and semiparametric regression models". In R. Blundell, W. K. Newey, and T. Persson (eds), *Advances in Economics and Econometrics: Volume 2*, pp. 312–57. Cambridge University Press.

Böckenholt, U. (1996). "Concomitant variables in latent change models". In J. Frost and R. Langeheine (eds), *Applications of Latent Trait and Latent Class Models in the Social Sciences*, pp. 361–9. Waxman.

Bowman, A. W. and A. Azzalini (1997). *Applied Smoothing Techniques for Data Analysis: The Kernel Approach with S-plus Illustrations*. Oxford University Press.

Breiman, L., W. Meisel, and E. Purcell (1977). "Variable kernel estimates of multivariable densities". *Technometrics* 19, 135–44.

Carrasco, M., J. P. Florens, and E. Renault (2007). "Linear inverse problems in structural econometrics: estimation based on spatial decomposition and regularization". In J. J. Heckman and E. E. Leamer (eds), *Handbook of Econometrics*, Volume 6. North-Holland.

Chernick, M. R. (2007). *Bootstrap Methods: A Guide for Practitioners and Researchers*. Wiley Series in Probability and Statistics.

Chu, C. K. and J. S. Marron (1991). "Comparison of two bandwidth selectors with dependent errors". *Annals of Statistics* 19, 1906–18.

Chui, C. K. (1992). *An Introduction to Wavelets*. Academic Press.

Claeskens, G. and I. Van Keilegom (2003). "Bootstrap confidence bands for regression curves and their derivatives". *Annals of Statistics* 31, 1852–84.

Cowell, F. A. and E. Flachaire (2007). "Income distribution and inequality measurement: the problem of extreme values". *Journal of Econometrics* 141, 1044–72.

Crowley, P. M. (2007). "A guide to wavelets for economists". *Journal of Economic Surveys 21*(2), 207–67.

Darolles, S., J. P. Florens, and E. Renault (2003). "Nonparametric instrumental regression". IDEI Working Paper no. 228.

Daubechies, I. (1988). "Orthonormal bases of compactly supported wavelets". *Communications on Pure and Applied Mathematics* 41, 909–96.

Daubechies, I. (1992). *Ten Lectures on Wavelets*. SIAM.

Davidson, R. and E. Flachaire (2007). "Asymptotic and bootstrap inference for inequality and poverty measures". *Journal of Econometrics* 141, 141–66.

Davidson, R. and E. Flachaire (2008). "The wild bootstrap, tamed at last". *Journal of Econometrics* 146, 162–69.

Davidson, R. and J. G. MacKinnon (2003). *Econometric Theory and Methods*. Oxford University Press.

Davidson, R., W. C. Labys, and J.-B. Lesourd (1998). "Wavelet analysis of commodity price behavior". *Computational Economics* 11, 103–28.

Davidson, R. and J. G. MacKinnon (2006). "Bootstrap methods in econometrics". In T. C. Mills and K. D. Patterson, *Palgrave Handbooks of Econometrics: Volume 1 Econometric Theory*, pp. 812–38. Palgrave Macmillan.

Davison, A. C. and D. V. Hinkley (1997). *Bootstrap Methods and their Application*. Cambridge University Press.

de Boor, D. (2001). *A Practical Guide to Splines*. Springer.

Delouille, V. (2002). "Nonparametric stochastic regression using design-adapted wavelets". Ph.D. thesis, Université Catholique de Louvain.

Dempster, A. P., N. M. Laird, and D. B. Rubin (1977). "Maximum likelihood from incomplete data via EM algorithm (with discussion)". *Journal of the Royal Statistical Society B* 39, 1–38.

Desdoigts, A. (1994). *Changes in the World Income Distribution: A Non-parametric Approach to Challenge the Neoclassical Convergence Argument*. Ph.D. thesis, Florence: European University Institute.

Desdoigts, A. (1996). "Smoothing techniques applied to a key economic issue: the convergence hypothesis". *Computational Statistics* 11, 481–94.

Diebold, F. X., J. H. Lee, and G. C. Weinbach (1994). "Regime switching with time-varying transition probabilities". In C. Hargreaves (ed.), *Nonstationary Time-Series Analysis and Cointegration*, pp. 283–302. Oxford University Press.

Dobson, A. J. (2001). *An Introduction to Generalized Linear Models*. Chapman & Hall.

Dolado, J. J. and R. M. María-Dolores (2006). "State asymmetries in the effects of monetary policy shocks on output: some new evidence for the euro-area". In P. R. C. Milas and D. van Dijk (eds), *Nonlinear Time Series Analysis of Business Cycles*, 276. Elsevier.

Donoho, D. L. and I. M. Johnstone (1994). "Ideal spatial adaptation by wavelet shrinkage". *Biometrika* 81, 425–55.

Donoho, D. L. and I. M. Johnstone (1995). "Adapting to unknown smoothness via wavelet shrinkage". *Journal of the American Statistical Association* 90, 1200–24.

Donoho, D. L. and I. M. Johnstone (1998). "Minimax estimation via wavelet shrinkage". *Annals of Statistics* 26, 879–921.

Donoho, D. L., I. M. Johnstone, G. Kerkyacharian, and D. Picard (1995). "Wavelet shrinkage: asymptotia". *Journal of the Royal Statistics Society*, Series B 57, 301–69.

Durlauf, S. N. and P. A. Johnson (1995). "Multiple regimes and cross-country growth behaviour". *Journal of Applied Econometrics* 10, 365–84.

Durlauf, S. N., P. A. Johnson, and J. R. Temple (2005). "Growth econometrics". In P. Aghion and S. Durlauf (eds), *Handbook of Economic Growth*. Elsevier.

Efromovich, S. (1999). "Quasi-linear wavelet estimation". *Journal of the American Statistical Association* 94, 189–204.

Efron, B. (1979). "Bootstrap methods: another look at the jacknife". *Annals of Statistics* 7, 1–26.

Efron, B. and R. Tibshirani (1993). *An Introduction to the Bootstrap*. Chapman & Hall.

Eilers, P. H. C. and B. D. Marx (1996). "Flexible smoothing with B-splines and penalties". *Statistical Science* 89, 89–121.

Eilers, P. H. C. and B. D. Marx (2004). "Splines, knots and penalties". Mimeo.

Epanechnikov, V. A. (1969). "Nonparametric estimation of a multidimensional probability density". *Theory of Probability and its Applications* 14, 153–58.

Eubank, R. (1999). *Nonparametric Regression and Spline Smoothing*. Marcel Dekker.

Everitt, B. S. (1993). *Cluster Analysis*. Edward Arnold.

Everitt, B. S. and H. Torsten (2006). *A Handbook of Statistical Analyses Using R*. Chapman & Hall/CRC.

Fan, J. and I. Gijbel (1996). *Local Polynomial Modelling and its Applications*. Chapman & Hall.

Fan, J. and Q. Yao (2005). *Nonlinear Time Series: Nonparametric and Parametric Methods*. Springer-Verlag.

Faraway, J. J. (2006). *Extending the Linear Model with R*. Chapman & Hall/CRC.

Filardo, A. J. (1994). "Business-cycle phases and their transitional dynamics". *Journal of Business and Economic Statistics* 12, 299–308.

Fiorio, C. V. (2008). "Analysing tax-benefit reforms using non-parametric methods". *Fiscal Studies* 29, 499–522.

Flachaire, E. (2005a). "Bootstrapping heteroskedastic regression models: wild bootstrap vs. pairs bootstrap". *Computational Statistics & Data Analysis* 49, 361–76.

Flachaire, E. (2005b). "More efficient tests robust to heteroskedasticity of unknown form". *Econometric Reviews* 24, 219–41.

Flachaire, E. and O. Nuñez (2007). "Estimation of income distribution and detection of subpopulations: an explanatory model". *Computational Statistics & Data Analysis* 51, 3368–80.

Florens, J. P. (2003). "Inverse problem and structural econometrics: the example of instrumental variables". In M. Dewatripont, L. P. Hansen, and S. J. Turnovsky, *Advances in Economics and Econometrics, Theory and Applications, Eight World Congress*, Volume II, pp. 284–310. Cambridge University Press.

Florens, J. P. and R. Lestringant (2007). "The practice of non-parametric instrumental variables estimation". Mimeo.

Florens, J. P., J. Johannes, and S. V. Bellegem (2005). "Instrumental regression in partially linear models". CORE Discussion Paper no. 2006/25.

Fox, J. (2002). *An R and S-Plus Companion to Applied Regression*. Sage Publications.

Fraley, C. and A. E. Raftery (2006). "MCLUST version 3: an R package for Normal mixture modeling and model-based clustering". Technical Report no. 504, Department of Statistics, University of Washington.

Frühwirth-Schnatter, S. (2001). "Markov Chain Monte Carlo estimation of classical and dynamic switching and mixture models". *Journal of the American Statistical Association* 96, 194–209.

Frühwirth-Schnatter, S. (2006). *Finite Mixture and Markov Switching Models*. Springer.

Frühwirth-Schnatter, S. and S. Kaufmann (2008). "Model-based clustering of multiple time series". *Journal of Business and Economic Statistics* 26, 78–89.

Gao, H.-Y. and A. G. Bruce (1997). "Waveshrink with firm shrinkage". *Statistica Sinica* 7, 855–74.

Gao, J. (2007). *Nonlinear Time Series: Semiparametric and Nonparametric Methods*. Chapman & Hall/CRC.

Gao, J. and T. Lee (2000). "Adaptative estimation in partially linear autoregressive models". *Canadian Journal of Statistics* 28, 571–86.

Gelfand, A. E. and A. F. M. Smith (1990). "Sampling based approaches to calculating marginal densities". *Journal of the American Statistical Association* 85, 398–409.

Gençay, R., F. Selçuk, and B. Whitcher (2001). *An Introduction to Wavelets and Other Filtering Methods in Finances and Economics*. Academic Press.

Geweke, J. and M. Keane (2007). "Smoothly mixing regressions". *Journal of Econometrics* 138, 252–90.

Ghosal, S. and A. W. van der Vaart (2001). "Entropies and rates of convergence for maximum likelihood and Bayes estimation for mixtures of normal densities". *Annals of Statistics* 29(5), 1233–63.

Gilks, W., S. Richardson, and D. Spiegelhalter (1995). *Markov Chain Monte Carlo in Practice*. Chapman & Hall.

Green, P. J. and B. W. Silverman (1993). *Nonparametric Regression and Generalized Linear Models*. Chapman & Hall.

Grün, B. and F. Leisch (2006). "Fitting finite mixtures of linear regression models with varying and fixed effects in R". In A. Rizzi and M. Vichi (eds), *Compstat 2006–Proceedings in Computational Statistics*, pp. 853–60. Physica Verlag.

Grün, B. and F. Leisch (2007). "Application of finite mixtures of regression models". <http://cran.r-project.org/web/packages/flexmix>

Grund, B., P. Hall, and J. Marron (1994). "Loss and risk in smoothing parameter selection". *Journal of Nonparametric Statistics* 4, 107–23.

Gu, C. (2002). *Smoothing Spline ANOVA Models*. Springer.

Hall, P. and J. L. Horowitz (2005). "Nonparametric methods for inference in the presence of instrumental variables". *Annals of Statistics* 33, 2904–29.

Hall, P., S. N. Lahiri, and J. Polzehl (1995). "On bandwidth choice in nonparametric regression with both short- and long-range dependent errors". *Annals of Statistics* 23, 1921–36.

Hall, P. and P. Patil (1996). "Effects of threshold rules on performance of wavelet-based curve estimators". *Statistica Sinica* 6, 331–45.

Hamilton, J. D. (1989). "A new approach to the economic analysis of nonstationary time series and the business cycle". *Econometrica* 57, 357–84.

Hamilton, J. D. (1994). *Time Series Analysis*. Princeton University Press.

Hamilton, J. D. and B. Raj (2002). "New directions in business cycle research and financial analysis". *Empirical Economics* 27, 149–62.

Härdle, W. (1989). *Applied Nonparametric Regression*. Econometric Society Monograph, Cambridge.

Härdle, W. and A. W. Bowman (1988). "Bootstrapping in nonparametric regression: local adaptative smooting and confidence bands". *Journal of the American Statistical Association* 83, 102–10.

Härdle, W. and E. Mammen (1993). "Comparing nonparametric versus parametric regression fits". *Annals of Statistics* 21, 1926–47.

Härdle, W. and J. S. Marron (1991). "Bootstrap simultaneous error bars for nonparametric regression". *Annals of Statistics* 19, 778–96.

Härdle, W., H. Lütkepohl, and R. Chen (1997). "A review of nonparametric time series analysis". *International Statistical Review* 65, 49–72.

Härdle, W., G. Kerkyacharian, P. Picard, and A. B. Tsybakov (1998). *Wavelets, Approximation, and Statistical Applications*. Lecture Notes in Statistics, volume 129. Springer.

Härdle, W., M. Müller, S. Sperlich, and A. Werwatz (2004). *Nonparametric and Semiparametric Models*. Springer-Verlag.

Hastie, T. J. and R. J. Tibshirani (1986). "Generalized additive models". *Statistical Science* 1, 297–318.

Hastie, T. J. and R. J. Tibshirani (1987). "Generalized additive models: some applications". *Journal of the American Statistical Association* 82, 371–86.

Hastie, T. J. and R. J. Tibshirani (1990). *Generalized Additive Models*. Chapman & Hall.

Hayfield, T. and J. S. Racine (2008). "Nonparametric econometrics: The np package". *Journal of Statistical Software* 27(5).

Heckman, J. J. and B. Singer (1984). "A method for minimizing the impact of distributional assumptions in econometric models of duration". *Econometrica* 52, 271–320.

Heiler, S. (1999). "A survey of nonparametric time series analysis". Working paper EconWPA Finance 9904005.

Horowitz, J. L. (1998). *Semiparametric Methods in Econometrics*. Springer.

Horowitz, J. L. (2000). "The bootstrap". In J. J. Heckman and E. E. Leamer (eds), *Handbook of Econometrics*, volume 5. Elsevier Science.

Horowitz, J. L. (2004). "Semiparametric models". In J. E. Gentle, W. K. Härdle, and Y. Mori (eds), *Handbook of Computational Statistics*, pp. 697–718. Springer.

Horowitz, J. L. and W. Härdle (1994). "Testing a parametric model against a semiparametric alternative". *Econometric Theory* 10, 821–48.

Horowitz, J. L. and W. Härdle (1996). "Direct semiparametric estimation of single-index models with discrete covariates". *Journal of the American Statistical Association* 91, 1632–40.

Hsiao, C., Q. Li, and J. S. Racine (2007). "A consistent model specification test with mixed categorical and continuous data". *Journal of Econometrics* 140, 802–26.

Ichimura, H. (1993). "Semiparametric least squares (SLS) and weighted SLS estimation of single-index models". *Journal of Econometrics* 58, 71–120.

Inclan, C. and G. C. Tiao (1994). "Use of cumulative sums of squares for retrospective detection of changes of variance". *Journal of the American Statistical Association* 89, 913–23.

Jones, C. I. (2001). *Introduction to Economic Growth*. W. W. Norton.

Kamakura, W. A., B. D. Kim, and J. Lee (1996). "Modeling preference and structural heterogeneity in consumer choice". *Management Science* 15, 152–72.

Keribin, C. (2000). "Consistent estimation of the order of mixture models". *Sankhyä Series A* 62, 49–66.

Klein, R. W. and R. H. Spady (1993). "An efficient semiparametric estimator of binary response models". *Econometrica* 61, 387–421.

Koop, G. (2003). *Bayesian Econometrics*. Wiley-Interscience.

Krolzig, H. M. (1997). *Markov-Switching Vector Autoregressions*. Springer-Verlag.

Le, N. D., R. D. Martin, and A. E. Raftery (1996). "Modeling flat stretches, bursts, and outliers in time series using mixture transition distribution models". *Journal of the American Statistical Association* 91, 1504–14.

Leisch, F. (2004). "FlexMix: a general framework for finite mixture models and latent class regression in R". *Journal of Statistical Software* 11(8), 1–18.

Lenk, P. J. and W. S. DeSarbo (2000). "Bayesian inference for finite mixtures of generalized linear models with random effects". *Psychometrika* 65, 93–119.

Leroux, B. G. (1992). "Consistent estimation of a mixing distribution". *Annals of Statistics* 20, 1350–60.

Li, J. and J. S. Racine (2006). *Nonparametric Econometrics*. Princeton University Press.

Lindsay, B. (1995). *Mixture Models: Theory, Geometry and Applications*. Regional Conference Series in Probability and Statistics. Institute of Mathematical Statistics.

Liu, R. Y. (1988). "Bootstrap procedure under some non-i.i.d. models". *Annals of Statistics* 16, 1696–708.

Loader, C. R. (1999a). "Bandwidth selection: classical or plug-in?". *Annals of Statistics* 27, 415–38.

Loader, C. R. (1999b). *Local Regression and Likelihood*. Springer.

Loretan, M. and P. C. B. Phillips (1994). "Testing the covariance stationarity of heavy-tailed time series: an overview of the theory with applications to several financial data sets". *Journal of Empirical Finance* 1, 211–48.

MacKinnon, J. G. (2002). "Bootstrap inference in econometrics". *Canadian Journal of Economics* 35, 615–45.

Mallat, S. G. (1989). "A theory for multiresolution signal decomposition: the wavelet representation". *IEEE Transactions on Pattern Analysis and Machine Intelligence* 11, 674–93.

Mammen, E. (1993). "Bootstrap and wild bootstrap for high dimensional linear models". *Annals of Statistics* 21, 255–85.

Mankiw, N. G., D. Romer, and D. N. Weil (1992). "A contribution to the empirics of economic growth". *Quarterly Journal of Economics* 107, 407–37.

Manski, C. F. (1988). "Identification of binary response models". *Journal of the American Statistical Association* 83, 729–38.

Marron, J. S. and H. P. Schmitz (1992). "Simultaneous density estimation of several income distributions". *Econometric Theory* 8, 476–88.

Marron, J. S. and M. P. Wand (1992). "Exact mean integrated squared error". *Annals of Statistics* 20, 712–36.

Marsh, L. C. and D. R. Cormier (2001). *Spline Regression Models*. Sage Publications.

McCullagh, P. and J. A. Nelder (2001). *Generalized Linear Models*. Chapman & Hall.

McFadden, D. and K. E. Train (2000). "Mixed MNL models of discrete response". *Journal of Applied Econometrics* 15, 447–70.

McLachlan, G. J. and K. E. Basford (1988). *Mixture Models: Inference and Applications to Clustering*. New York: Marcel Dekker.

McLachlan, G. J. and D. Peel (2000). *Finite Mixture Models*. Wiley.

Mincer, J. (1974). *Schooling, Experience and Earnings*. Columbia University Press for the NBER.

Murphy, K. M. and F. Welch (1990). "Empirical age-earnings profiles". *Journal of Labor Economics* 8, 202–29.

Nadaraya, E. A. (1964). "On estimating regression". *Theory of Probability and Its Applications* 9, 141–42.

Neumann, M. H. and J. Polzehl (1998). "Simultaneous bootstrap confidence bands in nonparametric regression". *Journal of Nonparametric Statistics* 9, 307–33.

Newey, W. H. and J. L. Powell (2003). "Instrumental variable estimation of nonparametric models". *Econometrica* 71, 1565–78.

Newey, W. K. and K. D. West (1987). "A simple, positive semi-definite, heteroskedasticity and autocorrelation consistent covariance matrix". *Econometrica* 55, 703–08.

Newey, W. H., J. L. Powell, and F. Vella (1999). "Nonparametric estimation of triangular simultaneous equations models". *Econometrica* 67, 565–604.

Opsomer, J., Y. Wang, and Y. Yang (2001). "Nonparametric regression with correlated errors". *Statistical Science* 16, 134–53.

Paap, R. and H. K. van Dijk (1998). "Distribution and mobility of wealth of nations". *European Economic Review* 42, 1269–93.

Pagan, A. and A. Ullah (1999). *Nonparametric Econometrics*. Cambridge University Press.

Park, S. (2003). "Semiparametric instrumental variables estimation". *Journal of Econometrics* 112, 381–99.

Percival, D. B. and A. T. Walden (2000). *Wavelet Methods for Time Series Analysis*. Cambridge University Press.

Pfann, G. A., P. C. Schotman, and R. Tschernig (1996). "Nonlinear interest rate dynamics and implications for the term structure". *Journal of Econometrics* 74, 149–76.

Phillips, A. W. (1958). "The relationship between unemployment and the rate of change of money wages in the United Kingdom, 1861–1957". *Economica* 15, 283–99.

Poulsen, C. S. (1990). "Mixed Markov and latent Markov modelling applied to brand choice behavior". *International Journal of Research in Marketing* 7, 5–19.

Powell, J. L., J. H. Stock, and T. M. Stoker (1989). "Semiparametric estimation of index coefficients". *Econometrica* 51, 1403–30.

Quah, D. (1993). "Empirical cross-section dynamics in economic growth". *European Economic Review* 37, 426–34.

Quah, D. (1997). "Empirics for growth and distribution: stratification, polarization, and convergence clubs". *Journal of Economic Growth* 1, 27–59.

Racine, J. S. and Q. Li (2004). "Nonparametric estimation of regression functions with both categorical and continuous data". *Journal of Econometrics* 119, 99–130.

Racine, J. S. and C. F. Parmeter (2008). "Constrained nonparametric kernel regression: estimation and inference". Paper presented at GREQAM, Marseille.

Ramaswamy, V. E. (1997). "Evolutionary preference segmentation with panel survey data: an application to new products". *International Journal of Research in Marketing* 14, 57–80.

Ray, S. and B. G. Lindsay (2005). "The topography of multivariate normal mixtures". *Annals of Statistics* 33, 2042–65.

Redner, R. and H. F. Walker (1984). "Mixture densities, maximum likelihood and the EM algorithm". *SIAM Review* 26, 195–239.

Robert, C. P. and G. Casella (2005). *Monte Carlo Statistical Methods*. Springer.

Robinson, P. M. (1988). "Root-*n*-consistent semiparametric regression". *Econometrica* 56, 931–54.

Ruppert, D. (2002). "Selecting the number of knots for penalized splines". *Journal of Computational and Graphical Statistics* 11, 735–57.

Ruppert, D., M. P. Wand, and R. J. Carroll (2003). *Semiparametric Regression*. Cambridge University Press.

Schwarz, G. (1978). "Estimating the dimension of a model". *Annals of Statistics* 6, 461–4.

Scott, D. W. (1992). *Multivariate Density Estimation: Theory, Practice, and Visualization*. John Wiley & Sons.

Sheather, S. J. and M. C. Jones (1991). "A reliable data-based bandwidth selection method for kernel density estimation". *Journal of the Royal Statistical Society Series B* 53, 683–90.

Silverman, B. W. (1986). *Density Estimation for Statistics and Data Analysis*. Chapman & Hall.

Simonoff, J. S. (1996). *Smoothing Methods in Statistics*. Springer Verlag.

Sims, C. A. and T. Zha (2006). "Were there regime switches in US monetary policy?". *American Economic Review* 96, 54–81.

Stărică, C. and C. Granger (2005). "Nonstationarities in stock returns". *Review of Economics and Statistics* 87, 503–22.

Summers, R. and A. Heston (1991). "The Penn World Table (mark 5): an expanded set of international comparisons, 1950–88". *Quarterly Journal of Economics* 106, 327–68.

Titterington, D. M., U. E. Makov, and A. F. M. Smith (1985). *Statistical Analysis of Finite Mixture Distributions*. Wiley.

Train, K. E. (2003). *Discrete Choice Methods with Simulation*. Cambridge University Press.

Venables, W. N. and D. M. Smith (2009). *An Introduction to R*. Network Theory Ltd.

Wahba, G. (1990). *Spline Models for Observational Data*. SIAM.

Wand, M. P. (2000). "A comparison of regression spline smoothing procedures". *Computational Statistics* 15, 443–62.

Wand, M. P. and M. C. Jones (1995). *Kernel Smoothing*. Chapman & Hall.

Watson, G. S. (1964). "Smooth regression analysis". *Sankhya*, Series A 26, 359–72.

Wedel, M. and W. A. Kamakura (1999). *Market Segmentation: Conceptual and Methodological Foundations*. Kluwer Academic Publishers.

White, H. (1980). "A heteroskedasticity-consistent covariance matrix estimator and a direct test for heteroskedasticity". *Econometrica* 48, 817–38.

Wong, C. M. and R. Kohn (2000). "A bayesian approach to estimating and forecasting additive nonparametric autoregressive models". *Journal of Time Series Analysis* 17, 203–20.

Wood, S. N. (2006). *Generalized Additive Models: An Introduction with R*. Chapman & Hall/CRC.

Wu, C. F. J. (1986). "Jackknife bootstrap and other resampling methods in regression analysis". *Annals of Statistics* 14, 1261–95.

Yatchew, A. (1998). "Nonparametric regression techniques in economics". *Journal of Economic Literature* 36, 669–721.

Yatchew, A. (2003). *Semiparametric Regression for the Applied Econometrician*. Cambridge University Press.

Yatchew, A. and Z. Griliches (1984). "Specification error in probit models". *Review of Economics and Statistics* 66, 134–39.

Index